W0091385

SAGE was founded in 1965 by Sara Miller McCune to support the dissemination of usable knowledge by publishing innovative and high-quality research and teaching content. Today, we publish over 900 journals, including those of more than 400 learned societies, more than 800 new books per year, and a growing range of library products including archives, data, case studies, reports, and video. SAGE remains majority-owned by our founder, and after Sara's lifetime will become owned by a charitable trust that secures our continued independence.

Los Angeles | London | New Delhi | Singapore | Washington DC | Melbourne

ADVANCE PRAISE

This book is a must-read for every Indian. It brings out the frightening growth of religious communalism in India, which threatens to tear apart the delicate fabric woven by the Indian people over the centuries. Yet the author is optimistic that what will endure is this very practice of the Indian people living together for centuries evolving a syncretic, plural, multi-cultural society which our nation builders tried to promote as the 'idea of India'.

**—Aditya Mukherjee, Professor of
Contemporary History, Centre for Historical Studies,
Jawaharlal Nehru University, New Delhi**

This is a searing exposé of the violence, hatred and narrow communal prejudices that are integral to the Hindutva DNA. In tracing the trajectory from Savarkar to Modi, Ziya Us Salam shows that nothing has changed and how, therefore, our secular nationhood is currently threatened. He sums up by explaining how the Muslim community might best meet this challenge through internal social reforms. A balanced account with a wise ending, I would highly commend the book to general and specialist readers.

**—Mani Shankar Aiyar, author of *Confessions
of a Secular Fundamentalist***

This book by Ziya Us Salam tells us about the twists and turns in the history of our country during the recent years, especially during the period of Modi regime. He has a lot to say about the Hindutva phenomenon, the issue of cow, mob lynching of Muslims, engineered communal riots, the Muslim identity, the politics of triple talaq and so on. The author has written about these and several other related issues with his characteristic elegance, felicity and persuasiveness.... The book is a must-read for understanding India's current predicament.

—D.N. Jha, Historian

Ziya Us Salam's *Of Saffron Flags and Skullcaps: Hindutva, Muslim Identity and the Idea of India* is a timely work which tries to grapple with a burning issue which is seminal to the survival of the concept of a secular nation as envisioned and guaranteed by the Constitution of India. Salam not only deals with the growth of Hindutva 'Nationalism' which in the present day is trying to appropriate some of the foundational philosophies of people like Sardar Patel, Bhagat Singh and Dr Ambedkar, but also exposes those who are trying to propagate a divisive agenda where the 'other' is tried to be demonized. Through this work Salam makes an attempt to put the 'idea of India' back on its secular rails and show how Muslims are an important component of this nation, historically and otherwise.

—Professor Syed Ali Nadeem Rezavi, Chairman & Coordinator, Centre of Advanced Study, Department of History, AMU, Aligarh

A thorough, multi-faceted and clear-eyed historical account of relations between Hindus and Muslims of the Indian subcontinent: Ziya Us Salam has produced a much needed up-to-date analytical narrative which, rightly, warns against the rise of majoritarian Hindutva under the garb of nationalism. A timely book to inspire all those who uphold India's traditional unity in diversity.

—Dilip Hiro, author of *Indians in a Globalizing World: Their Skewed Rise*

This book is a bold and frank account of the transformation of the relationship between Muslims and the Indian nation. It questions the civilized denial about the antagonistic othering of Muslims and their marginalization. It tells us that the disenfranchisement of Muslims and destruction of the secular project of the Indian freedom struggle did not happen overnight. Set in a period when the RSS started capturing all institutional, cultural and political spaces, the book observes and registers different episodes of the gradual decline and fall of the idea of India shaped by Gandhi, Nehru and Ambedkar.

—Apoorvanand Jha, Professor, Department of Hindi, University of Delhi

Of SAFFRON FLAGS
AND SKULLCAPS

Of SAFFRON FLAGS AND SKULLCAPS

Hindutva, Muslim Identity and the Idea of India

ZIYA US SALAM

Los Angeles | London | New Delhi
Singapore | Washington DC | Melbourne

First published in 2018 by

SAGE Publications India Pvt Ltd
B1/I-1 Mohan Cooperative Industrial Area
Mathura Road, New Delhi 110 044, India
www.sagepub.in

SAGE Publications Inc
2455 Teller Road
Thousand Oaks, California 91320, USA

SAGE Publications Ltd
1 Oliver's Yard, 55 City Road
London EC1Y 1SP, United Kingdom

SAGE Publications Asia-Pacific Pte Ltd
3 Church Street
#10-04 Samsung Hub
Singapore 049483

Published by Vivek Mehra for SAGE Publications India Pvt Ltd, typeset in 10/16 pt Georgia by AG Infographics, Delhi and printed at Chaman Enterprises, New Delhi.

Library of Congress Cataloging-in-Publication Data

Name: Ziya Us Salam, author.
Title: Of saffron flags and skullcaps: Hindutva, Muslim identity and the idea of India / Ziya Us Salam.
Description: New Delhi: SAGE Publications India; New York: SAGE Publications, 2018. | Includes bibliographical references.
Identifiers: LCCN 2018015540| ISBN 9789352807345 (print pb) | ISBN 9789352807352 (e-pub 2.0) | ISBN 9789352807369 (e-book)
Subjects: LCSH: India—Ethnic relations—Political aspects. | Hindutva—India. | Hindus—India. | Muslims—India—Ethnic identity. | Identity politics—India. | Hinduism and politics—India. | Racism—India.
Classification: LCC DS430 .Z59 2018 | DDC 320.550954--dc23 LC record available at https://lccn.loc.gov/2018015540

ISBN: 978-93-528-0734-5 (PB)

SAGE Team: Manisha Mathews, Alekha Chandra Jena, Kumar Indra Mishra and Ritu Chopra

To

Pappa

(known to the world as Dr Ausaf Saied Vasfi)

for his *ilm* and *qalam*.

Thank you for choosing a SAGE product!
If you have any comment, observation or feedback,
I would like to personally hear from you.

Please write to me at **contactceo@sagepub.in**

Vivek Mehra, Managing Director and CEO, SAGE India.

Bulk Sales

SAGE India offers special discounts
for purchase of books in bulk.
We also make available special imprints
and excerpts from our books on demand.

For orders and enquiries, write to us at

Marketing Department
SAGE Publications India Pvt Ltd
B1/I-1, Mohan Cooperative Industrial Area
Mathura Road, Post Bag 7
New Delhi 110044, India

E-mail us at **marketing@sagepub.in**

Get to know more about SAGE

Be invited to SAGE events, get on our mailing list.
Write today to **marketing@sagepub.in**

This book is also available as an e-book.

CONTENTS

FOREWORD

WRITER, FILM AND LITERARY CRITIC, social commentator and
a perspicacious journalist whose insights and ideas have
brightened the spaces of *The Hindu* and *Frontline* for
nearly two decades, Ziya Us Salam collates here a mar-
vellous set of thought-provoking ideas into an important
book, *Of Saffron Flags and Skullcaps*. I believe that apart
from its obvious literary merit, this book is significant as it
feeds extensively into the current narrative of India. While
underlining some of the uncomfortable truths of the present age, it also reinforces the original vision of India, the
republic that guaranteed fundamental rights and freedom
for all its citizens. Drawing from the author's experience
besides his writing for *The Hindu* and *Frontline*, as well
as a large original and fresh material, this book touches on
some important core values that this nation stands for—
secularism, equality, tolerance, diversity and plurality.
What is singularly obvious in this work is that the reflections and revelations are drawn from a vast exploration
of ideas, of actual experience and most importantly, from
his own practice of journalism, which in the author's own
words involves 'investigation, research, cross-questioning,
fact-finding and then putting all the details together'.

In this volume, the observations about society, politics, people and the multi-layered history of India are filled with an acuity and sharpness that reflect an in-depth understanding of the nature of contemporary India. The country's first Prime Minister Jawaharlal Nehru and other founders of the republic envisaged the nation as 'an ancient palimpsest', something upon which much has been inscribed without erasing anything that had been there before, thus strongly asserting the plurality of India. What is happening at present is the overriding of this vision, a rewriting of the nation's history and the distortion of the story of India and as the author quite correctly observes, 'politics ... is impervious to history'. In addition, of course (and this is all too obvious), is the fact that the contemporary sociopolitical realities do not mirror many of the values and ideals of the Indian republic, and it is this painful truth that this book captures through harrowing tales of loss, of alienation and the search and reaffirmation of identity in a beleaguered nation that seems to have lost its way.

Most central to the sense of disaffection is the perception of being the 'Other', experienced by many Muslims currently and reinforced by the blatant prejudice and bigotry of many sections of the majority community. What is increasingly dangerous is the often tangible support from the ruling or powerful elite especially from Hindu nationalist groups such as the Rashtriya Swayamsevak Sangh (RSS) which feeds directly into the ruling party's culture emphasizing its complicity in this ethos. The author traces the history of such prejudice in the rhetoric and tracts of Hindu nationalists such as M.S. Golwalkar, V.D. Savarkar and others whose inheritors are people such as Rajeswar

Singh of the Dharam Jagran Manch who, as late as 2015 was, the author says, 'emboldened enough to claim that the country would be rid of Muslims and Christians by 2021'. 'We have ensured "*ghar wapsi*" (reconversion) of three lakh Muslims and Christians back to Hinduism', he claimed, rejoicing in climbing a molehill before a mountain of 180 million Muslims and 27.8 million Christians!

Interestingly, the author points out that Savarkar, 'that icon of Hindutva', wrote an essay titled 'Care for Cows, Do Not Worship Them' and argued that 'considering the cow as divine is an insult to humankind'. However, Savarkar and Golwalkar modelled their notion of a new Hindu nation much as a replica of Hitler's totalitarian and fascist ideas. The author points out again that these ideas have spawned present-day right-wing ideologues who spew public invectives of hatred. He gives among various instances the example of the actor Anupam Kher who tweeted in Hindi that when pest control is used, cockroaches and vermin emerge from hiding and thus the house is cleansed. The actor in his not so veiled comment went on to suggest that pest control of the country is being done at present. The author points out, 'Kher's words were almost a reproduction of Hitler's who referred to Jews as insects, vermin and bacteria!' The wounds of a community are tangible and present in the scores of other examples that the author presents and the poignancy of it all summed up in one sentence: 'I have been here for almost 1,400 years. Yet I am the "Other"'.

The essays in this book traverse a range of subjects that stem from this kind of alienation, currently experienced by many members of the minority community in India. The author neatly juxtaposes actual fact with notions that have gained popular currency but have no basis in fact. For instance, the Muslim women's right to divorce called *khula*, which confers the same rights as in the case of Triple Talaq, is little known. There are other fallacies. He illustrates how Hindutva actually preceded the notion of Muslim appeasement and was one of the 'early shades of political expression' reaching millions of homes through magazines such as *Kalyan* of the Gita Press, retrograde in content and in essence opposing gender equality (for example, it was against the Sarada Act which put the minimum age of marriage for Hindu girls at 14) and also against the continuation of a pluralist society where all sections of the population would have equal rights.

The point of rallying support against the 'Other' is the spectre of terrorism using extremist outfits as the bogey, as the case in point and thereby forming private armies in places such as Meerut, Muzaffarnagar, Hanumangarhi, the *raksha dals* as has been reported in the media. The author painstakingly traces the historical roots of such phenomena and puts side to side the growing polarization between the majority and minority communities. The debate around topics such as the issue of conversions, the appropriation of Bhagat Singh and the subject of the RSS and the Tricolour are dispassionately framed in the book, and the personal delve into history and texts adds a poignant dimension to one's experience of the book.

There are also moving vignettes of individuals who are present-day pioneers; teachers such as Farhat Hashmi based in Canada, who despite opposition from conservatives within the fold devised a course that would lead to a better understanding of the Quran, especially for women, instead of the usual rote learning. Increasingly women were encouraged to attend these courses breaking traditional barriers that kept them to home study and even began to use CDs and pen drives to enhance their learning. Another chapter depicts an affecting account of the tribulations of Mohammed Aamir Khan whose book *Framed as a Terrorist*, co-authored with Nandita Haksar, recounted here makes harrowing reading. The abuse Khan underwent at the hands of the police and in jail after being framed in several bomb blast cases described in shocking detail underlines much of the suffering that innocent and powerless people experience in a democratic structure that is supposed to safeguard their civil liberties. In this chapter, however, a greatly redemptive light emerges through the character of Khan himself—for all the 14 years of unlawful imprisonment, despite the torture and mistreatment at the hands of the authorities, he remains 'a remarkably level-headed man' forging friendships across religions in his neighbourhood, assisting in the rehabilitation of prisoners into mainstream society through various civil society organizations and perhaps most importantly, his faith in this pluralist democracy remains unshaken. The author quotes Khan, 'For Indian Muslims, India is their country by choice—I am grateful to my ancestors for making that choice'. And as the author concludes, 'Therein lies the hope for continued shared living'.

The book is an important reading precisely because it discusses situations and people such as this one, lifting the veil on distortion, misinformation and manipulative politics that undermine the vision of a secular plural nation mandated by our Constitution. A distinctive feature of the Indian democratic experience is that despite the frequent assaults on the nation's edifice from reactionary and intransigent forces, it has continued to thrive and evolve, expanding the scope of individual freedom and strengthening the rights of all people. And as the author says, 'India is greater than the sum of its parts'.

Dr Nirmala Lakshman
Director
The Hindu Group

PREFACE

IT WAS APRIL 2011. An emergency meeting of imams was called at a prominent mosque in New Delhi. The agenda was different from the usual. There was no talk of Islam in danger, none of any police excesses or denial of rights to Muslims in a mofussil part of the country. Instead, the imams had gathered to take stock of the India Against Corruption movement that had rapidly gained traction, and attracted Indians across the barriers of religion or caste, gender or politics. The campaign led by Anna Hazare was beginning to catch international attention as thousands of young men and women moved on the streets of New Delhi, Mumbai, Pune, Kolkata, Bangalore and Chennai with special Anna Hazare caps on their heads. Hazare, an activist with limited popularity until then, was transformed into a cult figure, as he led the likes of Shanti Bhushan, Arvind Kejriwal, Kiran Bedi, Prashant Bhushan, and later Baba Ramdev to raise a cry for the appointment of Jan Lokpal. The appointment was then considered to be the panacea of all ills of corruption. To this, Ramdev added the demand for bringing back black money from Switzerland. And common Indians, for years living with the feeling of being constantly cheated by corrupt politicians, bought into the narrative. Hazare and his team got a lot of support from the Opposition political parties, although he did not allow members from the Bharatiya Janata Party and the Communist Party of India (Marxist) to share the stage with him. But Hazare, at least momentarily, taken as a New Gandhi, rattled the Manmohan Singh government. What made it worse was the presence of people of all religions at the Jantar Mantar protest. There were young boys, clearly Sikh by their appearance. There were girls, easily identified as Muslim because of their hijab. There were Buddhist monks and a few Christian priests too. They all lent a pluralist shade to the protest with the common Indian happy to don the Hazare caps irrespective of religious or caste affiliation. It was an enviably non-violent protest, replete with marches, rallies, dharnas and hunger strikes.

The imams too met at the conclusion of evening prayers and resolved to join the protest from next morning. 'The Quran has explicit verses against corruption. It asks man not to spread corruption on the earth. It is our duty to join this fight against corruption. Else we will be guilty of dereliction of duty on the Day of Judgement', concluded an imam, adding, 'We are going to purchase some Anna Hazare caps, and join the protest from tomorrow'. Not for a moment did it strike the imams that they were trading the skullcaps worn during prayer for the cap that had become a symbol of protest. The purpose was loftier than any symbol.

The fight continued with barely a few hiccups for a few months. After the first sign of assurance on forming a joint committee comprising members of civil society besides those from the ruling Congress-led alliance, Hazare called off the fast. It dented not a bit of his following among the common Indians keen to exorcise the ghost of corruption. His subsequent fasts only added to his aura; the only blip being Ramdev's midnight escape from the Ramlila Maidan protest after a police party raided the premises.

That was then, a time when religious identity was subservient to a national fight for a clean system. It was immaterial who led the fight or what religion he followed. What mattered was for every Indian to lend his shoulder to the movement. It was a unity that was to pick its biggest scalp soon—the UPA-II government whose fate was sealed much before the 2014 General Elections.

Cut to 2014. The government led by Narendra Modi assumed the reins of power with the best possible mandate and oft-repeated promise of '*Sabka saath, sabka vikas*' (Everybody's support, everybody's development). The nation watched with baited breath. A new dawn had arrived. Or so it seemed. The days of corruption would end soon. And all communities would take part in the promised unprecedented development of the country, people will have jobs, women will enjoy safety and inflation will be under control. 'I want to tell my fellow Indians that in letter and spirit I will take all Indians with me', Modi assured the countrymen. However, higher the hopes soared, the sooner they collapsed. For all his promise of taking everybody along the path of progress, the Prime Minister did not fail to mention, 'twelve hundred years of slavery' in his Motion of Thanks speech to the President's address to the joint session of the Parliament. 'Twelve hundred years?' one asked. It was only a little later that one understood what he meant. He fought the elections against the Congress, but now he trained his guns at Muslims, the community said to have ruled India for a thousand years, beginning 1193 with Muhammad Ghori, and ending in 1857 with Bahadur Shah Zafar. Add to that another hundred years under the British. With one sentence, he had equated the Muslims with the British colonial masters. It left many Indians fuming. Among them was noted historian Mushirul Hasan, who said, 'It is a complete falsification of history. The British did not make India their home, whereas Muslims, who came here, settled in India and contributed to the country's culture. That gave birth to the Ganga–Jamuni tehzeeb'.

The Prime Minister, however, was only technically guilty of deliberate miscalculation, but stayed true to his belief. After all, M.S. Golwalkar, the 'Guruji' of Hindutva forces, of which the Prime Minister was now the most popular face, had said something similar well before Independence. 'Ever since that evil, when Moslems first landed in Hindustan, right up to the present moment, the Hindu Nation has been gallantly fighting on to shake off the despoilers. The Race Spirit has been awakening'.

The Prime Minister got the desired response. He not only drew a wedge in the fight against corruption but also showed the way towards community-specific polarization in the days, weeks and months to come. The days of a united fight against corruption were over. The days of polarization had arrived.

His words were picked up by his followers. It was the beginning of the process of 'Othering' of Muslims. A Muslim, and his ancestors, could have lived here for hundreds of years, made it his home, participated actively in the freedom struggle, gone to jail fighting the British, helped with giving slogans such as Quit India or designing the national flag, but he was still the 'Other'. His patriotism doubted at the crucible of politics by those who played no role in the freedom struggle.

SEPTEMBER 2015

Fifty-two-year-old Akhlaq, father of an Indian Air Force personnel, is suspected of killing a calf, and storing beef in his refrigerator at his residence in Dadri. A mob attacks his house hours after Eid-ul-Azha festivities, drags him out of his bedroom, thrashes him to death. There is an outrage across the country. Most are shocked at the gory murder of Akhlaq. His IAF-employed son refuses to lose hope. On a television show, he appeals for peace, and rounds off his message, saying, '*Saare jahan se achcha Hindustan hamara*'. This from a young man whose father had been murdered by a bloodthirsty mob, egged on by local BJP leaders. Among the accused is the son of a BJP leader.

Two years later, one of the accused, Ravin Sisodia, dies in police custody, allegedly due to dengue. A union minister, Mahesh Sharma, wraps his body in the Tricolour, announces a compensation of ₹8 lakhs and a job for his wife. It is probably the only instance in the history of independent India that a murder accused is sent on his last journey in the national flag.

Other 15 murder accused, out on bail, are soon given a job at the National Thermal Power Corporation in Dadri. This follows a meeting at the BJP MLA Tejpal Nagar's residence with NTPC officials in attendance.

There have been killings in the past too, in the name of the cow as well. It is for the first time that a serving IAF man's father's murder accused are rehabilitated by the ruling political dispensation.

India is changing!

2016

A little more than a century ago when Abanindranath Tagore portrayed Bharat Mata as a four-armed Hindu goddess, little did he realize that one day the concept will be used to divide Indians in the name of the nation. A PIL under IPC Section 124A (Sedition) is filed against All India Majlis-e-Ittehadul Muslimeen chief, Asaduddin Owaisi, for refusing to chant '*Bharat Mata ki jai*'. Even as Owaisi, no soft-liner himself, expresses faith in Indian judiciary, BJP General Secretary Kailash Vijayvargiya says, 'Those who do not want to chant *Bharat Mata ki jai* have no right to stay in India'. It is also the time when certificates of nationalism and patriotism are being distributed by Hindutva hawks. Owaisi, Kanhaiya Kumar, Umar Khalid and others who question the government are branded traitors. Some are advised to migrate to Pakistan. Much like Giriraj Singh, the Bihar MP, had done earlier. The country is riven with 'we' and 'they' talk. Being Hindu is to be conferred the birthright to nationalism, unless, of course, one questions the government, such as Kanhaiya. There seems to be only one way of being an Indian, the PM's promise of taking everybody along notwithstanding. The famed pluralism of the country is under attack. The concept of unity in diversity is giving way to uniformity. Hindi, Hindu, Hindustan is the cry.

2017

If upcoming communist leaders, and the most out-spoken Muslim leaders, were in the firing line earlier, this year drags the majestic Taj Mahal into the debate. Sangeet Som, a BJP leader from western Uttar Pradesh, calls it a blot on the nation. 'It was built by traitor', he claims. In his loony-populated world, he claims, 'The Taj was built by a man who imprisoned his father and wanted to massacre Hindus'. Som clearly has never attended any history classes in school. Or gets confused between the father Shah Jahan and son Aurangzeb.

Som does not operate in a vacuum. Before his tirade against the Taj, his party's government in Uttar Pradesh stops giving models of the Taj to visiting dignitaries as the Taj 'does not reflect Indian culture'. Soon after, the Taj is dropped off a list of Uttar Pradesh Tourism Department's brochure. The attacks on the Taj are emblematic of the attacks on India's largest minority. Predictably, Hindutva hawk Vinay Katiyar advises Muslims to go to Pakistan.

It is also the year when Pehlu Khan is accused of smuggling cattle, and done to death by cow vigilante groups in Alwar, Rajasthan, in April. There is again an outcry against mob lynching. In his dying declaration, Khan names six individual for the attack. All six are cleared by the police. A few months later, in January 2018, the state government, files FIR against the dead!

In December 2017, Afrazul, a migrant worker, is burnt to death, his body mutilated in Rajsamand, Rajasthan. The accused is Shambhulal Regar. Hindutva lobby rises to Regar's defence, collects more than ₹3 lakh for the wife of the accused. The family of the deceased lives in fear.

India has changed!

A Muslim murdered on the road is dubbed a suspect. And mutilation and murder of another Muslim goes viral. The hawks whistle, clap and cheer. India has changed beyond recognition.

Meanwhile, the world of Muslims undergoes a churning too. From the frenzied participation in the anti-corruption movement to a more muted response to the killing of Afrazul, the community has undergone a transformation. At one end are the age-old Muslim bodies, notably Jamaat-e-Islami and Jamiat Ulama-e-Hind trying to find solutions within the Indian Constitution to the emerging problems of the community, on the other are preachers such as Abdullah Tariq and Aslam Parvaiz encouraging the community to read, understand and explore the meaning of the Quran. They seek to take the focus away from rote learning in which madrasas have specialized for hundreds of years. The new generation preachers want the community to move away from a cleric-centric approach

to religion. It is an approach that runs counter to the one taken by Tablighi Jamaat which regards Islam to be a set of rituals to be performed in a given manner.

Yet, unnoticed by many, the world of Indian Muslims is undergoing a quiet transformation. For proof, one just has to see the reaction of the members of All India Muslim Personal Law Board to the Supreme Court verdict invalidating Triple Talaq. The Board responded in a dignified, mature manner, accepted the verdict, and asked Muslim men to take a pledge that they will never end their marriage through Triple Talaq. It was ages removed from the fulminations that followed the Shah Bano judgement in 1986.

At another level are women like Farhat Hashmi seeking to spread the message of Islam, and Jamida who dared to lead the Friday prayers in Kerala in January 2018, becoming in the process the first woman in Asia to do so. She will always have her critics, as will the Board. But together the two have proved that the community is looking for fresh answers to emerging questions. The right answers may yet be only blowing in the wind though. Unless of course one reads the direction of the wind blowing from Asansol.

The Ram Navami procession in March 2018 throws up an unlikely hero: imam of Noorani Masjid in Asansol, the second largest city in Bengal. Imam Imadul Rashidi loses his 16-year-old son in the communal violence that follows a Ram Navami procession where provocative slogans are mouthed. The boy is killed in the communal frenzy. A little later, some 30,000 people gather for his funeral. Tension is writ large. Everybody is on tenterhooks. Until the boy's father, Imam Rashidi, forgets his own sorrow and appeals for peace. 'I have lost my son. I accept it. He was supposed to live only this long. But do not indulge in violence. No revenge will bring my son back. I do not want anybody to suffer. If anybody still wants to take revenge for the killing of my son, I will leave the masjid. I will move away from this city'. His words meet a desired response. Men, young and old, say the final prayer for his son, and disperse peacefully. The Lord Shiva temple in the vicinity of the mosque stands unharmed and secure, prompting the state BJP president to admit, 'The imam has set an example of communal harmony'.

Asked about his rare gesture, the imam says, 'I have done nothing out of the ordinary. I merely asked people to maintain peace, and not to indulge in rumour-mongering. The Prophet and his companions were tortured for 13 years but never retaliated. If I can do even a drop's worth of their effort, I will be happy. I drew strength from the example of the Prophet and his companions. I asked people not to pass on any piece of information they come across without verifying it as I remembered the Quran. Through Surah Hujurat we are asked not to believe every news we get without cross-checking. I was merely doing my duty'.

This simultaneous churning in the world of the faithful as also Hindutva hawks set me thinking. Are these two parallel tracks that shall always run together but never meet? Or, is India on the brink of a sociopolitical change, one that in the years to come will be marked by not only aggressive Hindutva but also the forces of Islam undergoing a transformation after some 1,400 years in the country?

ACKNOWLEDGEMENTS

THIS EXERCISE WOULD NOT HAVE BEEN POSSIBLE but for a visit to the World Book Fair 2018 in New Delhi where I met Manisha Mathews, Executive Editor, Commissioning, for the first time. Brimming with optimism, she urged me to finish the book in time. Never once did she waver in her commitment towards the book nor did she allow my enthusiasm to wane. Of course, I can never thank Aarti David enough. For years, she has been the face of SAGE for me. Quiet, graceful and honest, she never promised more than she delivered, never delivered less than she promised. But for these two women, *Of Saffron Flags and Skullcaps* would have remained just an idea whose time had come and gone.

The World Book Fair meeting was just the beginning. A few more chats, telephone calls and the book was on track. Thank you, wonderful ladies!

I owe more than a word of thanks to Dr Nirmala Lakshman, Director, *The Hindu* and the author of the bestseller *Degree Coffee by the Yard: A Short Biography of Madras*. She has done the 'Foreword' here, but actually, she has been the pivot of my journey with *The Hindu*.

As I wrote, along the way I dipped into my writings for *The Hindu* and *Frontline*, and happily gained from the experience of my colleagues R. Vijayasankar, Venkitesh

Ramakrishnan, John Cherian, Purnima Tripathi, T.K. Rajalakshmi, Divya Trivedi and Akshay Deshmane. Not to forget the good word of Vijay Lokapally, Anuj Kumar, S. Ravi and Madhur Tankha. Each one of them helped me in ways known only to them and me, as was the case with Anjana Rajan, who took time out to read a good part of the manuscript while on a whistle-stop tour to Kerala. Of course, my wife Uzma and kids, Maryam, Aliza, Juveria and Mishal, had to bear patiently many of the demands on my time through the process of putting it all together. Not to forget my sisters, Muslima and Sajida; nephews, Osama Jalali and Umair; besides friends such as Aslam Khan, Aftab Alam, Rashid Ali, Masroor Mian, Arif Ali Khan, Irfan Ahmed, Mansoor Ansari, Shabbir Ahmed, R.M. Singh and Robin Bose, who never read a word of my manuscript but kept asking me about its progress. It helped me stay focused. Grateful. As I sign off, I cannot forget my Chhoti Maa, known to the world as Mrs Natasha Raina Kanwar. Not a day passes when I do not think of her. Nor can I thank brother Khadim Hussain enough. Not a prayer is completed without remembering him. May it stay that way!

Hindutva

THE IDEA OF A HINDU NATION

HINDUTVA AND HINDU NATIONALISM

IF ISLAM BASHING IS A SURE SHOT WAY TO HIT HEADLINES, Kamlesh Tiwari is a predictable, almost inevitable hero. The incorrigible man unleashed the worst allegations against the Prophet, and soon found himself being the topic of discussions on television debates, newspaper editorials and drawing room exchange of views. Indeed, he became like a glue for the ummah, as the faithful came out in thousands to demand his arrest in places as far removed as Muzaffarnagar and Mumbai, Lucknow and Hyderabad. Until he uttered the unmentionable words about the Prophet, few had taken notice of him. A handful who did after he had announced *bhoomi pujan* for a Godse temple in Sitapur had either forgotten him or dismissed him as yet another eccentric attention seeker.

Yet Tiwari was not just another man hungry for publicity. He was a self-proclaimed president of Akhil Bhartiya Hindu Mahasabha; his repeated indiscretions forcing the Hindu Mahasabha to disown him. Remember, he was the one who announced the formation of a private defence army named after Nathuram Godse, the man who assassinated the Father of the Nation. Why, he even had the temerity to demand that Mahatma Gandhi's picture be removed from the currency notes! His antipathy towards Muslims seemed understandable, but why his hostility towards the Mahatma? Well, in Tiwari's scheme of things, the Mahatma was responsible for the creation of Pakistan, a state for Muslims! His brand of nationalism stemmed from communalism. Simply put, it was majority communalism masquerading as nationalism.

Disconcerting though Tiwari's views were, what was more unsettling was that he claimed to be from a body that has for more than a century sowed seeds of disaffection and disunity. And all in the name of the nation! One is referring to the Hindu Mahasabha, a body known for its distrust of everything non-Hindu, a party well known for its role in exacerbating communal tension in parts of North India. Revelling in the 'we' and 'they' divide, the Mahasabha always painted the 'other' with the tar of treachery and sedition. In this scheme of things, there was place only for those minorities which could fit under the Hindu umbrella, notably Buddhists, Jains and Sikhs. These were religions which originated from the country. There was no space for other minorities such as Christians and Muslims, as they could not be subsumed under the Hindu umbrella. Their birthplace and sacred place were different; *janmabhoomi* and *punyabhoomi* were not one and the same. They were independent streams of thought with little in common with Hinduism. Also, they were the ones who had to periodically prove their loyalty to the nation, their patriotism, as the Hindus, by virtue of having 'lived in the country "since times immemorial" were part of a "national society", and since the "same Hindu people" had built the "life values, ideals and culture" of the country, their nationhood was "self-evident"'.

Although its early sympathizers, such as Madan Mohan Malaviya, Lala Lajpat Rai, etc., were also members of the Congress, it was essentially a contra culture group, one that vied with the Muslim League in the politics of exclusion. As pointed out by Ishita Banerjee-Dube (2014),

> The Mahasabha, formed in 1915 as a part of the Congress but with radical Hindu nationalist objectives, emerged as a strong critic of the Congress in the 1920s.... The Mahasabha had a very limited base in its initial phase; it was composed almost entirely of upper-caste and upper-class Hindu males and had branches only in a few towns and cities of north India.

Interestingly, the Muslim League composition was on similar lines too. Noted author Jyotirmaya Sharma laid bare any claims to justice and fairness of the Mahasabha through a scathing portrait of its principal ideologue Vinayak Damodar Savarkar, often called Veer Savarkar by the proponents of the right-wing ideology. Turns out, he was not exactly veer (brave) as his apologies from the Andamans prove. Nor even a nationalist; the stokes of Hindu Rashtra consumed him. Incidentally, he is said to have added the prefix 'Veer' to his name himself through a biography he himself authored. Called *Life of Barrister Savarkar*, the book came out a couple of years after Savarkar was released from prison. The book was like a paean to Savarkar, extolling him for his courage. The second edition of the book came out in 1987. It was published by Veer Sarvarkar Prakashan, the official publishers of Savarkar's writings. Ravindra Ramdas revealed in its preface that 'Chitragupta is none other than Veer Savarkar' (Kulkarni 2017).

A little after Tiwari was arrested, perchance I laid my hands on Sharma's book. Let me make a confession here: It is not often that I start a book with the last chapter, but I made an exception here, thanks to Tiwari—I was curious to know just from where does he get his ammunition for sustained hatred. Surely constant vitriol would need replenishment, I reckoned. The chapter in question, 'Vinayak Damodar Savarkar', is all about the founder of the Mahasabha, the man about whom Sharma (2011) writes, 'Even today, Savarkar remains the first, and most original, prophet of extremism in India'.

> Savarkar was the original ideologue of Hindutva. Golwalkar and others borrowed the idea from him. He was the one who gave the idea of *pitrabhoomi* and *punyabhoomi* whereby only a person whose birth-land and sacred land happened to be here could claim to be Indian. (Sharma 2011)

Even before I picked up Sharma's book, I was reasonably aware of the actions of Savarkar though. There was a feature film on him by the name of *Veer Savarkar* by Ved Rahi. The 2001 film sought to impart a halo around the founder of Hindu extremism. It had a well-earned limited run at the box office, then slipped from public memory. Yet Savarkar's entry into the world of 'we' and 'they', 'self' and 'other' has undoubted recall value. In his biography of Savarkar, Dhananjay Keer recounts an incident in which a 12-year-old Vinayak Damodar Savarkar leads a march of his schoolmates to stone the village mosque following rumours of cow slaughter and attendant riots. This was

Savarkar's revenge against the 'atrocities' committed against Hindus during the Hindu–Muslim riots. Sharma (2011) writes about the incident,

> Savarkar's own account of this act speaks of his rage against the deeds of physical violence committed against the Hindus by Muslim rioters. (For him, it was always the Muslims who initiated a riot.) So, when Hindus killed Muslims in acts of retribution, Savarkar and his friends would dance with joy.... Savarkar's description of raiding the mosque has a chilling echo to events of 6 December 1992: We vandalized the mosque to our heart's content and raised the flag of our bravery on it.

Is anybody reminded of Uma Bharati's infamous line, '*Ek dhakka aur do*', even as she sat watching the Babri Masjid being demolished, brick by brick by the so-called *kar sevaks*? Or even Narendra Modi's action–reaction remark following the Gujarat 2002 violence?

The seeds of Hindutva were laid in that attack on that mosque, what one saw in the demolition of the Babri Masjid was merely the fruition of that process. Savarkar paved the way for the modern-day Togadias and Bharatis. He always talked of revenge, counter violence, aggression, seldom, if ever, of peaceful coexistence. Unless, of course, the minorities were subsumed by the majority whole. Sharma (2011) writes,

> His writings are replete with terms like *pratishodh* and *pratikaar*, all synonyms for revenge, retribution and retaliation—not unlike the utterances of the BJP, the VHP, the Bajrang Dal, Narendra Modi and Praveen Togadia. As the progenitor and most eloquent theoretician of political Hindutva, Savarkar formulated his entire world-view in terms of well-entrenched, non-negotiable

binary oppositions. His universe is strictly divided into 'friends' and 'foes, 'us' and 'them', 'Hindus' and 'Muslims' ... 'righteous' and 'wicked'.

Interestingly, as recalled by P.N. Chopra in *A Comprehensive History of India*, Savarkar is reported to have said, 'We Hindus are a Nation by ourselves. Hindu nationalists should not at all be apologetic to being called Hindu communalists'. Savarkar's words were very similar to those of Golwalkar who said during our freedom struggle, 'We Hindus are at war with the Muslims on the one hand and the British on the other'. Hindu nationalists were actually naked communalists then. As is the case now.

At war with Muslims, Savarkar certainly was. While at the beginning of his career, he was a nationalist, soon his vision of Hindu Rashtra subsumed everything, including India's struggle for Independence.

> While Savarkar was certainly part of the nationalist movement, his commitment to the creation of a *Hindu Rashtra* superseded the goal of political independence for India. The very definition and conception of *Hindu Rashtra* depended entirely on its relation with its primary non-self, the Muslims. (Sharma 2011)

That Savarkar had succeeded in setting the template for future practitioners of Hindutva became clear just a little later. The baby steps Mahasabha took enabled the RSS to come into being in 1925. The body remained without a name for a couple of years. No name, no flag, nothing, but it revelled in symbolism. Founded on the Vijay Dashami day, the day Ram prevailed over Ravan in the age-old story of good prevailing over evil, the body was christened thus two years later in 1927. It also happened to be the year when it charted its future course of action. The mould was ready.

As nationalist leaders sought to boycott the Simon Commission in 1927 for being an all-white men delegation, the members of the RSS were involved in a communal riot in Nagpur. Their provocative words and actions as facilitators earned the then young Hindutva body many popular points. The RSS version of the riots is given by C.P. Bhishikar in *Khaki Shorts and Saffron Flags* by Tapan Basu, Pradip Datta, Sumit Sarkar, Tanika Sarkar and Sambuddha Sen (1993). Bhishikar writes of Muslim aggression and the Hindu retaliation, a template which has been used countless times by the so-called Hindu nationalists until today.

Stones were thrown at Doctorji's house [K.B. Hedgewar, one of the five founders of the RSS; the others being Dr B.S. Moonje, Dr L.V. Paranjpe, Dr B.B. Thalkar and Baburao Savarkar who was Vinayak Damodar's brother]. He was also receiving letters threatening to kill him. And the Muslims hatched a conspiracy to bring out a massive procession on September 4, 1927 (Mahalakshmi Puja day) and indulge in rioting. The procession was scheduled for the afternoon, a time during which Hindus would be resting after lunch. The Sangh workers got wind of the plan, and we knew that the procession was going to be attended by riot. Doctorji was personally out of Nagpur on that day. The procession was to pass through the Mahl area, an educated middle class locality. On both sides of the route there were a number of narrow lanes. The processionists were equipped with *lathis*, javelins, knives, daggers. Those who wanted to indulge in violence and loot indulged in thunderous slogans of 'Allah ho Akbar' and 'din, din' and attacked a house situated in front of the narrow lane. But at the entrance itself, they got a thorough beating.

Thereafter, they got thrashing at every lane entrance. Several rioters had their heads broken. The procession broke up, and people began to run. The fleeing goondas beat up the lone Hindus they found in the way. After the first retaliation against the Muslim intrusion, several Hindus left their lunch unfinished in anger and came out; by the evening they beat back the invaders. (Basu et al. 1993)

In this narrative, certain things are omitted while others are highlighted. For instance, the response to 'Muslim aggression' lay in 'Hindu militancy'. At another, a Muslim fleeing for his life is still a 'goonda' (sic) and an 'invader'. What is left unexplained is how did the Hindus organize themselves? What were the members doing at the entrance of each lane? How did they procure weapons to take on a mob armed with '*lathis*, javelins, knives, daggers'? Of course, the leader (Hedgewar) was provided an alibi too; he was said to be out of station. Thus, no accountability, no responsibility for what his flock did in his absence. It is the same narrative that was later used by Hindutva practitioners with the law of marginal returns yet to set in. Of course, its members who later maintained a stony silence when Mahatma Gandhi's Dandi march galvanized the nation, spread their version of history to impressionable youth: How the brave Rana Pratap (addressed as Maharana Pratap) and Veer Shivaji beat back the 'foreign' challenge; read Akbar and Aurangzeb. Looked at a bit carefully, it was the same principle at work: Hindus were 'We', Muslims 'the Other'. From kings to common man, that the idea transcended generations was realized when at the height of Babri Masjid–Ram Janmabhoomi controversy in the late 1980s and early 1990, the foot soldiers of the Hindutva lobby (the BJP–VHP–Bajrang Dal combine) went village to village, lane to lane in cities mouthing a slogan, '*Musalman ke do hi sthaan, Pakistan ya qabrastan*' (Muslims have only two places, Pakistan or cemetery). With a single slogan, the divorce of Muslims from India was pronounced. What was left unsaid was that India belonged to the Hindus. Just as Savarkar wanted.

Coming back to the Mahasabha. If the RSS used its template to the last letter in 1927, Savarkar himself went from being principally anti-British in his early years to a votary of a Hindu nation. As Sharma writes,

> Savarkar's early anti-British record is unimpeachable and heroic; it is difficult to make a similar statement about his activities in the mid-1920s, after he had evolved into the principal ideologue of Hindutva and become the leader of the Hindu Mahasabha. Mahasabha members of local bodies, legislatures and services were urged by Savarkar to 'stick to their posts and continue to perform their regular duties' during the 1942 movement, and his wartime slogan, 'Hinduize politics and militarize Hinduism' meant in practice a combination of virulent anti-Muslim propaganda and full collaboration with the British.

Meanwhile, the RSS, for all its latter years' antipathy towards Savarkar, copied his teachings faithfully. For instance, Savarkar wanted the Hindu society to organize itself, be militant and ready to take on any aggressor. The RSS did the same in its *shakhas*.

> The ... words justifying the Hindu martial strain were an outcome of Savarkar's denunciation of Gandhi and his philosophy of ahimsa, non-violence. Savarkar calls it 'the monomaniacal principle of absolute non-violence'. Absolute non-violence in the face of incorrigible aggression was immoral. It was not 'an outcome of

any saintliness but of insanity'.... Ahimsa was the other non-self that Savarkar's Hindu Self had to contend with. (Sharma 2011)

It is a thought Tiwari had inculcated profoundly, resulting not just in his hostility towards the Mahatma but an unrelenting animosity towards Muslims, and all things they hold dear.

I think yet again of Tiwari and his hatred of Gandhi, his disrespect towards the Prophet, and his intolerance towards everything non-Hindu. In his reasoning, only the Aryans who came here at the beginning of the Vedic civilization belong here. Rest are all invaders, a fallacy repeated a million times. But, didn't the Aryans succeed the Indus Valley civilization? If, so, weren't they immigrants too? Isn't everybody an immigrant here? All that matters is how far back you go in time. Some put 1947 as the cut-off date; others, like Prime Minister Narendra Modi who referred to a thousand years of foreign rule in his address to the nation following his victory in 2014, put the time roughly around the age of the invasions of Mahmud of Ghazni, thereby equating India with Hindus. They believe that whosoever came after Ghazni, namely, the Sultanate rulers, the Mughals and the British, were all outsiders, never mind if millions made it their home, contributing to its life and culture, indeed its freedom from colonial rule. They argue that those who came here earlier, such as, say, with the Aryan invasion around 1500 BC were the original settlers of the land. Hence, the assertion that India is a Hindu Rashtra.

But, what if you take time back all the way to 3000 BC? Or bring it forward to 1857? Or even 1947? Then who is an immigrant? And whose *rashtra* is it? Does India belong to us all? Or only to those who would wish away those not like them?

HINDUTVA PRECEDES APPEASEMENT

In 2014, when some Muslim women filed a petition in the Supreme Court demanding entry to all mosques in the country, they set the cat among the pigeons. The fact that their action coincided with Hindu women calling for an end to the ban on their entry into the select temples meant they got more media coverage than would have otherwise been possible. The response was on expected lines: Several women organizations were quick to speak up for them, notably, Zakia Soman, co-founder of the Bharatiya Muslim Mahila Andolan, along with Noorjehan Safia Niaz. Others feared a comeback of sorts to the murky politics played after the Shah Bano judgement. Worse, many dreaded a more belligerent Hindutva, arguing that it was after Rajiv Gandhi's government had overturned the Shah Bano judgement that Hindutva really took off, that *mandir* politics occupied centre stage. That every Indian who was not Hindu began to feel uneasy and insecure—sounds familiar these days? Considering the Babri Masjid–Ram Janmabhoomi actually occupied mind-space in the days following the Shah Bano judgement, their fears seem to have some reason. More so, when one considers that it led to the demolition of the Babri Masjid besides taking lives of hundreds of innocent in communal riots across large parts of North and West India. Indeed, in its manifesto in 1991, Bharatiya Janata Party talked of taking the nation '*Ram Rajya ki Ore*', a politically correct euphemism for Hindu Rashtra.

However, if one is prepared to cast the net wider, surprises lie in wait. Yes, Hindutva raised its more aggressive head during the Ayodhya agitation with provocative slogans and pamphlets being found across Hindi-speaking belt. But it was not the time when seeds of Hindutva were sowed. The fruit had merely ripened in the 1980s. The seeds were laid in the pre-Independence time, in 1920s, to be precise, thereby making Hindutva among the early shades of political expression; that it found far greater popularity than came the way of the Communists who started around the same time, is another story.

It all started with V.D. Savarkar and Gita Press. While Savarkar's role in laying the foundation of Hindu Rashtra is well documented, what has slipped in under the radar is the Gita Press from Gorakhpur with publications as impervious to notions of gender equality as they were opposed to the idea of pluralist society and polity. With its low cost fare ably distributed, it became a household name, and in many ways acted as a perfect companion to Hindutva leaders, men like Savarkar, Hedgewar and later Madhok, etc., who believed that only Indians who called the land their *pitrabhoomi* and *punyabhoomi* were deserving of any rights or concessions; the rest could stay at the sweet will of the majority with no rights; it is the Hindu majority that will decide the concessions to the minority. What Savarkar and others said through their speeches, Gita Press, through its monthly magazine *Kalyan*, reached millions of middle-class Hindu homes, thereby subtly indoctrinating them. While themes ranging from '*gau mata*' to 'Bharat Mata' were covered in each issue, *Kalyan* also made sure that the debate was within the rarefied concerns of Hindu society, and conducted within the fold of Hinduism. It was happy to deride Dr B.R. Ambedkar, a low caste man, for marrying a Brahmin woman. It expressed itself on subjugation of women, underlying their traditional roles and propagating stereotypes. Not surprisingly, it opposed the Sarda Act which sought to put a minimum age for marriage for Hindu girls at 14.

For decades, Gita Press conducted its publication business with remarkable clarity of thought and consistency of principles. So much so that when noted journalist Akshaya Mukul came out with a painstakingly researched 540-page book titled *Gita Press and the Making of Hindu India*, it acted as quite an eye opener for the English press. The fact that Mukul got access to rare private papers of Hanuman Prasad Poddar, the man behind Gita Press since inception to his death in 1971 meant authenticity was never given a go by. Brick by brick, layer by layer, sentence by sentence the deeply symbiotic relationship that existed between the RSS and the Gita Press—founded in 1925 and 1923, respectively—is revealed. Although both Gita Press and the RSS claimed to work for the uplift of Sanatan Hindu dharma, their hidden agenda of making India a Hindu Rashtra on independence did not remain hidden for long. In fact, well before the Independence, Golwalkar had conceded that the Hindu society faced two opponents: the British and the Muslims and Christians, thereby making clear that there was no space for Muslims and Christians in his scheme of things once the British left India. Although technically, Gita Press and RSS were independent entities, they followed the same goal and frequently converged on issues of interest to the Hindu society.

The beginnings were all austere. Gita Press, for the first couple of years, concentrated on publishing only the Gita with a Hindi commentary. But the Hindutva project lurked round the corner, and first raised its head in 1926 during a debate between Gandhians such as Jamnalal Bajaj and G.D. Birla on one side and the likes of Hanuman Prasad Poddar on the other. Soon, like modern-day resistance to the entry of Dalits into temples, Poddar too found himself unable to toe Mahatma Gandhi's instructions on the Temple Entry Movement. Although it initially meant little, over a period time, it reinforced the age-old belief that Gita Press was all for perpetuation of the traditional four-fold caste system. In fact, *Kalyan* was founded with the idea of opposing any threat to the traditional Hindu dharma. In the past lay the seeds of future. As Mukul (2015) writes,

> For Poddar, bhakti through recitation of God's name was the ultimate recipe to deal with the trials of life and ensure continued divine beneficence. When a woman who had been raped at a family wedding sought his advice, Poddar lamented the decline in morality among men and told her not to reveal the fact to her husband. For herself, she should recite the name of Rama at the rate of a hundred *malas* daily for a year.

Predictably, if in the early years of Independence, it supported the cow protection movement, in the 1980s, it espoused the cause of the Ram Janmabhoomi movement. Interestingly, Poddar not only presided over a meeting to welcome Golwalkar after he was released from jail in 1949, he was also on hand for a public meeting with Atal Bihari Vajpayee after the Nehru government lifted the ban on the RSS. And like modern-day *bhakts*, Poddar was clear in his mind about the possible provocation for any communal riots.

> Born in the middle of this surcharged decade (1920s), Kalyan was clear from the start about its stand on the Hindu-Muslim question. Poddar's editorial in the inaugural issue put the blame for the riots squarely on the Muslims, bemoaned Hindu inaction, called for sanghbal (unity of strength) and invoked co-religionists not to turn the principle of non-violence into cowardice. Hindu involvement in the riots was considered an act of defending the religion. (Mukul 2015)

For Poddar, for Gita Press, the blame for riots was always laid at the door of 'others'. Much like what Savarkar did, and what Golwalkar did. The words do not change, nor do the notes. If a few years before Independence, the RSS men recalled the Nagpur riots and the aggressive Hindu response following provocation by the Muslims, it was the same around the time of Independence.

> Interestingly, the December 1939 issue of Kalyan carried a piece by leading Hindi writer Ramnaresh Tripathi, where he recounted the personal encounter with a Muslim tongawala of Bareily in January that year. The UP town was rife with communal tension when Tripathi landed there in the middle of the night. The writer deliberately hired a tonga whose driver had a moustache. 'During communal riots, Muslim tonga-drivers become merchants of death. So I hired someone who has a moustache thinking he would be a Hindu.' Tripathi's story then descends into the usual stereotypes about Muslim looks and character.... The incident narrated in Kalyan was meant to show how God had saved the writer, but the underlying communal tenor in the unverifiable tale is unmissable. Similar stories that raised questions about the personal integrity of Muslims appeared in various issues of Kalyan. (Mukul 2015)

Does it not carry a stark resemblance to the narrative we are witnessing these days, from a union minister like Katheria talking of Hindu *sangathan* (organization) in Agra to a Lavanya talking of retaliation, only the names of the principal characters have changed. The message of hatred and hostility continues unabated. The yesteryear *mlecchha*, and *yavanas* are today's minorities for them. Indeed, as Mukul (2015) concludes, 'No other publishing house in India has marketed religion so successfully. And despite claiming to maintain a safe distance from politics, Gita Press has regularly taken political stands', much like the RSS today or Doctorji in pre-Independence India. The emphasis is always on duality of being involved but not so, of being a director but only tacitly so.

Now who needs a Triple Talaq verdict or a Haji Ali Dargah incident to stoke up Hindutva embers? Or even calls for banning azaan in mosques? Poddar and company have done it for ages. Undiluted Hindutva precedes any possible Muslim appeasement. Or even the myth of it all.

URA: HINDUTVA AND HIND SWARAJ

In the age of Right to Information, we are denied the right to introspection. A society pledged to development has no compunctions in passing off the greed of the vast multitudes as their need. A nation drunk to the potion of growth cares little for shadeless roads, chopped trees and smog-filled sky. It is the same overweening desire to possess, to attain which collectively propelled Narendra Modi to the august office of the Prime Minister.

Indeed, at a time when the nation has all but forgotten Naroda Patiya, it is futile to look for Mahatma Gandhi of Noakhali. The dead of Gujarat were just puppies that came under the wheel of the car, deserving of no rituals. Modi's politics is not about moderation, but exclusion. As Shiv Visvanathan says so succinctly in the foreword to U.R. Ananthamurthy's (URA hereafter) *Hindutva or Hind Swaraj*, Modi's nationalism is about elimination of opposites, not accommodation of differences.

> Modi is not the liberal mind, wondering how to deal with all the vexations: the Dalit vexation, the Muslim vexation, the cosmopolitan vexation. Like the liberal, he does not fear he might lose his morality trying to manage these tensions. Such sensitivity is unnecessary for those who manage the nation. Nationalism eliminates opposites. Like Mao. Like Stalin. Like Napoleon. Like Modi.

19

Throughout this wonderful book, hurriedly penned by URA in his last days, Modi comes across as an ideological offshoot of Savarkar. And URA, one of the first to speak up for the soul of India when Modi's victory seemed inevitable, again and again warns the nation that if in today's battle stakes Savarkar wins, Godse wins. It is important to secure victory for Gandhi, the man who thought of the nation state as evil, as opposed to Modi who sees it as god.

As Visvanathan reminds us,

> URA claims that Gandhi and Godse were dealing with two separate notions of evil. For Godse, evil was external. For Gandhi, evil was encompassed in the textures within. For Gandhi and Tagore, the nation state was the unfolding of evil. For Godse and Modi, it was both God and the ultimate good. (Ananthamurthy 2016)

Step by step, word by word, the soul of the nation is laid bare. Although he had written this 'manifesto' in the autumn of his life, he manages to paint with words. And quietly, almost imperceptibly, he paints a portrait of Modi:

it is a portrait Modi, just soaking in the adulation of his wax peer, won't be very proud of. URA begins with the past, not out of nostalgia but a dispassionate observation facilitated by the passage of time.

> When I was growing up in the pre-war years, we complained that goods 'Made in Germany' were difficult to get, and dismissed as 'Made in Japan' all the shiny, cheap items that we actually used.... Today all that glitters is 'Made in China'. America is incapable of manufacturing even a pin or a shirt. What it can produce are weapons of war and supercomputers.

Soon, he comes to the main subject: Hindutva and Modi. Here he first talks of Godse, who

> recognising the strength of Gandhi, assassinated him while he was on his way to pray to the Almighty for the well-being of the country rather than his own. The Hindutvavadi Godse's action, committed with utmost detachment and in cold blood, was the sacrificial offering made at the *yajna* of nation building. And Savarkar's ideology was the text for this *yajna*. Only in a democratic system does this sentiment, latent in all of us, find expression in the smooth-tongued Modi raising *aarti* to the holy Ganga.

There is more. URA touches upon the issue of Israel too, and is happy to connect it to the Modi government's change in policy with the state. When the Western world created Israel by banishing the local people, Gandhi opposed it as he felt that the Jews should accept the land where they lived as their own. Savarkar, of course, considered him a traitor due to 'his indifference to the nation state'. 'The Modi Government, inspired by Savarkar's idea of a Hindu state on the lines of Israel, is clearly aligned towards Israel. Modi, who was like a "brahma" during the Gujarat *yajna*, differs from the stand taken by the Vajpayee government'.

Having used his pen like a scalpel on the issue of Israel, he returns to the artist in him. Outlining that Mahatma Gandhi's concept of Hind Swaraj would have been a fine alternative to the much hyped Hindutva today, URA writes,

> He who does not dream is not human. One dreams of the well-being of mankind, a green earth and a clear sky. A dream of Gandhi's ahimsa. A dream where man works for a living, uses the benefits of science wisely and makes sure the environment is not destroyed. Gandhi's Hind Swaraj envisaged such an India. Modi's victory is in direct opposition to that dream. His triumph has moved closer to Savarkar's idea of Hindutva, without actually saying so.

Pertinently, URA draws attention to Mahatma Gandhi's response to violence at the time of Partition. When Sardar Patel broke the news to him that Delhi was not the Delhi of old and thousands of Hindus had occupied mosques while Muslims had fled to Karachi, Gandhi asked him to 'immediately remove the Hindus who were occupying the mosques. He urged Patel to bring back the Muslims who had fled to Karachi and reinstate them in their homes'. About Gujarat 2002, he leaves the answer blowing in the wind. Ah, the joy of the unsaid!

Reason enough to read URA, among the first to speak up about the challenges that were likely to confront India post-Modi's victory. He famously pledged to leave India if Modi won, something the Hindutva elements did not tire of reminding him. A few days of Modi's rule and God took that decision out of the equation for him. Long may URA be read! Longer still may he be heeded!

HINDUTVA AND WOMEN

Sadhvi Niranjan Jyoti was appointed Minister of State for Food Processing Industries in November 2014. She took little time to grab national headlines. It had nothing to do with her ministry. Within a week of becoming a minister, Jyoti, the BJP lawmaker from Fatehpur in Uttar Pradesh shocked the nation with her comments at an election rally in Delhi. At Dwarka, a middle-class colony, she allegedly told the masses that they had to choose between *Ramzaade* and *Haraamzade*, the sons of Ram and illegitimate sons, respectively. It resulted in a logjam in Parliament with the Opposition parties asking for her resignation. Jyoti soon apologized from 'her heart'.

Sadhvi Savitri Phule, a BJP MP from Bahraich in Uttar Pradesh, is touted as the new Dalit face of the party in Uttar Pradesh. She too addressed *jan sabhas* in Delhi before the elections to Delhi Assembly in 2015. Unlike Jyoti, she refrained from courting controversy, preferring to arouse Dalits' conscience; the idea being to bring them under the larger Hindu umbrella. Phule has eight criminal cases and claims to have been a child bride who walked out of her in-laws' house some 20 years ago and joined Jan Sewa Ashram in Bahraich. Following successive victories in *zila* panchayat elections, she rose to be an MLA from Balta (reserved) constituency in Uttar Pradesh before becoming an MP during the Modi wave in 2014.

These women, regarded as emerging voices of Hindutva, constitute what is often dubbed as the anonymous fringe element of the ruling dispensation. 'Enough of sakshis, sadhus and sadhvis' has been an oft-heard lament in secular circles. The complaint would not have been needed had the RSS founder, K.S. Hedgewar, had his way. Back in 1925, when RSS was launched, it was an all-male world—celibacy was a virtue, women, quite obviously superfluous beyond their role as mothers or sisters. Indeed, even when V.D. Savarkar sought to unite the Hindu society beyond the divides of caste, even seeking to bring in those beyond the direct umbrella of Hinduism into the fold, he only addressed men directly, harping on purity of the Aryan blood. In the initials years of the RSS, Hedgewar had even refused to consider a women's wing of the organization. Some 11 years after the RSS was founded, Rashtra Sevika Samiti was established following the constant urging of Lakshmibai Kelkar. It, however, continued to be a token body, more like a little gesture to appease some vocal women. Tanika Sarkar in her essay, 'The Gender Predicament' which is part of an anthology *The Concerned Indian's Guide to Communalism*, writes,

The Rashtrasevika Samiti was founded in 1936 with daily shakhas that provided physical, martial arts as well as ideological or *boudhik* training. It remained, however, a small and low-keyed affair. Though the second oldest women's organisation affiliated to a political body, it was overtaken and completely overshadowed by nationalist and Left women's movements. It participated in no mass struggles—anti-colonial or for women's rights—and it was not foregrounded by the RSS in any of its own activities. The second *sarsanghchalak* and supreme ideological guru of the RSS, M.S. Golwalkar, saw no reason to specify a distinctive role for it within the Sangh complex. His strictures to the women of Sangh families taught them how to run their homes and to bring up their children on the correct Sangh values. The Samiti was not required to play a significant part in RSS self-fashioning.

So, today when Mohan Bhagwat addresses Hindu women in the same vein, one knows where it is coming from. It should not have shocked anybody when he emphasized the domestic role of women. Bhagwat said at a rally in Indore a little more than a year before the Modi government was sworn in,

> A husband and wife are involved in a contract under which the husband has said that you should take care of my house and I will take care of all your needs. I will keep you safe. So, the husband follows the contract terms. Till the time, the wife follows the contract, the husband stays with her, if the wife violates the contract, he can disown her.

Interestingly, the RSS turned a blind eye to Golwalkar's vision for women during the time of the Babri Masjid–Ram Janmabhoomi agitation. That was a rare occasion when women occupied special place in the scheme of things of the RSS. As Sarkar writes,

> Around 1989–90, in a sudden and dramatic spurt of activities, the Sangh parivar threw up a large number of women's organisations and women leaders into dazzling prominence—the BJP Mahila Morcha, the VHP Matri Mandal and Durga Vahini with their different regional versions. Thousands of *kar sevikas* participated in the attacks on the Babri Masjid and in its demolition and their role was highlighted in the Sangh media products—the Jain Studio video films, the VHP fortnightly magazine Hindu Chetna, Hindi video newsmagazines like Kalachakra. On 6 January 1993, a month after the demolition of the Babri

Masjid, a women's celebratory demonstration was held at Ayodhya where Sadhvi Rithambhara was a guest of honour. Women were active and prominent in the bloody riots that swept across India in the course of the Ram Janmabhoomi movement ... the role of Rithambhara's audiocassetted speech and Uma Bharati's propaganda tours in stoking ferocious anger and aggression against Muslims was memorable.... I observed at that time that the Samiti had come a long way from the parameters laid down by Golwalkar about pure domesticity. The women of the Sangh come from conservative, domestic urban, middle-class and upper-caste backgrounds... Although the primary focus remained on women within the home, for a new generation of more active women, it could impart self-confidence and competences. (Sarkar 1999)

Not surprisingly, these women encountered opposition. Some old-timers within the Sangh had reservations and warned against their disruptive influence. Once the heady days of the Ayodhya agitation were over, the Samiti, which had enthusiastically used the eight-armed icon of Durga carrying weapons, confined itself to its routine meetings, bringing out *Jagriti*, a monthly magazine that provided orientation course of sorts for wives of RSS men who had come from non-RSS families. Over a period of time, these activities waned; times of peace did not seem to present the same challenge to them. 'Muslims as the enemy' replaced by marked westernization, the latter not having the same ring to it. The twice-daily meetings were replaced by twice-a-week meetings. The monthly journal, *Jagriti*, was replaced by annual sheet called *Sevika*. However, the body has not so much as faded away, as assumed new responsibility. Today, it acts as a feeder of stories 'about Muslim and Christian "atrocities" among Hindu women'.

This depiction of the allegedly helpless Hindu women at the hands of Muslims out to increase their numbers by marrying Hindu women is a far cry from the days of Ayodhya agitation when the favourite slogan of Samiti members was *'Hum Bharati ki nari hain, hum phool nahin chingari hain'*.

It is this feed that fuels the Love Jihad trail. It is also the more passive role of the Samiti during peaceful times that leads Bhagwat to emphasize their domestic respon-sibilities. And pray how do the Sadhvis such as Niranjan and Savitiri keep busy? Well, there is always that issue of lineage, the former's *Ramzaada* versus *Haraamzaada* was only an uglier manifestation of what has been cloaked in the Sangh history—those whose *pitrabhoomi* and *punyabhoomi* being one and the same, and those whose *punyabhoomi* lies beyond the *pitrabhoomi*.

HINDUTVA AND DALITS

To mark the first Gandhi Jayanti since he took over as the Prime Minister, Narendra Modi launched the Swachh Bharat Abhiyan. The campaign, covering 4,041 cities and towns, is aimed at getting rid of open defecation by 2 October 2019 which will mark the 150th birth anniversary of the Father of the Nation. Under the campaign, around 12 million toilets are to be constructed. As soon as Modi launched the campaign by picking up a broom to sweep away a few autumn leaves, the media was agog with his photographs. The pictures spoke a thousand words. On the face of it, they were all for Clean India. If you went a bit deeper though, it seemed a statement against the well-entrenched caste system, a system under which a Dalit ends up doing the cleaning up operation for the larger society. With the Prime Minister of the country picking up the broom, there could not have been a more powerful statement against age-old injustice; a system under which a man is denied the right to explore his potential, prove his worth and merely follow what his ancestors had been doing. To the impressionable, it appeared that the proponents of Hindutva had turned a new leaf—Dalits' caste origin was no longer their primary identity or hereditary vocation their only mode of earning a livelihood.

Yet the more pictures circulated, the more the irony of it all struck me. Modi with a broom seemed at odds with Modi the author. As the Prime Minister, he had come up with a rare, if symbolic, statement against the caste system. Cleanliness was the responsibility of each one of us, he seemed to cry from newspapers, magazines and billboards. But as the author, he had said quite the opposite. Much before he became the Prime Minister, Modi had penned a 101-page book, *Karmayogi*, in 2007 where he defended the vocation and questioned the claims of those who felt the Dalits worked as scavengers due to the absence of other avenues for earning a livelihood. He even hinted at a spiritual purpose behind it all. The book, a collection of his lectures, is no longer in circulation. However, when the book first hit the headlines, it was greeted with protests by Dalits in Tamil Nadu and Maharashtra, with many wondering how could the Chief Minister of a state—Modi was the Chief Minister of Gujarat then—virtually legitimize the discriminatory caste system? Although 5,000 copies of the book were withdrawn, Modi's defence of the vocation continued. Even in 2009, he sought to draw a parallel between the work of a priest and that of a scavenger, arguing that the priest cleans the temple before a pooja. And a Dalit cleaned the city like a temple. The hint at spiritual association with the vocation was unmistakable. Although the book is no longer available, an extract from *Karmayogi* has been reproduced in *Ambedkar and Hindutva Politics* by Ram Puniyani, former professor at IIT, Mumbai, who took voluntary retirement to work for communal harmony. The extract reads,

> I do not believe that they (Valmikis) have been doing this job just to sustain their livelihood. Had this been so, they would not have continued with this type of job, generation after generation.... At some point of time, somebody must have got the enlightenment that it is their (Valmikis) duty to work for the happiness of the entire society and the Gods, that they have to do this job bestowed upon them by Gods, and this job of cleaning up should continue as an internal spiritual activity for centuries. This should have continued generation after generation. It is impossible to believe that their ancestors did not have the choice of adopting any other work or business.

Indeed, Modi's words stemmed from his understanding of the scriptures. The Narayana Samhita says that Dalits have to clean human excreta, clear dead bodies, remove carcasses. And a Dalit who does this is only doing his dharma, his duty. The famous ideologue of the RSS, Deendayal Upadhyay, too upheld the caste system when he talked of integrated humanism. He wrote, 'In our concept of four castes, they are analogous to the different limbs of Virat Purusha, the primeval man whose sacrifice, according to the Rig Veda, gave birth to society in the form of the *varna vyavastha*'. Yet in a country where the Constitution has abolished untouchability and granted equal rights to all Indians without discrimination on the basis of caste or religion, Modi's words were not exactly palatable. And as the talk about Swachh Bharat Abhiyan gained ground, it left me wondering how could a man who defended manual scavenging pilot a programme to the contrary? More so, as the Abhiyan aims to construct 12 crore dry latrines by 2019. Who will clean these dry latrines? Who will clean the septic tanks? Will the government find new workers to do the needful or will it trust those who have been doing it for centuries without ever getting a chance to do anything else; those whose spiritual lot it was, as once argued?

Manual scavenging is a reality in rural parts of the country, particularly states such as Uttar Pradesh, Bihar, Rajasthan and parts of Karnataka and Andhra Pradesh. It involves removing by hand human excrement from dry latrines and carrying the same in wicker baskets to a disposal site. According to the statistics quoted by Safai Karamchari Andolan headed by Magsaysay Award winner Bezwada Wilson, there are around 180,000 Dalit households in the country who clean the 790,000 public and private dry latrines across India. Most manual scavengers are women and paid a pittance. Over the past three decades, many of them burnt their wicker baskets without alternative sources of income, thus proving wrong Modi's assertion that it is impossible to believe that they had no other avenues for income and did the job for spiritual elevation. Pertinently, many Dalits converted to Christianity and Islam to avoid the caste inequities. Most of them continued with the vocation in the initial days after conversion. However, in the absence of a sermon from a church or mosque in justification of the abominable practice, they succeeded in picking up other jobs and find acceptance in the larger society. It was not the same with the Dalits who did not step out of the *varna* (caste) system.

Manual scavenging is an organized disorganized industry. After 1993, when the Employment of Manual Scavengers and Construction of Dry Latrines (Prohibition) Act was passed, not a single person has been punished across the country. Yet the practice continues in defiance of the Constitution.

Finally, though a ray of hope is there. It comes not from the Swachh Bharat Abhiyan or Prime Minister wielding the broom, but from the oppressed Dalits of Gujarat. Following the Una lynching incident in which seven members of a Dalit family were stripped to the waist, tied to a car and flogged in public after being accused of skinning a dead cow, the Dalits refused to carry the cow carcasses for a few days, arguing that if the cow was a mother to upper caste Hindus when alive, it should not be the Dalits' responsibility to clear the body once the Gau Mata died. As the community marched hand in hand for kilometres, the Dalits found their voice. And silenced that of Hindutva forces bent on perpetuating the centuries-old caste hierarchy.

Meanwhile, the Prime Minister kept quiet, failing to criticize those who assaulted the Dalits. Was it the man who had piloted the Swachh Bharat Abhiyan who was staying silent? Or was it the Gujarat leader who had penned *Karmayogi* around a decade earlier? Either way, it became clear that Hindutva reiterated caste hierarchy. If in 1925, it was caste driven, it was the same in 1992 and in 2007, as also in 2017.

REDISCOVERING NATIONAL ICONS

INTEGRATING SARDAR PATEL

Muslim share of population up 0.8%, Hindus' down 0.7% between 2001 and 2011

The Muslim population in India grew by 24.6% between 2001 and 2011 while the decadal population growth for Hindus stood at 16.8% during the same period. Though Muslims' all-India decadal growth is less than the 29.3% recorded between 1991 and 2001, their state-wise decadal growth rate was higher than that of Hindus in all 35 states and Union Territories in 2001–11.

The Times of India (TOI), 27 August 2015

Muslim population growth slows

India's Muslim population is growing slower than it had in the previous decades, and its growth rate has slowed more sharply than that of the Hindu population, new Census data show.

The decadal Muslim rate of growth is the lowest it has ever been in India's history, as it is for all religions.

The numbers show that the sex ratio among Muslims, already better than among Hindus, has further improved.

The Hindu, 27 August 2015

WAS THE *TOI* HEADLINE an attempt at stoking up old fears among the Hindus? Was it an attempt to tell the majority community that the largest minority, albeit by a huge margin, is likely to catch up with it shortly? That Hindus, sometime in the foreseeable future, would be reduced to a minority in India? With no definite answer available, it sent my mind racing back to the late 1980s and 1990s. Those were the days when the Babri Masjid–Ram Janmabhoomi agitation was at its peak. And anything L.K. Advani touched brought an electoral harvest for the BJP. While Muslims were almost on a daily basis reminded of their only two possible destinations with a slogan *'Musalman ke do hi sthaan, Pakistan ya qabrastan'*, Hindus were exhorted to give away their sons for the cause of the birthplace of Ram, *'Bachha bachha Ram ka, Ram Janmabhoomi ke kaam ka'*. Groups of volunteers of Rashtriya Swayamsevak Sangh (RSS) toured across the northern and central states of Uttar Pradesh, Rajasthan, Madhya Pradesh and Bihar, etc., exhorting people to come to the *shakhas*, join hands for a grand Ram temple in Ayodhya. Such was the cry for the Ram temple that for a few years Ram seemed to overshadow other 33 crore deities. And even the customary greeting 'namaskar' was replaced in public with 'Jai Sri Ram'. I happened to attend such a meeting in Noida. Little more than a callow youth then, I was horrified at the mix of lies and poison used to indoctrinate young, impressionable minds by speaker after speaker. A speaker told the audience, *'Ek musalman ki char-char patniyan hain. Ek saal mein char-char bachhe karte hain'* (A Muslim has four wives and gives birth to four kids in a year). But the rate of polygamy among the Muslims is lower, I wanted to counter, but kept my counsel—by the way, now I know from where did the Union Minister Giriraj Singh draw his inspiration for his alleged comments on controlling the Muslim population in Bihar. Soon, another speaker took over. After claiming that Mahatma Gandhi was a coward who gave to Muslims what they wanted (read Pakistan), he screamed, *'Hindu kayar hai, musalman gunda hai. Talwar uthhao. Raksha karo maa–behnon ki'* (The Hindu is a coward. The Muslim is a scoundrel. Pick up your sword. Defend your mother–sisters).

A little more than a decade later, Narendra Modi, then the Chief Minister of Gujarat, used similar language in election campaign in September 2002. Alleging that refugee camps were baby-producing factories, he mocked, *'Hum panch, hamare pachhees'* (We five, ours twenty-five). It was a shrewd allusion to the alleged four wives which a Muslim man had and then the burgeoning numbers. The speech attracted the attention of the National Commission for Minorities (NCM) besides widespread flak. But the damage was done. Modi had reinforced the age-old stereotype that Indian Muslims are prolific, and soon would overtake Hindus. The *TOI* headline was more of the same. Interestingly on the same day, using the same Census figures, *The Hindu* sought to put things in perspective. The headline, 'Muslim population growth slows' said it all.

Be that as it may, it did set me thinking, why an Indian Hindu should feel insecure, why should any politician try to play with words and figures to generate fear among the majority community. Considering approximately four out of five Indians are Hindus, the fears seem unfounded. But then such attempts to capitalize on the innate insecurity of the common man are neither new nor aberrations. It was the same in the early years after Independence when the RSS hawks tried to sell the lie for the first time. So much so that the Home Minister, Sardar Vallabhbhai Patel, had to step in to quell such fears. Patel, who is now sought to be appropriated by votaries of Hindutva, warned those who raised the cry of Hinduism being in danger, 'I warn you all against any such false cry being raised. We have paid enough for such things in this land. Do not do anything of the kind any more. Let us—Hindus, Christians, Parsees, Jews and Muslims—who are here, live in peace and harmony and let us try to be happy. Let us conserve what is good in society and let us build for future well being of society'. The words were quite becoming of the man who sheltered Muslims in the Red Fort when Partition violence threatened to go out of control, the man who visited Nizamuddin Auliya's Dargah.

Patel was at his wits end when confronted with statements about Hinduism being in danger in India. He said,

> The other thing which has pained me considerably in this Union is that for the first time now I hear the cry on this side that Hinduism is in danger. Where is it in danger? Are the Hindus being coerced, are they being terrorised and oppressed? Is there any obstruction for them in following their own religion? Why create imaginary picture of fright? Is it in order to create splits, groups or capture vote? Can you capture power by that method? (Chopra 2015)

Patel also saw the dangers of parties being formed on religious lines.

> It is equally dangerous to form a party or to lay down a programme on a religious basis. The days of religious bigotry are gone in this world. It would not pay. Now that the country has got freedom for anybody to say that any religion is in danger is a very dangerous precedent to set up.... People who say that Hinduism is in danger do not realise that Hinduism is in danger because Hindus have not followed Hinduism. They take wrong means. (Chopra 2015)

He saw the danger within, not without. The biggest challenge to Hinduism, according to Patel, whose 182-metre tall statue is being built near Vadodara in Gujarat, came not from the alleged growth of Muslims but untouchability within the Hindu fold. He wrote, 'because of that crores of Hindus have left their religion and have embraced other religions'.

Ironically, the people behind Patel's Statue of Unity, to be the tallest in the world on completion, are the ones who have forgotten Patel's lessons in pluralism, his warning against creating an atmosphere of fear and distrust. No wonder, we have the Hindutva hawks telling us every other day that Hinduism is in danger, that Hindus are going to be outnumbered by Muslims. Those ready to buy the Sangh lies about Hindus and Muslims would do well to remember what Patel had said after the assassination of Mahatma Gandhi. 'The objectionable and harmful activities of the Sangh (RSS) have, however, continued unabated and the cult of violence sponsored and inspired by the activities of the Sangh has claimed many victims. The latest and the most precious to fall was Gandhiji himself', lamented Patel. The RSS was then banned.

Today, the same RSS and its various affiliates seek to appropriate Sardar Patel. Like in all other things, the appropriation too is selective. No fond embrace, just a convenient pick and choose policy to fill in the gap in its own narrative. Remember the contrast between what Modi did after the Gujarat violence. And what Patel did after the Partition violence. Their respective responses say it all.

APPROPRIATING BHAGAT SINGH

Some poor, really poor, students are attempting to reinvent history. The Hindutva brigade, now acutely aware of the total absence of its ideological guru, RSS, from the freedom struggle, is on a mission to borrow, acquiesce, accommodate. And ultimately present a national hero as one of its own. The effort started in the second decade of the new millennium when Sardar Patel, whose aversion to all things RSS, is well documented, was sought to be accommodated by the BJP in the run-up to 2014 General Elections with Narendra Modi talking of building a colossal statue of the first Home Minister in Gujarat. What was sought to be swept under the carpet is the fact that Patel questioned the nationalistic credentials of the RSS and, as the Home Minister, had even banned the organization.

A similar effort was made to 'accommodate' Bhagat Singh when the Vajpayee government was in power. Attempts were made then by right-wing outfits to project Bhagat Singh in saffron hues, highlighting his Arya Samaji roots. The Vajpayee government was voted out of power in 2004 and Bhagat Singh as a Hindutva hero was put in cold storage, only to be revived in 2014 when it became clear that the next government at the Centre would be formed by the BJP. Suddenly, posters were put up in crowded streets of Old Delhi, near Delhi University and Jamia Millia Islamia—they left JNU then—that called him *desh bhakt, rashtra bhakt*, even *virat purush*. The terms were suspiciously close to those used by right-wing activists for their political heroes. Then came attempts via newspapers, news channels, radio and, in early 2015, through WhatsApp, to 'remind the nation' that 'we' had 'forgotten the sacrifice of Bhagat Singh, Sukhdev and Rajguru' even as we celebrate Valentine's Day! Excuse me, Valentine's Day and Bhagat Singh? Yes, that was the canard first used in 2014, and subsequently repeated each February. The Hindutva proponents' hostility to the con-cept of the Valentine's Day is well known. So, in a sharp move, the sacrifice of Bhagat Singh, Sukhdev and Rajguru was 'shifted' from 23 March to 14 February! Neat sleight? Not quite. For we all have read in history books that the three of them were hanged by the British Government in 1931 on 23 March, not Valentine's Day. This association of Bhagat Singh with Valentine's Day is an innovation not supported by history. Oh! Didn't we say these guys are poor, really poor students of history?

For those who came in late, noted historian Bipan Chandra (2015) wrote more than 30 years ago,

> Bhagat Singh was not only one of India's greatest free-dom fighters and revolutionary socialists, but also one of its early Marxist thinkers and ideologues. Unfortunately, this last aspect is relatively unknown with the result that all sorts of reactionaries, obscurantists and com-munalists have been wrongly and dishonestly trying to utilize for their own politics and ideologies, the name and fame of Bhagat Singh and his comrades such as Chander Shekhar Azad.

Bhagat Singh himself wrote in *Why I Am an Atheist,*

> My atheism is not of so recent origin. I had stopped
> believing in God when I was an obscure young man.... I
> was rather a boy with a very shy nature, who had certain
> pessimistic dispositions about the future career and in
> those days I was not a perfect atheist. My grandfather
> under whose influence I was brought up is an orthodox
> Arya Samajist. An Arya Samajist is anything but an athe-
> ist.... Later on I began to live with my father. He is a liberal
> in as much as the orthodoxy of religions is concerned. It
> was through his teachings that I aspired to devote my life
> to the cause of freedom. In the Non-Cooperation days, I
> joined the National College. It was there that I began to
> think liberally and discuss and criticise all the religious
> problems, even about God ...

Thus began the transformation of Bhagat Singh. Later,
when waiting for the noose to be tightened around his
neck, he wrote,

> In God man can find very strong consolation and support
> ... I know the moment the rope is fitted round my neck
> and rafters removed, from under my feet. That will be
> the final moment. That will be the last moment. I, or to be
> more precise, my soul, as interpreted in the metaphysical
> terminology, shall be finished there. Nothing further ...
> God was brought into imaginary existence to encourage
> man to face boldly all the trying circumstance, to meet all
> dangers manfully and to check and restrain his outbursts
> in prosperity and affluence.

Talking of Bhagat Singh's execution, there is a school of
thought which believes that Bhagat Singh's execution
and indeed that of Sukhdev and Rajguru could have been
averted. Noted scholar Chaman Lal pointed out in an interview with *The Hindu,*

There was tremendous pressure on Mahatma Gandhi to make clemency for three revolutionaries a condition in Gandhi-Irwin talks. Nehru-Subhas and more were pressing for it inside Congress party, but Mahatma Gandhi while pleading for leniency to Viceroy Irwin in this matter, was not inclined to make it a condition. On the other hand, Bhagat Singh himself was insistent to get executed to awaken Indian masses from slumber! Mahatma Gandhi failed to stand on his own principle of being against capital punishment in this case, as he did not assert his opposition to three executions on his principled stand. He did suggest Irwin for leniency, nothing more. (Salam 2016)

Incidentally, in 1909, Gandhi had voiced disapproval of the act of Madan Lal Dhingra, a revolutionary who had killed William Curzon. He was a follower of Savarkar. And Gandhi is reported to have said, 'My Dhingra's defence (by Indian revolutionaries) was inadmissible. He was egged on to do this act by ill-digested reading of worthless writings. It is those who incited him to do this that deserve to be punished'.

Mahatma's failure apart, even Bhagat Singh's execution proves he was as far apart from the right wing which stands for 33 crore gods and goddesses as any man could get. And pretty close to what young Karl Marx wrote in 1844,

Religion is the general theory of that world, its encyclopaedic compendium, its logic in a popular form, its spiritualistic point d'honneur, its enthusiasm.... Religious distress is at the same the expression of real distress and also the protest against real distress. Religion is the sigh of the oppressed creature, the heart of a heartless world.

Incidentally, Bhagat Singh's own writings were replete with quotations from Marxist classics. His involved study of Marx, Engels, Lenin and Trotsky, etc., showed his ideological preference and development. His court statements, writings such as '*Letter to Young Political Workers*' (Singh 2007), reading Lenin minutes before leaving for gallows, his explanation of the meaning of '*Inquilab*' in court, all clearly indicated his ideological position. In fact, newspaper reports of 1929–31 identify him as 'Red' as earlier Marx was referred in his contemporary newspapers!

This should keep Bhagat Singh safe from 'usurpation' by believers. If not, here is a reminder of what M.S. Golwalkar (1966), the revered ideologue of the RSS, wrote in *Bunch of Thoughts* when he decided to express himself on the sacrifice of Bhagat Singh, Sukhdev and Rajguru:

> There is no doubt that such men who embrace martyrdom are great heroes and their philosophy too is pre-eminently manly. They are far above the average men who meekly submit to fate and remain in fear and inaction. All the same, such persons are not held up as ideals in our society. We have not looked upon their martyrdom as the highest point of greatness to which men should aspire. For, after all, they failed in achieving their ideal, and failure implies some fatal flaw in them.

This from a man who shared ideological affinity with V.D. Savarkar, who filed repeated mercy petitions to the British, even promising to work for the perpetuation of the British Empire! Then there was K.B. Hedgewar, Sarsanghchalak of the RSS from 1925 to 1940, who claimed, 'Patriotism is not only going to prison. It is not correct to be carried away by such superficial patriotism'.

Such poor students of history! Such innovation. Such a travesty!

CO-OPTING DR AMBEDKAR

In March 2016, Prime Minister Narendra Modi laid the foundation stone for the Dr Ambedkar National Memorial, to be built at 26, Alipur Road in Delhi. It is said to be the place of Mahaparinirvan of Dr Ambedkar. Drawing a parallel with Martin Luther King, Modi wondered why it had taken the nation 60 years for a memorial to be dedicated to the architect of our Constitution, saying 'Perhaps this was written in my fate. Perhaps I had blessings of Baba Saheb on me'. In the second half of 2015, he had inaugurated Dr Ambedkar Memorial in London at the place where Dr Ambedkar had stayed for two years. In fact, in 2015, the government made concerted attempt at appropriating the glory of Dr Ambedkar, all the time belittling Nehru. The Directorate of Advertising and Visual Publicity gave 156 full-page colour insertions in newspapers across the country to observe his 125th anniversary. Also, on 6 December 2015, the Ministry of Social Justice and Empowerment issued a full-page colour advertisement to mark the 60th Mahaparinirvan Diwas of Dr Ambedkar.

On the face of it, the two inaugurations and a glut of media advertisements seem a belated attempt at righting a historical wrong—remember how in 1949, the RSS burnt effigies of Dr Ambedkar when the Hindu Code Bill was taking shape and Dr Ambedkar was keen to get it passed as soon as possible. It is, however, no belated realization of truth or even Dr Ambedkar's worth. It is a natural progression from around a decade ago when the RSS sought to see in Dr Ambedkar a Hindu icon, drawing parallels between Dr Hedgewar and Dr Ambedkar, arguing that the two doctors knew the pulse of the nation. Today, if you look closely, you will find this is, at the very least, an attempt to smother with affection.

It reminds faintly of the early attempts by Hindutva icons such as Dr Hedgewar and Guru Golwalkar to draw an umbrella of religions which originated here (Hinduism, Buddhism, Jainism and Sikhism) leaving the rest (Islam, Christianity and Judaism) as the 'other'. Some would argue that this appropriation of Dr Ambedkar is nothing but a wilful muzzling of a critical voice, a voice that fought against the inequities of the caste system, a man who famously said, 'I am born a Hindu. I will not die as one'. He lived up to his word.

Yet today the youngsters are sought to be indoctrinated by the Hindutva brigade that all Dr Ambedkar wanted was reform within the Hindu society! It is akin to saying that the man who brought with him a spell of fresh rain seeking to clean every nook and corner of the society essentially engineered nothing more than a storm in a teacup. How disrespectful to the memory of Dr Ambedkar! What a travesty! And to think he was the man responsible for including safeguards in the Constitution for the minorities, reservation for Scheduled Castes and Scheduled Tribes, etc., Much before the RSS started the campaign to accommodate Dr Ambedkar, post 1990, when V.P. Singh unleashed a social storm by accepting the recommendations of the Mandal Commission, he had written, 'I am disgusted with Hindus and Hinduism because I am convinced they cherish wrong ideals and live a wrong social life'. At a time when a debate around conversions is raging, it is important to remember what Dr Ambedkar said about the phenomenon. He saw conversion as important for Dalit society as self-government for India.

For a true understanding of what Dr Ambedkar stood for, and how far away was he from the right-wing forces, one only need to read his book, *Pakistan or The Partition of India*. While he takes on communal elements among Hindus and Muslims with equal disdain, it is his words on Hindutva that, in retrospect, appear to be a warning for the nation; more so when we hear calls about India being a Hindu Rashtra every other day. Dr Ambedkar wrote,

> If Hindu Raj does become a fact, it will, no doubt, be the greatest calamity for this country. No matter what the Hindus say. Hinduism is a menace to liberty, equality and fraternity. On that account it is incompatible with democracy. Hindu Raj must be prevented at any cost. (Ambedkar 1975)

According to him, the pet slogan of Hindutva, 'Hindustan for Hindus' was more than just arrogant. He later took to task V.D. Savarkar for advocating the cause of Hindu Rashtra, calling the Muslims as the 'other', yet denying them the right to their own separate nation.

Dr Ambedkar believed that Hindutva only helped reaffirm the power structure within Hinduism, enriching the rich, denying the poor. It also excluded the 'other' from a share of the resources.

> They have a trait of character which often leads the Hindus to disaster. This trait is formed by their acquisitive instinct and aversion to share with others the good things of life. They have a monopoly of education and wealth, and with wealth and education they have captured the State. To keep this monopoly to themselves has been the ambition and goal of their life. Charged with this selfish idea of class domination, they take every move to exclude the lower

classes of Hindus from wealth, education and power.... This attitude of keeping education, wealth and power as a close preserve for themselves and refusing to share it, which the high caste Hindus have developed in their relation with the lower classes of Hindus, is sought to be extended by them to the Muslims. They want to exclude the Muslims from place and power, as they have done to the lower class Hindus.

Little wonder, the Hindutva brigade, so bereft of icons in freedom struggle, is keen to appropriate Dr Ambedkar as one of its own, somebody who denounced M.A. Jinnah. What is easily forgotten is the parallel he drew between Jinnah and Savarkar. He saw little difference between Jinnah and Savarkar, even criticized Savarkar when he opposed Jinnah.

> Mr Savarkar's attitude is illogical, if not queer. Mr. Savarkar admits that the Muslims are a separate nation. He concedes that they have a right to cultural autonomy. He allows them to have a national flag. Yet he opposes the demand of the Muslim nation for a separate national home. If he claims a national home for the Hindu nation, how can he refuse the claim of the Muslim nation for a national home? ... Mr. Savarkar will not allow the Muslim nation to be co-equal in authority with the Hindu nation. He wants the Hindu nation to be dominant nation and the Muslim nation to be the subservient one. (Ambedkar 1975)

Also sought to be consigned to dustbin of forgotten history are the Ambedkar effigies the organization burnt on the issue of the Hindu Code Bill. The same RSS today seeks to absorb him within the pantheon of Hindu social reformers. In reality, he was far from it. Dr Ambedkar was quite critical of the religion which had a clear hierarchy, a segmentation which the upper castes were only too keen to perpetuate. He wrote,

> Hinduism and social union are incompatible. By its very genius Hinduism believes in social separation which is another name for social disunity and even creates social separation. If Hindus wish to be one, they will have to discard Hinduism. They cannot be one without violating Hinduism. Hinduism is the greatest obstacle to Hindu Unity. Hinduism cannot create that longing to belong which is the basis of all social unity. On the contrary Hinduism creates an eagerness to separate. (Ambedkar 1975)

Incidentally, in telling developments between the two inaugurations by the Prime Minister, a Dalit old man was charred to death in Hamirpur for seeking to visit a temple where Dalits were barred from entry, and a 28-year-old 'child', as the HRD Minister Smriti Irani referred to Rohith Vemula, committed suicide in Hyderabad Central University. After both tragedies, Dalit organizations along with various minority bodies organized protests at Jantar Mantar in New Delhi to make themselves heard.

It all left me wondering who is following Dr Ambedkar, who is merely appropriating. Yes, as a title of a booklet on the subject says it, 'Ambedkar can neither be adopted nor appropriated'.

PANDIT DEENDAYAL UPADHYAY: NOT QUITE AN ICON

For long years, Pandit Deendayal Upadhyay had slipped from pubic memory. Barring the die-hard RSS workers, he mattered little to an average Indian. Boys and girls born after 1980 had heard of him only in passing. Although a contemporary of former Prime Minister Atal Bihari

Vajpayee, he had somehow slipped under the radar, partly because he did not live as long—he passed away in 1968 in a mysterious train accident. All this was sought to be changed with a single stroke when the Prime Minister Narendra Modi mentioned him and Mahatma Gandhi in the same sentence in one of his public addresses in Kerala. This seemingly gentle, even innocuous, comparison was a breakthrough moment. At one go, he was being considered at par with the Mahatma. And the BJP, desperate to have a national icon to call its own, raised Upadhyay in public imagination as a philosopher, activist, economist and a spiritual guru rolled into one to mark year-long centenary celebrations—he was born on 25 September 1916 in Mathura.

Just one mention, and people scurried to read up about the theoretician of the Sangh, the man who guided the earlier avatar of the BJP, the Jana Sangh, the man who talked of political enfeeblement for Muslims as a necessary route to their gradual assimilation into the fold of Bharat Mata. The BJP got down to implementation of his advice on political marginalization in earnest post 2014. First tickets to Muslim candidates were cut down, then, in a state such as Uttar Pradesh, no Muslim contested as a BJP candidate in the 2016 Vidhan Sabha elections. By early 2017, out of BJP's 1,386 MLAs across the country, only four were Muslims.

Upadhyay was one of the early practitioners of the deeply divisive 'we' and 'they' philosophy, a man who never quite accepted our Constitution, a man who was ready to tolerate the minorities only if they ceased to be one, that is, adopt the Hindu way of life, distinguished only by a private mode of worship, if at all. He stood for Akhand Bharat not as a geographically cohesive unit with different streams of religion and culture, but one Hindu monolith, which was tolerant of very little that was different, accepting of hardly any. It was, to use a contemporary expression, 'my way or the highway' ideology, a one-size-fits-all principle.

Incidentally, so distrustful of Muslims was Upadhyay that he proposed a 10-mile corridor on the Indo-Pak border where the community was not to be allowed to settle. Within the Hindu fold, he was a votary of the caste system as an essential tool for social cohesion. Views that fit in nicely with our Constitution? Far from it. Little wonder, he wrote, 'Our Constitution should be unitary instead of federal. Bharat culture, like Bharat varsha is one and indivisible'.

For the non-RSS society, Upadhyay was no longer on the outer. Rather his ideology was being followed by the Prime Minister as became clear when Modi invoked Upadhyay while addressing the BJP's National Council in Kerala in September 2016. Modi reminded the party that it should not treat Muslims as different people. 'Do not treat them as vote banks', he said. Well, that is not something new. The BJP has been mouthing those lines for years. It is what he added after this sentence that got a section of the media excited, and more discerning listeners clearly perturbed. 'Do not regard them to be an object of hate', he reminded them, adding, 'Do not shun them (*tiraskrit mat karo*). Do not reward them (*puraskrit mat karo*) but purify them (*parishkar*), consider them your own'. That Modi mentioned Muslims by name for the first time since assuming the office of the Prime Minister in May 2014 seemed reason enough to gloat for gullible few.

Indeed, a section of the media went to town with head-lines such as 'Modi asks Muslims to be encouraged' and 'PM wants Muslims to be adapted'.

Some read in it the party's age-old cry against the alleged appeasement of Muslims, but a more careful look proved that Prime Minister was invoking the ideology of Pandit Deendayal Upadhyay, not merely quoting him. It brought back memories of Dayanand Saraswati's Shuddhi movement, which was about the 'purification' of Muslims, who were then welcomed into the Hindu fold. Or *ghar wapsi* (back to home), as some recent event managers have termed religious conversion exercises. Upadhyay, it may be recalled, stood for assimilation of Christians and Muslims in the national mainstream if they gave up their distinct characteristics and admitted to their Hindu ancestry. Upadhyay once elaborated on the subject, 'No sensible man will say that six crores of Muslims should be eradicated or thrown out of India, but then they will have to identify themselves completely with Indian life'. For him the word Indian was interchangeable with Hindu. The minorities were to be tolerated if they gave up their distinct way of life and agreed to live under the umbrella of Hinduism, as maybe just another sect like Mohammadiya sect or Jesuit sect. 'There exists only one culture here. There can be no separate cultures here for Muslims and Christians. Culture is not related to mode of worship or sect. It is related to the country. Kabir, Jayasi and Raskhan should serve as models for Muslims', he said. His words after that tell us that the template of those who doubt the patriotism of Muslims comes from him. 'Today, their centre of loyalty is outside Bharat. The Muslims must completely change their sentiment and view'.

On the one side, such a communal mindset made patriotism the unique monopoly of Hindus; on the other, it equated Muslims with Pakistan, something that was done at a popular level in the Hindi film *Gadar: Ek Prem Katha* (2001). In the film, directed by Anil Sharma, known for peddling pulp patriotism, the hero, a Sikh, is asked to pronounce the Kalima by the Muslim heroine's father. Upon doing so, he is asked to hail Pakistan. He does so too. Then he is asked to denounce India. And hell breaks loose in typical Hindi film style. Something at a more serious level was passed at the Jana Sangh resolution back in 1965.

> As long as Partition exists, there will be no peace between Bharat and Pakistan. It is because of our submission to *goondaism* of Pakistan and our policy of appeasement that the rift between the two has widened. Many Muslims of Bharat have emotional affinity for Pakistan. Twofold efforts shall have to be made to change the situation. Firstly, a policy of tit for tat should be adopted in our relations with Pakistan.... Secondly, there should never be any bargaining with Muslims of Bharat with a view to appeasing them. All their rights are protected in the non-communal State of Bharat. But, while not tolerating the pro-Pakistan tendencies of Muslims, every effort shall have to be made to change their outlook and make it Bhartiya. (Kelkar 2014)

And pray what did Modi say? He asked the party to make 'extra efforts to take everyone along, especially the poor and the downtrodden'. Quoting Upadhyay, he said, 'Deendayalji used to say that if equality has to be achieved, people at the higher level have to bend down and support those who have been exploited and neglected'.

Deendayal Upadhyay all over again. For better. More likely, for worse.

MADAN MOHAN MALAVIYA: EARLY HINDU NATIONALIST

In March 2015, Hindu Mahasabha completed a centenary, low key, almost quiet, but not insignificant. Without saying as much, the Government of India recognized the contribution of the Hindu extremist organization by conferring Bharat Ratna on one of its founders, Pandit Madan Mohan Malaviya. The award did not come as a surprise; his grandson, J. Girdhar Malaviya, was one of the proposers of Narendra Modi's candidature from Varanasi during 2014 General Elections. Probably Modi was merely reciprocating the gesture. More likely, it was a warm embrace of the Hindutva espoused by Malaviya, who, ironically, was the president of the Indian National Congress four times. Yet, he also happened to be the voice of Hindutva within and outside the party. A rare man who happened to be the president of the Hindu Mahasabha as well, Malaviya's life was but a bundle of seeming contradictions; he had learned Bhagavad Gita recital at home; in 1911, he gave up his practice as a lawyer to take to the life of a sanyasi, surviving on society's generosity. Yet, he did come out of renunciation, took part in the freedom struggle and even took up the case of the accused in the Chauri Chaura incident in 1922. He saved 156 people from being sent to the gallows. A little before that though, he had opposed Congress' participation in the Khilafat (Caliphate) movement. Then in the 1930s, he advocated Hindu–Muslim unity. In 1933, in his presidential address at INC's Calcutta session, he stated,

> I implore all Hindus and Mussalmans, Sikhs, Christians and Parsees and all other countrymen to sink all communal differences and to establish political unity among all

sections of people. In the midst of such darkness, I see a clear vision that the clouds which have been hanging over our heads are lifting. Let every son and daughter do his or her duty to expedite the advent of dawn of the day of freedom and happiness.

He did not live to see that day, having passed away in 1946.

This was a marked departure from what Malaviya had said as a recipe for a lasting unity between Hindus and Muslims as the president of Hindu Masabha in early 1920s. In another presidential address, he stated, 'If the Hindus made themselves strong and the rowdy section among the Mahomedans were convinced that they could not safely rob and dishonour Hindus, unity would be established on a stable basis'.

Yes, along with the likes of Lala Lajpat Rai, he was responsible for the upsurge in Hindu nationalism in 1920s. The man who did not want the Congress to take up the cause of Khilafat movement to bring in more Muslims to the freedom struggle, started in 1919 Prayaga Seva Samiti to serve the pilgrims at the Kumbh Mela.

He followed what historian Bipan Chandra refers as 'liberal communalism'. Motilal Nehru minced no words about his role. Pushed to the edge, he wrote to Jawaharlal Nehru on 2 December 1926,

It was simply beyond me to meet this kind of propaganda started against me under the auspices of the Malaviya– Lala gang (Lala Lajpat Rai). Publicly, I was denounced as anti-Hindu and pro-Mohammedan but privately almost every individual voter was told that I was a beef-eater in league with the Mohammedans to legalise cow slaughter in public places at all times.... Communal hatred and heavy bribing of the voters was the order of the day. I am thoroughly disgusted and am now seriously thinking of retiring from public life. What is worrying me is how to occupy my time. I am waiting for the Congress Session at Gauhati and keeping mum in the meanwhile. The Malaviya–Lala gang aided by Birla's money are making frantic efforts to capture the Congress. They will probably succeed as no counter effort is possible from our side.

They succeeded no doubt as there was infusion of the Hindu Right in the Congress over the next few years.

The establishment of the Banaras Hindu University (BHU) too was considered a platform for Malaviya to propagate his political ideas about Hindu society. Indeed, a careful perusal brings out only one note: he was a Hindu nationalist who often put the community's interest ahead of the nation. For him BHU was all about propagation of the Hindu identity.

An Italian scholar, Casolari (2002) observed,

The foundation of the BHU was the accomplishment of Malaviya's efforts to strengthen the Hindu sense of identity and cohesiveness. The BHU thus became the public platform from which Malaviya propagandised his political ideas. His was a two-pronged approach. As a prominent member of the Hindu Mahasabha, of which he was President in 1923, he could finally extend his programme of reorganising Hindu identity and society to the national level. Founding Hindu primary schools with Hindi as official language, and grass roots level Hindu organisations, as well as participation in the 'shuddhi' movement, were the main lines of Malaviya's political involvement. I do not agree with the interpretation according to which 'the Hindu Mahasabha was the daughter of the movement for the creation of the BHU'. I think it was just the opposite;

the BHU was the result of the increasing sense of militancy in the Hindu segment of Indian society. Ultimately, Malaviya's project of founding a Hindu University was part of a wider project for the promotion of Hindu education, and it also attracted many other organisations and supporters in other parts of northern India. He was part of a political milieu that considered Gandhian non-violence a form of cowardice and harmful to Hindu Society.

Gradually, the university became one of the centres for the construction of politicized Hindu identity. And Malaviya served as its Vice-Chancellor for 20 years, beginning 1919. This term coincided with the rise of the Mahasabha and the birth of the RSS. Malaviya helped in both. Although he was not an RSS *pracharak* (propagandist), he allowed the body to grow roots on the campus. He encouraged his students to take part in its drills. And gave ample space to the body on the BHU campus to attract the young; the RSS always concentrated on younger men, arguing that married men are too well set in their thought process, and too tied down with family responsibilities to take up the cause of the Hindu society. Incidentally, M.S. Golwalkar studied here and joined the RSS here in 1931.

For Malaviya, BHU was the crowning achievement in a career that covered the ripples and waves of the Hindu Right. It all started early. Sample this: In 1880s, he was associated with the activities of Prayag Hindu Samaj in Allahabad. The body was not above posturing and concentrated on highlighting the Hindu interest. It supported training Hindus to resist enemies. Malaviya was an important cog of this wheel as he relentlessly sought to promote Hindi as a national language, and creating more Hindu educational institutions. Prayag Hindu Samaj was only one of the many similar organizations Malaviya either founded or was a member of. In fact, he even edited journals on the same lines. In 1884, he became a member of the Hindi Uddharini Pratinidhi Sabha, and, three years later, in 1887, he founded Bharat Dharma Mahamandal. This was aimed at propagating Sanatan Dharma and Hindu culture. Hindu Samaj, Hindu University, Hindi Sabha. There was a lot more Hindu than Indian in the politics of Malaviya, a fact no doubt reinforced by the developments post-2014 elections. As Bipan Chandra had stated,

Hindu communalism did not lag behind. Its political trajectory was different. The two main liberal communal leaders during the 1920s were Lajpat Rai and Madan Mohan Malaviya. Lajpat Rai died in 1928 and Malaviya finding himself in 1937 in the sort of situation which Jinnah found himself in the same year, decided to retire from active politics, partly on grounds of health. But Hindu communalism would also not commit suicide; it too advanced to the extremist of the fascist phase. (Chandra et al. 1988)

Indeed, Malaviya did within the Congress what the likes of Savarkar, Hedgewar and Golwalkar did as full-fledged founders/members of the Mahasabha, the RSS, etc., He paved the way to modern day upsurge of Hindutva in independent India.

UNDERSTANDING RSS AND FRINGE ELEMENTS

RSS AND NATIONALISM

ON 19 FEBRUARY 2016, Assistant Sub Inspector Yunus Sheikh and his colleague K. Awaskar prevented around 25 youth belonging to the little known Shivaji Jayanti Mandal from hoisting a saffron flag at the Ambedkar Chowk, a communally sensitive point in the township in Latur, Maharashtra. The next day, a mob of around a hundred laid siege to the police *chowki*. Sheikh was coerced out of the premises. Forced to carry a saffron flag, he was made to march across the township, chanting 'Jai Bhawani' slogans. His colleague Awaskar was spared. There was not a voice from Nagpur or Jhandewalan in defence of Sheikh who was being punished by the mob for merely doing his job. Or was he? Well, in the Hindutva scheme of things, he had far exceeded his brief. As a Muslim, he could live and work solely at the pleasure of the Hindus. His job was not to uphold the Constitution that gave every Indian equal right but to protect the Hindu interests.

Something to that effect was said by M.S. Golwalkar, the ideological fountainhead of Hindutva forces. While referring to the Nazis of Germany he once wrote,

> It is worth bearing well in mind how these old Nations solve their minorities problem. They do not undertake to recognize any separate element in their polity. Emigrants have to get themselves naturally assimilated in the principal mass of the population, the National Race, by adopting its culture and language and sharing in its aspirations, by losing all consciousness of their separate existence.... If they do not do so, they live merely as outsiders, bound by codes and conventions of the Nation, at the sufferance of the Nation. (Golwalkar 2006)

So there it is. Sheikh and his ilk could hope to live in India only after being assimilated in totality, no separate faith, no language, no culture. If not, then they could live as outsiders, with no rights, only responsibilities. I was reminded of the words of former RSS chief K.S. Sudarshan, who aimed at de-Islamicization of Indian Muslims. Back in 2006, while addressing Hindu priests in Dangs district in Gujarat, he had said, 'Because we cannot throw the Muslims and Christians into the sea, we have to Indianise (read Hinduise) them'. Sudarshan's plea was neither the first such call nor a lone voice. Much earlier, Swami Shradhanand had advocated a policy of muzzling the minorities with affection, a policy under which they had to agree to lose their way of worship, merge their language and culture with the mythical national mainstream. He suggested voluntary installation of a statue of the Prophet in temples if the Muslims agreed to give up their special identity. Interestingly, this offer of Swami Shradhanand stemmed from history. Much before the Muslims set foot here, Gautam

Buddha was accommodated as an avatar of Lord Vishnu by the Hindus, clearly rattled by Buddha's appeal for an egalitarian society. What they could not eject, they assimilated. The same strategy was revived when it came to tackling Christians and Muslims. Sudarshan took a clue from Swami Shradhanand's words. Just as former HRD Minister Murali Manohar Joshi had done when he claimed all Indians were Hindus, the only difference being that some were Mohammadiya Hindus or Jesuyia Hindus. Others were just Hindus. Sudarshan even suggested a pattern of names such as Muhammad Prasad or Muhammad Das! Clearly, for him, India belonged to the Hindus. And there was only one way of being an Indian—Hindu!

It is the same mindset that manifested itself when the Jawaharlal Nehru University controversy erupted in the spring of 2016. With members of its students union in jail for allegedly anti-national speeches, the students of the university took to the streets, demanding the release of their president, Kanhaiya Kumar, besides asking the police to find out another member Umar Khalid who had gone missing. The students, asking for the release of Kanhaiya shouted, 'Fascism down, down', followed by shouts of 'Sanghis, down, down'. Then there were noises of 'Manuvad down down'. It seemed an all-encompassing cry.

It was followed by a counter march a day later wherein the right-wing activists agitated more vehemently, with a lawyer threatening to use petrol bomb on Umar Khalid. It was sickening. They wanted to bomb the man, a self-confessed atheist because he had a Muslim name! And they were ready to use force against those opposed to their idea of the nation, 'one religion, one nation, one language, one culture', template! Anybody who did not agree was anti-national. Never mind if one sang 'Saare

Jahan Se Achcha'. These men proved their patriotism by merely singing 'Vande Mataram'. Not surprisingly, they all drew their strength from the RSS, the very body that for more than half a century refused to hoist the Tricolour, the organization that stood opposed to India being a 'sovereign, socialist, secular, democratic republic', and even now wants India to be a Hindu Rashtra.

Today, self-confessed perjurers are claiming monopoly over nationalism. Right-wing prejudice cannot pass off as the thought of the nation. Reading Golwalkar is far from exhilarating. It is demanding, requiring both an open heart and a level head. In the end though, it is worth it.

RSS AND THE TRICOLOUR

On 26 January 2015, there was a news item buried in the inside pages of some newspapers, others choosing to ignore it. Meerut-based Akhil Bhartiya Hindu Mahasabha boycotted the Republic Day celebrations, preferring instead to observe it as a mourning day. Waving black flags in protest, the body pledged to make India a Hindu Rashtra. The Mahasabha's action was not surprising. After all, the body had earlier floated the idea of building a temple dedicated to Nathuram Godse! The latest action was in direct contrast to what its ideological partner RSS had said earlier in the month. The RSS urged the madrasas or Islamic seminaries to hoist the Tricolour on Republic Day. The advice was repeated on Independence Day in 2017 when the Uttar Pradesh Chief Minister Yogi Adityanath issued instructions to all madrasas to fly the national flag, and also make a video recording of the same. For once, it seemed perfectly sensible advice. But coming from the RSS, and a Chief Minister wedded to Hindutva ideals, it was rich. Isn't RSS the body which has for years been accused of not flying the national flag on its premises? Worse, did not its volunteers make shrill noises for Bhagwa Dhwaj (saffron flag) to be chosen as the flag of independent India rather than the Tricolour? For believers of India-is-a-monolith philosophy, the Bhagwa Dhwaj, same as the one associated with Ram, stood for the valour of the nation, not the Tricolour.

That the body was not in favour of the Tricolour even after 50 years of Independence became clear in 2001 when three activists of Rashtrapremi Yuwa Dal along with others entered the RSS premises and forcibly hoisted the national flag there mouthing patriotic slogans. The media then reported that the in-charge of the premises, Sunil Kathle, first tried to stop them from entering the premises and later tried to prevent them from hoisting the Tricolour. The activists, contending that the RSS had never hoisted the Tricolour on Republic Day, initially told the RSS men there that they had come to pay homage to the RSS founder Dr Keshav Hedgewar but soon took out banners and flag.

Incidentally, at the time of India's Independence, the RSS considered the Tricolour with three different strands less than auspicious as the numeral three was said to be evil. Its own mouthpiece, *Organiser*, had written then,

The people who have come to power by the kick of fate may give in our hands the Tricolour but it never be respected and owned by the Hindus. The word three is in itself an evil, and a flag having three colours will certainly produce a very bad psychological effect and is injurious to a country.

Incidentally, M.S. Golwalkar too had opposed our national flag. In the essay 'Drifting and Drifting' in *Bunch of Thoughts*, Golwalkar wrote,

> Our leaders have set up a new flag for our country. Why did they do so? It is just a case of drifting and imitating. Ours is an ancient and great nation with a glorious past. Then, had we no flag of our own? Had we no national emblem at all these thousands of years? Undoubtedly we had. Then why this utter void, this utter vacuum in our minds. (Golwalkar 1966)

A little after Independence, the body was banned following reports of its activists trampling the Tricolour in the wake of Mahatma Gandhi's assassination. And Prime Minister Jawaharlal Nehru was quick to take note of the lack of respect shown towards the national flag by some miscreants. In a speech on 24 February 1948, he noticed that 'at some places members of the RSS dishonoured the national flag. They know well that by disgracing the flag they are proving themselves as traitors....' Indeed a little later when there was talk of the ban being lifted, Home Minister Sardar Vallabhbhai Patel made respect towards Tricolour a precondition. He warned anybody who sought to supplant the national flag with any other flag.

Indeed, these statements by our prime minister and home minister had to be made because historically the organization had exhibited little faith in the flag. A passage in *Khaki Shorts Saffron Flags* (Basu et al. 1993) lucidly brings it out while talking of Gandhiji's Civil Disobedience Movement.

> Three months later Gandhi started his Dandi March and the Civil Disobedience Movement was born. The RSS, as

usual, remained deafeningly silent—except for a single, though interesting circular issued by Hedgewar as sarsanghchalak concerning the Congress decision to observe 26 January 1930 as Independence Day. The circular audaciously claimed that 'the Indian National Congress too had adopted our goal of Independence'. RSS shakha should therefore celebrate Independence Day—but through 'worship of the national flag, that is, the bhagwa jhanda'. Not, it needs to be noted, the Tricolour. 1930, in any case, remained the only year when the RSS celebrated 26 January, even though such a celebration became a standard feature of the freedom movement, and often came to mean confrontations with the colonial police. The RSS preferred to conserve its martially trained cadres for other objectives.... Hedgewar personally joined the Satyagraha movement, and briefly went to jail, but otherwise the Civil Disobedience of 1930–31 is a non-event in RSS history. (Basu et al. 1993)

Incidentally, the flag was not first hoisted by Madam Cama in Germany, as often claimed by some. It is said to be designed by P. Venkayya, a Congressman, although some give credit to Suraiya Tayyabji, arguing that Venkayya's flag had 'charkha' in the centre, not Asoka's wheel. Either way, the idea of the Tricolour was first mooted around 1920; Venkayya is said to have raised the question at various sessions of the Congress. It was initially to have a red strand to represent Hindus, green for Muslims and white as a symbol of peace as well as representation of other religions. Also, Gandhiji was in favour of the white strip at the top and red at the bottom. In the design offered by Venkayya, charkha was to cover all three segments. As we inched towards Independence, red was replaced by saffron and also placed on top. The charkha became smaller, now confined to the white middle strip. As Independence beckoned, our Constituent Assembly replaced the charkha with Asoka chakra as the former was identified too closely with the Congress. This Asoka chakra in the centre is said to have been designed by Tayyabji. Gandhiji was persuaded to accept the change; all leaders accepted the Tricolour. Not so the RSS. Sectarian allegiances were paramount, spirit of the nation secondary for some.

Hardly a surprise then that the RSS is all for hoisting the Bhagwa Dhwaj from the ramparts of the historic Red Fort in Delhi but would like to hoist the Tricolour in Srinagar—remember how in 1991 for a supposedly Ekta Yatra, Murli Manohar Joshi, later to be the HRD minister, went to unfurl the Tricolour at Lal Chowk in Srinagar, and Uma Bharti, then very much a firebrand leader, carried the national flag to Idgah which was then being targeted by the Hindutva brigade. Neither thought it wise to do the same at the RSS headquarters!

Interesting then that when the Uttar Pradesh Chief Minister issued instructions on Independence Day in 2017, he targeted the madrasas, asking them to hoist the Tricolour and record the proceedings. Non-compliance ran the risk of de-recognition. Almost every madrasa happily agreed; many even sent video recordings of the proceedings of the function to local district magistrate. However, there was no such circular issued to the RSS shakhas in the state or even to the schools it runs across Uttar Pradesh. Is that because the government knew that compliance might not be easy, given the track record of the first 50-odd years after Independence? Or was the government trying to send in a message to the RSS and the Mahasabha activists? The answer, in this case, blows not in the wind, but history.

THE MYTH OF THE HOLY COW

In May 2016, four men in district of Chittorgarh in Rajasthan were chased down by *gau rakshaks* (protectors of cows). The mcn were said to be 'transporters of cow'. They were allegedly ferrying 50 cows in Chhoti Sadri when they were first intercepted, then thrashed and stripped naked. The *gau rakshaks* made a video too of the entire incident, absolutely confident that they won't be hauled up for taking the law into their hands. The confidence was not misplaced either. As the video showing a Muslim man stripped to bone and lying on the ground with one of the *gau rakshaks* keeping his foot over his head went viral, one noticed the presence of a policeman in the frame as well. The policeman was seen as just an idle onlooker who does absolutely nothing to control the raging men or rescue the helpless. Later, a case was registered against the accused with the attackers going scot-free. The *gau rakshaks* celebrated their 'achievement' by sharing online more photos of the incident. Later, they released similar pictures of their 'work' in Aligarh in Uttar Pradesh.

Shockingly, the *gau rakshaks* left their phone numbers with the video and photos online. The police did nothing to arrest them. Rather, in the FIR filed, the four men who were assaulted were identified with their complete names, their father's name. Their religion was written as 'Muslim'. Although the incident shocked many, it did not get the kind of media coverage that came the way of the unfortunate Dalit victims in Una, Gujarat, or later Pehlu Khan in Rajasthan itself. The thrashing of innocent men in Chittorgarh, besides raising questions about the safety of the minorities in the country, also brought to fore the hideous hold Hindutva proponents had over the masses. Through careful and persistent indoctrination, these young men had started to believe the vitriol against Muslims. Worse, they had forgotten what Hinduism stood for. Not one of the attackers had read the Vedas to discover the real status of the cow in their faith. Political leaders for the past hundred years or so had been telling them that the cow was sacred to Hindus. And they had meekly believed, with their spirit of exploration, question and curiosity kept in cold storage. Yet the truth is very different from the hype. The good old cow was not held sacred in ancient India. And for all the shrill claims today, the same cow is just a political animal. If at one time, it was identified as part of the diet of the lower caste Hindus, today it is an instrument to persecute the Muslims. The believers know little. They have been told little. Unless of course one picks up the works of veteran historian D.N. Jha, who has been arguing for a few decades now that the cow was sacrificed in ancient India to please the gods and goddesses and its meat was distributed to all after the sacrifice. His book *The Myth of the Holy Cow* (Jha 2009) not only lives up to its name but also exposes arguments about the cow as both shallow and motivated.

As the Bharatiya Janata Party upped the ante on cow protection—it was in favour of beef ban in North India and Maharashtra but had no problems with beef eating in Kerala or the Northeast where in the 2017 elections it was at pains to allay the fears of the local population—I discovered that more than 70 communities in Kerala prefer cow flesh to mutton or chicken. So beef eating was not confined to Muslims or Christians. Or even the people of the Northeast, including Bengal.

So when did the cow become sacred? *The Myth of the Holy Cow* gives a delicious reason to stick to non-vegetarian diet—not just human beings even deities ate meat. Writes Jha (2009),

> Animal sacrifices were very common, the most important of them being the famous *aśvamedhá* and *Rājasūya*. These and several other major sacrifices involved the killing of animals, including cattle, which constituted the chief form of the wealth of the early Aryans. Not surprisingly, they prayed for cattle and sacrificed them to propitiate their gods. The Vedic gods had no marked dietary preferences. Milk, butter, barley, oxen, goats and sheep were their usual food, though some of them seem to have had their special preferences. Indra had a special liking for bulls. Agni was not a tippler like Indra, but was fond of the flesh of horses, bulls and cows. The Pūṣan, the guardian of the roads, ate mush as a Hobson's choice. Soma was the name of an intoxicant but, equally important, of a god, and killing animals (including cattle) for him was basic to most of the Ṛgvedic *yajñas*. The Maruts and the Asvins were also offered cows. The Vedas mention about 250 animals out of which at least 50 were deemed fit for sacrifice, by implication for divine as well as human consumption. The *Taittirīya Brahmana* categorically tells us, 'Verily the cow is food' (*atho annam vai gauh*) and Yajnavalkya's insistence on eating the tender (*amasala*) flesh of the cow is well known.

He cites examples from the Mahabharata and Ramayana to drive home the point—life was incomplete without a non-vegetarian meal for deities and *dasas* alike. He reminds that 'the Mahabharata also makes a laudatory reference to the king Rantideva in whose kitchen two thousand cows were butchered each day, their flesh, along with grain, being distributed among the Brahmanas'.

Similarly, Valmiki's Ramayana tells us of the dietary tradition of the gods and goddesses—Ram was born after his father, Dasharatha, performed a big sacrifice involving the slaughter of a large number of animals declared edible by the *Dharmashastras*. Sita assures the Yamuna, while crossing it, that she would worship the river with a thousand cows and a hundred jars of wine when Ram accomplishes his vow. Her fondness for deer meat drives her husband to kill Maricha, a deer in disguise.

Indeed, whether it was the Age of the Mauryan Empire, including the period of Asoka or the Gupta Age, animal sacrifice as also eating of the flesh was very much prevalent. For instance, ceremonial welcome of guests was considered complete only with honey, curd and flesh of cow or bull. Even the sacred thread ceremony for its part was not all that sacred, for it was necessary for a *snataka* (a Brahman) to wear an upper garment of cowhide and the dead too were sent away with animals. The thick fat of the cow was used to cover the corpse and a bull was burnt along with it to enable the departed to ride in the nether world. Interestingly, even the arrival of Buddhism and Jainism with their clear non-violent principles and practices did not put a full stop to animal slaughter. Buddha himself is said to have died after consuming a meal made of pork. Also, Manu provided a list of creatures whose flesh was considered edible. In the list, he exempted camel from being killed but not the cow.

So, just when did the cow become sacred? The answer came towards the end of the 19th century when Dayanand Saraswati started a movement for cow protection. Of course, a beginning was made earlier. In medieval India, it was considered a low caste practice to eat beef. The upper castes preferred fish or mutton. Indeed, the cow was never used for spiritual elevation. It is only around 1882 that it became a glue to mobilize the Hindu masses for political purposes. Dayanand Saraswati's lead was taken up by the RSS and the humble cow became a tool for political ambition: It was not the love of the cow that was driving the right-wing politics but a hatred of the Muslims and the Dalits. They started claiming that the cow was always a sacred animal. Or at least one until the arrival of the Muslims. The historical evidence though goes against this reasoning. If in ancient India cows were killed and the Brahmins ate cow meat, a little later the practice became so popular that an honourable guest was always served cow meat.

If one looks at the Vedas or the Dharma Sutras, cow killing was fine. After the Mauryan period, references to cow slaughter do become less widespread. Towards the beginning of the first millennium AD, this change took place, mainly in northern India. One cannot give the exact date. It may have taken several centuries. One reason for the change was economic. As more and more land came under cultivation, the economic importance of the cow increased. The Brahmins said, 'Okay, our cows won't be killed, but cows will be killed and the lowest in the caste order can kill but we will not kill'. They, therefore, associated beef-eating with the Dalits. This process was gradual, very slow, involving hundreds of years. But it does not deny the fact that Brahmins got their *dakshina* (honorarium paid to the priest for conducting a ritual) in cattle in the ancient India.

Also, none of the Brahmanical texts mentions cow-killing as a major crime. In traditional Indian literature, crime is classified as major and minor, *mahapataka* and *up-pataka*. Cow killing is *up-pataka*. It is stated that it is as bad as cleaning your teeth with your fingers. The *Dharmashastras* state that the food touched by a cow is impure. It has to be purified. The Brahmins cannot eat that food. So what are the *gau rakshaks* actually trying to defend?

COW PROTECTION MOVEMENT

Summer of 2017 arrived with grave foreboding for merchants of meat across Uttar Pradesh. Among the first decisions of the BJP government in the state was the closure of slaughterhouses. Ostensibly targeted only at those slaughterhouses which were functioning without a licence, the move impacted thousands of blue collar workers who assist at these slaughterhouses or innumerable local meat shops across cities and townships of the state. As supplies from the abattoirs reduced to a trickle, the activists of various Hindu outfits, notably Hindu Yuva Vahini, took it upon themselves to force closure of all meat shops, not just beef shops across the state. Even chicken and fish sellers were ordered to close down.

The closure of abattoirs was accompanied by the Central government decision to ban the sale of cows, buffaloes and camel for slaughter through animal markets. The decision hurt millions of poor farmers across religions besides Muslims involved as foot soldiers in meat trade and tanneries. The decisions, first the closure of slaughterhouses, then the virtual ban on cattle trade, had a Hindutva stamp. The calls for a ban on slaughterhouses—the BJP President Amit Shah had called for a ban on slaughterhouses in the UP election campaign earlier in the year—have invariably been accompanied or followed by cow protection movement. The slaughterhouses which deal in goat, sheep and buffalo trade and slaughter are all termed dens of cow slaughter, and forced to shut shop.

While the Central government gradually made trade in animals possible after hundreds of dairy farmers left their aged cows, beyond the age of giving milk, tied to a school in Uttar Pradesh, and perched outside a police station in Alwar, things have rarely been smooth in meat trade.

Back in 1966, sadhus from across the country gathered near Parliament House demanding a ban on cow slaughter. Before that, around 1947, there were calls for shutting down slaughterhouses and asking the Constituent Assembly to make cow slaughter illegal.

Although one tends to see a demand for a ban on cow trade and slaughter with respect to Hindu–Muslim conflict, it has not always been so. The cow protection movement has been a vexed issue for a long time. It did not have anti-Muslim ramifications initially. At the height of freedom struggle, it had definite anti-Muslim sentiment, but just a little before that, things were totally different. In the mid-19th century, the cow protection movement caused concern to the British ruling over India. In *British Origin of Cow Slaughter in India*, authors Dharampal and T.M. Mukundan write,

> The enormity of this movement and the threat it posed to the British may be gauged by the statement of Viceroy Lansdowne when he said that: 'I doubt whether, since the Mutiny, any movement containing in it a greater amount of potential mischief has engaged the attention of the Government of India'. They point out that a huge number of cattle were slaughtered daily by the British for their army and civilian personnel in India, yet very little is known, even to most scholars and historical researchers on India, about this India-wide Anti-Kine-Killing Movement against the British during 1880–1894. Even the scholars who have taken note of this movement have treated it as a Hindu–Muslim conflict. But such was not

the case, as many Muslims as well as the Parsis and Sikhs actively participated in the movement. The fact that the movement was directed against the British and not against the Muslims, as commonly believed, was clear to Queen Victoria and her officers. Queen Victoria said in a letter to Viceroy Lord Lansdowne, 'Though the Muhammadan's cow killing is made the pretext for the agitation, it is, in fact, directed against us, who kill far more cows for our army, etc., than the Muhammadans'. Faced with a challenge, the British did what they were best at: divide and rule. They soon spread the rumour that the Muslims were cow-eaters, and ably turned what was a political movement against the British into a communal issue between the two leading communities. Writing in Indian Nationalism and the Early Congress, John McLane said, 'The heart of the protection movement in the Gangetic districts which experienced rioting in 1893 was neither the occasional Congress lawyer or *zamindar* nor the wandering sadhus but rather the local *gaurakshini sabhas*. The *sabhas* were an expression of Hindu revival and anxiety. By focusing people's attention on the status of the cow, they communicated a concern for the preservation of one of Hinduism's oldest, commonest, and most reassuring symbols. At the same time, by giving Hindus concrete economic goals to fulfill in protecting cattle, the *sabhas* were appealing to sentiments in favor of modern material improvements and philanthropy'.

The point was reiterated by historian Mohammad Sajjad who talked of cow protection and riots in his book *Muslim Politics in Bihar*: 'The Hindu–Muslim conflict around cow was absolutely unknown before India became a British colony'. Indeed, a number of historians have elaborated upon the fact that with the publication of Dayanand Saraswati's pamphlet, *Gaukarnanidhi*, in 1881, *Gaurakshini sabhas* (cow protection society) and

Gaushalas (ranch) spread. With his supporters, Dayanand Saraswati travelled across the cow belt, demanding an end to the practice. Over a period, the voice became more shrill and it brought them into direct confrontation with Muslims and Dalits, said to be the chief consumers of the cow meat in North India. The ritual of worshipping the cow did not start as anti-Muslim. If one reads *The Collected Works of Vivekananda*, one finds that cows were eaten in ancient India. Their meat was served to guests too. Over a period of time, it was felt necessary to protect the cow, as we were an agrarian economy. Economic need became religious creed. One must de-link religion from the cow. Having created God out of the cow, the Hindutva forces went about using it for political benefit. By late 19th century, it was converted into an anti-Muslim issue.

Across Uttar Pradesh and Bihar, there were number of violent clashes and killings in the name of protecting cows. The *gau rakshaks* imposed fines, social exclusion against those who did not subscribe to their ideology. Even a short notice was enough to mobilize violent mobs coming on horses, elephants (and even on bicycles in 1920s–30s). These societies were funded by big landlords and *banias* (community of merchants, bankers, money-lenders, etc.). Advocates and schoolteachers indulged in campaigns through pamphlets, handbills. These conflicts also spread to annual cattle fairs. The dispute was manufactured around the issue if the village or locality had precedence of cow sacrifice or not. Another occasion was to prevent cow slaughter on the festival of Bakrid. Importantly, almost invariably, the *gau rakshaks*, taking law into their hands and killing people, were allowed to go scot free. They were not made to face police and court of law.

The Hindu–Muslim clashes became far too frequent. As written by noted historian Sumit Sarkar (1983) in *Modern India: 1885–1947*:

> A rash of rioting over cow slaughter spread over much of northern India. Gerald Barrier mentions 15 major riots of this type in the Punjab between 1883 and 1891, and such disturbances reached their climax in eastern U.P. and Bihar between 1888 and 1893, the districts worst affected being Ballia, Benares, Azamgarh, Goraphpur, Arrah, Saran, Gaya and Patna. Serious riots occurred also in Bombay city and a number of Maharashtrian towns between 1893 and 1895.

It is pertinent to remember that the British were never attacked. The Hindutva forces remained loyal to them. Mahatma Gandhi himself could see through the duplicity of the whole affair. In December 1915, he said, 'I have never been able to understand the antipathy towards the *Musalmans* [on the issue of cow]. We say nothing about the slaughter that takes place on behalf of Englishmen. Our anger becomes hot when a *Musalman* slaughters a cow'.

The cow came to be regarded as sacred across the whole of North and West India. In the run-up to India's Independence, senior Congress leader Pattabhi Sitarammaya wrote in an article in Gita Press' *Gau Ank* (1945) that India was nurtured by three mothers—*gau mata* (cow), *bhu mata* (mother earth) and *Ganga mata*. The votaries of cow protection did not confine themselves to a few write-ups in widely circulated magazines and journals. They sent telegrams too to Dr Rajendra Prasad, president of the Constituent Assembly, and soon to be the first President of India, calling for cow slaughter ban. They took the demand to the masses as well. As the nation prepared to keep its tryst with destiny,

cow defenders organized anti-cow slaughter day on 10
August 1947.

GAURAKSHINI SAMITIS TURN SENAS

For a little over a hundred years now, cow has evoked
sustained interest in sociopolitical circles. While the RSS
and its ideological partners have periodically sought a
ban on cow slaughter, the seeds for the movement were
laid soon after the foundation of Arya Samaj in 1875.
Within a few years, calls were made for cow protection
and *gaurakshini samitis* (cow protection societies) and
sabhas came up in North and West India. The earliest
samiti came up in 1882 in the Punjab, followed by others
in Maharashtra, Gujarat and Uttar Pradesh. The purpose then seemed pretty harmless—no violence, just an
emphasis on the unique status of the cow and an attempt
to build a shelter for the animal. Food, water and medical care were on the agenda. These cow protection bodies
were the brainchild of Dayanand Saraswati. Gradually, as
the Arya Samaj (again founded by Dayanand Saraswati)
spread its wings, the *gaurakshini sabhas* spread too.

That the cow protection movement divided the society
was beyond doubt. It was proven by the fact that songs
written for Ganapati Utsav in Maharashtra in the late
19th century urged the Hindus to boycott the Moharram
events. The Hindus, it may be recalled, participated freely
in Moharram processions which were then organized on a
bigger scale than Ganapati Utsav. Inflammatory slogans
were coined, one of them being, 'What boon has Allah
conferred upon you/That you have become Mussalmans
today? Do not be friendly to a religion which is alien....
The cow is our mother, do not forget her'.

Although the Brahmins as well Kshatriyas venerated the cow during the second half of the 19th and early 20th centuries, the Yadavas (a caste in India) took the lead in the cow protection movement. The early *gaurakshini sabhas* were formed by them. But they were not alone. Behind them was the support of the Marwaris (an ethno-linguistic group that originates from the Marwar region of Rajasthan). Well-heeled but still looking for social accept-ance, the Marwaris spent money in building shelters and looking after the cows who were injured or ailing. What money could not buy, cow made it possible. Their task was made easier by a magazine such as *Kalyan* that in 1920s and 1930s came up with special editions dedicated to the cow. In fact, what the Hindutva forces were doing at the ground level, *Kalyan* sought to do in academic circles and middle-class drawing rooms. It was not unusual for a middle-class Hindu man, otherwise well-read and pretty tolerant of other faiths, to subscribe to *Kalyan*, even if the magazine often reiterated its support to caste system, and similarly sought to draw a halo around the cow. All of it was accepted as part of a conservative Hindu society.

Although steadfast support for the cow protection was there since a few years after the First War of Independence in 1857, there was nothing by way of aggression, or vigi-lantism. Even during the freedom struggle, cow protection was never quite a national issue, and Savarkar is known to have expressed his reservations about the cow being a sacred animal since time immemorial. The change came about after Independence when some slaughterhouses were closed. Then in 1966 sadhus from across the country gathered near Parliament House demanding a ban on cow slaughter. This cow protection movement was led by Jan Sangh, the precursor of the BJP. Although Indira Gandhi turned it down, it left an impression on the mind of the common man. Slowly, the RSS whipped up support in the name of *gau mata*. Admittedly, this support grew but slowly when the Congress government was in power, but by leaps and bounds when the BJP-led NDA assumed the reins of the government. More so, after Narendra Modi came to power with a thumping majority. *Gau rakshaks*, a term which did not occupy the mindspace of an average English newspaper reader until then, suddenly became the talk of the social media with reports of *gau rakshaks* attacking cow traders in Rajasthan, Haryana, Himachal Pradesh, Gujarat and Uttar Pradesh. If Muslim men were attacked for transporting cows, Dalits were thrashed for skinning dead cattle. Importantly, most *gau rakshaks* were unemployed youth cutting across the caste barrier; there were no Dalit *gau rakshaks* though. These *gau rakshaks* were nothing but self-styled vigilante groups who took the law into their own hands, often dishing out on the spot punishment to any truck driver found ferrying cattle. They were emboldened enough to often shoot the videos of their adventure and put them up online. It usually took only a few hours for the video to go viral. In one video, they were shown stripping a cattle trader naked, and kicking him. In another, two men are force fed cow dung mixed with urine. In yet another, seven members of a Dalit family were assaulted for allegedly skinning a dead cow. Then four Dalit boys were stripped to their waist, tied to a vehicle and thrashed in public with belts and iron rods in Una. Earlier, of course, Akhlaq, father of an Indian Air Force personnel, was killed at home in Dadri on allegation of storing beef in his fridge. Amazingly, the policemen who went to investigate the crime did not bother to find out who entered Akhlaq's premises, whose finger prints were found on his body, door, etc. Rather the emphasis was on meat in the fridge—was it beef or mutton? Shockingly, an FIR was filed against Akhlaq's family members under the Cow Slaughter Act. And when one of the men accused of killing Akhlaq later died of illness in police custody, the casket was wrapped in the Tricolour. The marriage of *gau rakshaks* with the soul of India was complete!

Around the same time, the state of Haryana constituted Gau Raksha Task Force for the protection of the animal. And young men registered as *gau rakshaks* in other states too, including Rajasthan and Gujarat. With the newfound aggression in the behaviour and action of *gau rakshaks*, *gaurakshini sabhas* and *samitis* gave way to Gau Sena and Gau Raksha Dals. In almost all instances of violence around the cow, these *senas* and *dals* were involved. Also, unlike the animal activists who come to rescue stray dogs, these *senas* and *dals* have not been known to take stray cows home, or to aid the ailing ones. Their job seems less about cow protection, more about aggression in the name of the pacific animal. Cow has clearly become a political animal.

The latest example coming from New Delhi's Fleet Street where within days of the Modi government assuming power, a gaushala came up in front of media houses, and at a distance of around a 100 metres from the police headquarters. With no permission, cows were brought to the pavement, tied to trees around the place. Arrangements were made for the hay, water and shelter. And within 48 hours, a gaushala came up. Soon, even passers-by started stopping to feed the animals. The movement started in an obscure village of Punjab by Dayanand Saraswati had reached the corridors of power. Cow may or may not be sacred, but it certainly is the political animal of India in 2018!

RAKSHA DALS, THEN AND NOW

Private armies may not usually make much noise but when an English daily (*TOI* 20 January 2016) came up with a news item on the formation of 'dharma *sena*' on the outskirts of Delhi, it shocked even the unflappable ones. Ostensibly formed to counter the danger of ISIS, the Hindu Swabhiman Sena, according to the report, has 15,000 'soldiers' ready to die to safeguard their faith. The challenge, as the freshly recruited boys and girls were told, is to come up shortly in the form of the advance of ISIS to Uttar Pradesh–Uttarakhand! 'The ISIS will occupy western UP by 2020', the 'soldiers' have been told by their bosses, among them an ex-serviceman, and a former politician, now a spiritual guru of sorts.

According to the report, there are 50 training camps in Dasna, Meerut and Muzaffarnagar area where boys and girls, men and women are told to be ready 'for when the enemy strikes'. Among those undertaking training to use lathis and swords, pistols and guns are boys as young as eight years old; child soldiers, if one may call them. Indeed, the motto of the self-styled Sena is to catch the recruits young. It facilitates their indoctrination. The youngsters are not given firearms or military training initially. Instead, they are told to read the Gita to make sure that they are ready to sacrifice their life for the sake of their faith. It is an indoctrination based on the doctrine of the Other—the Other, as in the years past, is provided by Muslims. The ISIS, often in media headlines despite little presence in the country, provides an easy point to rally again; the most visible face of an imagined adversary. Once the youngsters are won over mentally, arms training is provided.

Some local wrestlers lend a helping hand. The ideological fuel is provided by Swami Narsinghanand Saraswati. According to the report, he stays in the temple where a board proclaims, '*Yeh teerth Hinduon ka pavitra sthal hai. Musalmanon ka pravesh varjit hai. Aadesh Mahant Baba Narsinghanand Saraswati*'. (This temple is a holy place of Hindus. Entry of Muslims is prohibited. By order of the head priest Baba Narsinghanand Saraswati.) That this happens barely a few kilometres from the Capital does not in any way affect him. Saraswati is at ease with the founding of the new militant body.

> I think an extremist outfit, like the ISIS, should exist for the Hindus. The only answer to the ISIS is an HS—a Hindu State. We want to match their level of extremism and fight fire with fire. I don't have the means to build an organization of that scale but with the help of Hindus, who believe in my cause, I will achieve it soon. We have pistols and they have rocket launchers. We need better weapons so that our army can be trained. That is how the ISIS got so big. Local business leaders helped them. Hindus from all over the country will help us too. (*TOI* 20 January 2016)

According to him, there is a mass contact programme underway. 'We have been addressing two panchayats per month, on an average. At the panchayats, I ask my Hindu lions to be brave and make sure they keep weapons with them at all times' (*TOI* 20 January 2016). Saraswati, pointing to a slogan on the wall, '*Hindu sheron, shaan se jeena hai toh shaan se marna seekho.* (Hindu lions, if you want to live with pride then learn to die with pride)', ends with a chilling finality, 'I am preparing my people for civil war. Neither the state government nor Narendra Modi can stop the civil war from coming. It is better to die fighting to protect our loved ones'.

Shocking as this formation of illegal dharma *sena* is, it is rooted in history. From the time the Hindu Mahasabha was founded to Independence, and even beyond, frequent calls were given by the Mahasabha members to Hindus to arm themselves. The calls were not to fight the British but 'enemy within', the 'Other', the not so veiled references to Muslims. Similarly, the RSS, even in the first two years when it had no name, no logo, it still concentrated on martial arts, the idea being in case of a communal riot, Hindu young men should be able to protect themselves, and instil fear in the minds of the adversary. In his book, seasoned journalist–author Akshaya Mukul talks of the role played by the Mahasabha as well as Gita Press with its organs such as *Kalyan* magazine in fuelling hatred. Mukul writes,

79

> Poddar proposed a twelve-point solution that included formation of a Raksha Dal (defence force) in each city and village to instil a feeling of confidence and security among the Hindu community, and to augment its strength so that the other side would not think of attacking.... Women should be trained to defend themselves, so that they would have the power of great women warriors.... Of course, there was Poddar's ultimate recipe for all situation—recitation of God's name, study of the *shastras*, Gita and Ramayana, and conducting *yagnas* (sacrifice). Throughout the

1940s and for some years in the next decade, a militant
approach in public coupled with recitation of God's name
(jap) in private and at community level would be Gita
Press's prescription for the problems of rapidly changing politics and society. [In fact,] Poddar envisioned
the setting up of a nationwide Rakshak Dal, a kind of
Hindu militia, of five million youth. In this context
Poddar praised the work of the RSS and encouraged
Hindu youth to participate in its programmes…. In his
convoluted fashion, Poddar told readers to replace the
word 'Muslims' with 'Hindus' in a speech by Jinnah
delivered in Delhi that read: 'We do not want to fight.
We want to live peacefully. But to save ourselves from
any attack we should conserve our energy so that the
other side should realize doing anything against Muslims
would cause more harm to them and would be suicidal'….
Hindu women were asked to be alert, not to venture out
unnecessarily, to carry a knife. (Mukul 2015)

Similarly, just before Independence, at the Gorakhpur
session of the Hindu Mahasabha in December 1946, L.B.
Bhopatkar, who presided over the session, gave a call to
all Hindus to 'take up arms in defence of their religion and
culture'. The formation of the Hindu National Guard was
mooted at the same session and women advised to carry
daggers. A little later, the RSS *pracharak* Krishna Gopal
Rastogi wrote in his autobiography, *Aap Beeti*, while
describing an incident where he personally led a mob of
armed Hindus against Muslims in Kaliyar, a town between
Roorkee and Hardwar,

> I organised 250 people, including known gangsters and
> raided Kaliyar. Then a strange thing happened. While we
> had been killing men, in one of the houses, we spotted a
> very beautiful young girl. The assailants led by me were

instantly enamoured. They even started fighting among themselves to take possession of the girl. The girl had to be eliminated. I took my gun and shot her.

Rastogi was to later rise to be on two committees of the HRD ministry when Murli Manohar Joshi was the HRD minister under Atal Bihari Vajpayee, and had the preface of his book done by K.S. Sudarshan, then the chief of the RSS. Indeed, the old order shows no signs of changing. Soon after Republic Day celebrations in 2018, it announced, 'The RSS has the ability to prepare an "Army" to fight for the country within three days, if such a situation arises. The Sangh will prepare military personnel within three days which the Army would do in six-seven months. This is our capability'. Now to think that the RSS is a self-proclaimed cultural body!

MAJORITARIANISM AND NATIONALISM

Soon after Narendra Modi took over as the Prime Minister in 2014, a new definition of nationalism emerged. He who adhered to the viewpoint of the fringe element was declared a nationalist. He who did not wear his nationalism on his sleeve was declared anti-national and advised to go to Pakistan. Nationalism lay in mouthing a slogan. That's all. If at one place students of a madrasa in Delhi were waylaid and asked to pronounce 'Bharat Mata ki jai', at another place, anti-national charges were levelled against students who took part in the campaign for the release of Kanhaiya and Umar Khalid, office bearers of the JNU students' union. Certificates in nationalism were doled out by those who believed in street justice, no court, no hearing, just instant verdict. In almost all such cases, the rallying point was Bharat Mata, and the attendant slogan of '*Bharat Mata ki jai*'. Yes, the same Bharat Mata that according to Hindutva ideologues was the timeless Bharata, the first civilization on earth. Never mind that the term Bharat too was absent from the vocabulary of the Aryans and the earliest reference comes only around 500 BC when the Bharata tribe was mentioned in Panini's *Ashtadhyayi*. Even then, Bharata was a small territory, a *janapada*, not quite the subcontinent we take it to be. The expression Bharatvarsha though was used in the Puranas, the word being used to denote territories of different shapes. The Puranas talk of Bharat divided into nine *dwipas* (islands), each separated by a sea.

Bharat as a mother did not exist until just over a hundred fifty years ago: In 1866, there was a Bengali book called *19th Purana or Unbeens Purana*. It talked of Bharat Mata. The book was later adapted to a stage play by Kiran Chandra Bannerjee in 1873. It coincided with a Hindu Mela by Tagore's family. The play was staged there. Then came K.C. Bandopadhyaya's Bharat Mata in early 1880s.

Until then there was a concept of Bharat, but not of a Mata. Bharat manifested itself in the description of Jambudwip, a term used by the Mauryan king Ashoka. The first reference to Bharat as a territory comes later through Kharavela's inscription in 1st century BC.

But until the late 1880s, the term Mata was not added to Bharat. It came with the release of *Anandmath*, and later the painting of Bharat Mata in 1905 by Abanindranath Tagore. He showed Bharat Mata as a four-armed goddess in saffron robes. The goddess held manuscripts, sheaves of rice besides a white cloth and a mala. Incidentally, Bharat Mata started off as Bang Mata as the work talked of the division of Bengal in 1905. Later, as part of the national movement, Bang Mata became Bharat Mata. The flag too was added later. In Tagore's painting, Bharat Mata was a simple lady without any ornamentation. She was shown as a frail, plain woman.

All these finer details did not matter to men who were intolerant of both opposition to their version of nationalism and any plurality. Anybody who did not agree with them was dubbed anti-national. Forgotten amid all this was a simple fact: Chanting 'Bharat Mata ki jai' was everybody's right, but not a duty. The image of Bharat as a deity went against the belief of Muslims and Christians. Bharat, to them, could be a motherland to be loved, admired, protected, but not a deity to prostrate in front of. What was being imposed upon was not nationalism but majoritarianism, worse, majority communalism masquerading as nationalism. In this ideology, there is no space for non-Hindus, particularly the followers of those religions which originated in West Asia. Hence, deliberate mixing of matters of Hindu faith with those of the nation.

It is under the same plan that many slogans came up on public walls around the same time across India. It was hardly unusual to see a slogan such as 'Gau mata ko rashtriya pashu banao' (declare mother cow the national animal) or 'Gau mata ke hatyaro ko phaansi do' (hang the murderers of mother cow). Then there was another one. It said, 'Jo gau hit ki baat karega wohi rashtra par raaj karega' (The one who will talk of protecting the mother cow will rule the country). Incidentally, gau mata and Bharat Mata are of almost the same vintage, the former having been conferred this status soon after the establishment of the Arya Samaj, the latter just a couple of years later. The messages were not-so-subtle attempts at making majoritarianism interchangeable with nationalism, taking my mind to the age-old debate of majority communalism passing off for nationalism. The phenomenon is neither new nor even recent.

Many summers ago, it raised its head during the Babri Masjid–Ram Janmabhoomi struggle, but actually dates back much further in time. Until the 1980s, school students were taught by history teachers how the use of Hindu symbols by the Bal-Pal-Lal—Balgangadhar Tilak, Bipin Chandra Pal and Lala Lajpat Rai—triumvirate post the partition of Bengal in 1905 alienated Muslims from the freedom movement, something which was sought to be redressed by Mahatma Gandhi's espousal of the Khilafat cause in 1919. Gandhi's support to Khilafat proved a masterstroke, bringing many more Muslims into the freedom struggle and allaying their fears of majoritarianism.

Incidentally, our freedom movement spearheaded by the moderates of the Indian National Congress had a parallel Hindu awakening movement. This had less to do with hostility towards Muslims, more to do with recapturing the Hindu past, real or imaginary. For instance, as recalled by Girilal Jain (1994),

> Bankim Chandra Chatterjee synthesized the Western secular concept of nationalism with the tradition and needs of Hindus even if he was thinking in terms of Bengal and not India when he wrote his famous novel *Anandmath* which contained the patriotic poem 'Bande Mataram' that became the national anthem during the struggle for freedom.

In a telling comment on the state of the society–polity post Independence, the song was replaced by Rabindranath

Tagore's 'Jana Gana Mana' as India moved away from religious patriotism, all along assuaging the sentiments of those whose *devabhoomi* and *janmabhoomi* were separate entities unlike the Hindus or Sikhs for whom *devabhoomi* and *janmabhoomi* were the same.

During the freedom struggle, although, there were several shades of Hindu revivalism which merged with nationalism but steadfastly stayed away from the latter-day idea of communalism.

As 'Bande Mataram', the extremist paper edited by Bipin Chandra Pal and Aurobindo Ghose explained: 'Swaraj as a sort of European ideal, political liberty for the sake of political self-assertion, will not awaken India. Swaraj as the fulfillment of the ancient life of India under modern conditions, the return of the Satyayuga of national greatness, the resumption by her of her great role of teacher and guide, self-liberation of the people for the final fulfillment of the Vedantic ideal in politics, this is the true Swaraj for India ... the groundwork of what may well be called the composite culture of India is undoubtedly Hindu'. Though the present Indian nationality is composed of many races, and the present Indian culture of more than one world civilization, yet it must be admitted that the Hindu forms its base and centre.... The dominant note of the Hindu culture, its sense of the spiritual and universal, will, therefore, be the peculiar feature of this composite Indian nationality. (Jain 1994)

Jain believed that the replacement of the Mughal rule by the British brought a little advantage to Hindus in terms of revival of their language.

The use of Sanskrit and Persian as languages of education would have perpetuated the Hindu-Muslim cultural stalemate, with the balance in favour of Muslims in view of the existing status of Persian as the language of administration even in non-Muslim states such as those of the Peshwas in Pune and of the Sikhs in Lahore. The changeover to English tilted the balance in their favour but involved the risk of the continued subordination of their culture and civilization to an alien one. (Jain 1994)

Now juxtapose those sentiments with the recent attempts at promotion of Sanskrit, marginalization of foreign languages and you know where it is stemming from. Similarly, the new laws safeguarding cattle. That is just another attempt at infusing a Right-wing Hindu element in the polity. Never mind that historians like Romila Thapar and D.N. Jha have categorically regarded the cow to be a unit of exchange for economic transactions in ancient India rather than a sacred being. Or the stray remarks by Right-wingers about India's soul being Hindu or every Indian being a Hindu. These comments only appear to be stray or intemperate. They actually all draw from the rivulet of majoritarianism.

However, unlike the spiritually driven movement of the 19th and 20th centuries with luminaries such as Raja Ram Mohan Roy and Sri Aurobindo, the present one is fuelled by hatred, intolerance and bigotry.

NATION FROM THE HISTORICAL LENS

M.S. GOLWALKAR AND IRFAN HABIB

JUST AS SPACE FOR DEBATE AND DISSENT is being encroached upon in our society, there are some old-school proponents of pluralist society who keep reminding us of our shared past; of the days when battles were political and boundaries of empires had little to do with religion; of the times when Alauddin Khilji ruled much of India, contracted many alliances, engaged in combat, but all actions were independent of religion. In fact, Alauddin knew little about Islam. He, in many ways, was responsible for the country we are. He had, after all, defeated the Mongols twice when they attacked India. The Mongols were known to follow a scorched earth policy, and Khilji, with his dare and wisdom, saved the country that faith. In fact, far from being a bloodthirsty tyrant, Khilji was a man ahead of times. His decisions on economy continue to impact us to this day.

The revival of Khilji in social discourse was caused largely by the controversy around a Hindi film, *Padmavati*, later released as *Padmaavat*, by director Sanjay Leela

Bhansali. A Rajput outfit, Karni Sena, objected to the film, and to the projection of Rajput queen, Rani Padmini, wife of Raja Rattan Singh. It led to a series of violent incidents, the worst of them being the attack on the eve of the film's release in January 2018 on a school bus in Gurugram in Haryana by hooligans claiming to be members of Karni Sena. Amid all the violence, the focus was lost from Malik Mohammed Jayasi, the 16th century scholar, poet, Sufi, who had penned *Padmavat* in 1540 wherein he talked of Padmavati. The poem was fictional in nature, but it did not stop right-wing outfits from appropriating the Rajput princess. The director too was guilty. He had hoped to reach a harvest at the box office by showing Khilji, a Muslim ruler from early medieval ruler, as a bloodthirsty tyrant, driven by lust. The Muslim community refused to get provoked by the projection of Khilji—Bhansali's was after all a fictional saga. Not so the Rajput bodies, one of whom demanded the head of the director, and the lead actress, Deepika Padukone.

Coming back to Jayasi, he was the 'good Muslim' referred to by the Hindutva leaders in the late 1980s up to the end of the century. At the height of the Babri Masjid controversy, Muslims were advised to take lessons from the likes of Jayasi, Raskhan and Kabir, and let go of Babur. But by 2018, all that he stood for too was consigned to the dustbin of history. The debate of 'Good Muslim—Bad Muslim' was revived a little before the Khilji controversy. While Bhansali was ready to overlook all the good Khilji did to project him in negative hues to appease the Hindutva lobby, the doors of this debate were thrown open in 2015 when in a classic case of Good Muslim versus Bad Muslim, New Delhi's age-old Aurangzeb Road was renamed after late President Dr A.P.J. Abdul Kalam. Mahesh Sharma, Union Minister, took the discourse to a new nadir by stating, 'Dr Kalam was a nationalist despite being a Muslim'. In the mind of the minister, nationalism was a monopoly of a certain religion!

Khilji–Jayasi, Aurangzeb–Kalam, the debate has been raging for long. It is, however, only in recent years that secular India is beginning to make itself heard again. While attempts have been made to project the positive side of the reigns of Khilji and Aurangzeb, historians are coming out in social sphere and out of their classrooms to talk of history lessons. They point out, for instance, that the Chittor battle between Akbar and Rana Pratap had nothing to do with religion, and all to do with political ambition. Likewise, Shivaji's fight with Aurangzeb was just another territorial clash. Shivaji's forces had Muslims in several key positions. Likewise, Aurangzeb had Rajputs in positions of authority.

All this talk of politics overpowering religion sent me in search of answers beyond what I had heard about Hindu generals/Muslim generals in Mughal/Maratha armies. First, I read about Irfan Habib's quite cogent views on Bhagwan Dass and Man Singh fighting Rana Pratap on behalf of Akbar. If such strongmen of the Rajputs were fighting on behalf of the Mughal emperor, it could not have been a *dharmyudh* (crusade), I reasoned. Habib's views, however, have been known for a long time. I needed to know more, and from other sources.

The answer came from the unlikeliest quarter: Madhav Sadashiv Golwalkar's age-old book *Bunch of Thought* (1960). The book is not easily available off the shelf but the thoughts are. So, I decided to dig a few. The reason could be different but imagine Habib and Golwalkar being on the same page! But that is exactly what I discovered as I sat down reading his work, tedious and challenging, as it is.

In the chapter, 'The Nation and Its Problem', Golwalkar wrote,

> The Muslims enjoyed perfect freedom and equality in the powerful Hindu empire under the Vijaynagar Kings or in the Punjab under Sikh heroes. The latest Hindu Power, which rose under the great Shivaji, too, did not discriminate against Muslims on the score of religion.... To cite a few instances, the naval chief of Chatrapati Shivaji, Darya Sarang, was a Muslim, and two of his main lieutenants were Ibrahim Khan and Daulat Khan. At the time of the grim encounter with Afzal Khan, out of the ten trusted bodyguards who accompanied Shivaji, three were Muslims. Again, the 18-year old lad who accompanied Shivaji to Agra and who played a key role in the thrilling escape of Shivaji from the grip of Aurangzeb was Madari Mehtar, a Muslim. Countless instances are there of Shivaji gifting land and annual grant to masjids and dargahs. He even made arrangements for the offering of worship according to Islam to the tomb of Afzal Khan on Pratapgadh. Even the most fanatic Muslim chroniclers of those times have noted with admiration that Shivaji treated with utmost respect their Koran, masjids and dargahs, their holy men and their womenfolk. (Golwalkar 1966)

A little later in the book, Golwalkar indirectly questions the division of history into religious segments. He wrote, 'Even later on, on the battlefield of Panipat in 1761, in the crucial struggle for the survival of Swaraj, the key position of the Artillery Chief on the side of the Hindus was held by Ibrahim Gardi, who ultimately fell fighting on the battleground'.

So be it Akbar versus Rana Pratap or Aurangzeb versus Shivaji, Khilji versus Rattan Singh, *dharmyudh* was not quite on their mind. Territorial supremacy yes, pursuit of glory, maybe. But a crusade? Never. Habib has always said that. Turns out even Golwalkar said the same.

Here is to some moments of peace and quiet.

CONFLICT AND CONCILIATION: BIPAN CHANDRA'S WORLD

On 11 July 1988, we were all strangers to each other as we sat together in a history class. There were around 30 students, some assembled in and out as they tried to complete last minute formalities. With us were three teachers, each of whom would go on to play a role in our lives in the years to come. Two of them introduced themselves, gave plastic smiles and excused themselves—their roles subsequently were as brief. One of them with short hair, a sleeveless blouse to go with her cotton sari stayed on. She was to teach us about medieval India and warmly recommended reading Irfan Habib's book on early medieval India. We happily jotted down the name. It took us another year to realize what an insightful book she had recommended. Habib talked of *qasbahs* and villages, old names for new townships and the like.

Realizing that the first day was not the best time to start the syllabus, she decided to relate a story to students on the brink of leaving teenage. It was a lesson that has lasted with me to this day.

Our history is like an unreserved railway compartment. You could call it a sleeper coach too. The moment a train arrives at the railway station, there is commotion. People rush in to grab a seat while those already inside try to defend their territory. There is a conflict and competition for the limited space available. As the train starts from the station, this conflict is replaced by an element of cooperation as new passengers request the earlier ones to please 'adjust'. First a little edge of the seat is conceded, then a little more.

A few minutes of stony silence, then the conversation starts. By the time the train arrives at the next station, these passengers would have opened their tiffins, asked each other to taste their food, exchanged notes on families and festivals. Conflict is replaced by conciliation and cooperation. Before getting down, they would have exchanged phone numbers! It is the same with our history. First the Aryans invaded. The Indus Valley people opposed, then conceded. Soon elements of the Indus Valley civilization brimmed over to the Vedic civilization. Then came Ghaznavi, the Ghoris. Conflict again. Resolved soon after with the setting up of the Delhi Sultanate in 1206. Then the Mughals attacked. The Lodis resisted. The Mughal prevailed. Again a period of hostility replaced by one of peace and progress.

It was a new way of looking at history, something our school teachers had totally missed in their quest for finishing all the chapters. We were advised to read Romila Thapar for ancient India and Bipan Chandra's *India Struggle for Independence* for modern India. Today, I seldom lose sight of Thapar's book with its invitingly yellow pages. The pages of Bipan Chandra's book though have yellowed only around the edges and do not always make the crackling sound I would like to get from my old, familiar, favourite books. Never mind. The loss is minor.

Like my lecturer, Chandra too opened a completely new window of looking at the past, not just for me or my generation but also for the family members of a freedom fighter such as Bhagat Singh. Until I read Chandra in college, modern history was all about black and white compartments—moderates, extremists, Gandhiji, the British. It is here that I discovered the vast passages of grey. Nobody was perfect. Not even Gandhi. Not Sir Syed Ahmed Khan. Not Netaji.

Today as I read the book (Chandra 1988), certain passages seem to have a contemporary ring to them. It is like they were written yesterday with tomorrow in mind. Sample this:

> The liberal communalist argues that India consisted of distinct religion-based communities which had their own separate and special interests which often came into mutual conflict.... Extreme communalism was based on the politics of hatred, fear psychosis and irrationality. The motifs of domination and suppression, always present in communal propaganda, became the dominant theme of communal propaganda. A campaign of hatred against the followers of other religions was unleashed.... Phrases like oppression, suppression, domination, being crushed, even physical extermination and extinction were used. The communalists increasingly operated on the principle: the bigger the lie the better. They poured venom on the National Congress and Gandhiji.

Chandra was writing about the 1930s. He could as well have been writing about 2017 or 2018 when venom was poured on him for using the term 'revolutionary terrorist' to describe Bhagat Singh, Surya Sen of the Chittagong Armoury Raid fame and others with some political leaders demanding a ban on the book! It mattered little that the term had been used for freedom fighters who were not averse to the use of bombs and weapons for ushering in

Independence, and to think that his nephew Jagmohan Singh did not find anything amiss in the term! 'It is because of Professor Bipan Chandra that I could collect all possible documents on the history of the Indian Independence movement from the family, co-patriots and other living freedom fighters and thus have the benefit of appreciating this great heritage', Singh said, shutting the controversy. Of course, it mattered little to those bent on vilification of Chandra that he had described 'revolutionary terrorist' Bhagat Singh as 'giant of an intellectual' and Surya Sen as 'unpretentious, soft-spoken person'.

Or sample this:

> Ironically, communalism in India got its initial start in the 1880s when Syed Ahmed Khan counterposed it to the national movement initiated by the National Congress.... He and his followers gradually laid down the foundation of all the basic themes of the communal ideology as it was propagated in the first half of the 20th Century.... Simultaneously, Hindu communalism was also being born. The Punjab Hindu Sabha was founded in 1909. Its leaders, U.N. Mukerji and Lal Chand, were to lay down the foundations of Hindu communal ideology and politics. They directed their anger primarily against the Congress for trying to unite Indians into a single nation and for 'sacrificing Hindu interests' to appease Muslims.... 'A Hindu', Lal Chand declared, 'should not only believe but make it a part and parcel of his organism, of his life and of his conduct, that he is a Hindu first and an Indian after'.

Chandra goes on to talk about action–reaction theory subscribed to by proponents of competitive communalism.

In fact, Chandra suffered for his frank views on the subject. A few months after he had breathed his last, National Book Trust decided to stop the Hindi print of his book *Communalism: A Primer* (Chandra 2016). Here, Chandra argued,

> Communalism is very often equated with religious fundamentalism, it actually represents an ideology. To counter it successfully, communal thinking has to be uprooted from people's minds. The struggle against communalism has to recognize the century-old heritage of inculcation and spread of communal ideology among the masses. Once the ideological character of communalism is recognized, combating it would require a dual-pronged strategy at both the political as well as the ideational level.

He described members of the Rashtriya Swayamsewak Sangh as extreme communalists.

Again, Chandra was talking of the days well before India kept its tryst with destiny. But such was the power of his skills as a historian, and of history as a subject, that he could be talking of today.

We all know history repeats itself, but Chandra had alerted us decades ago.

What we are witnessing today could do a soothsayer proud, if it were not so dismaying and disappointing. It seems the names of the players have changed, but their dialogues, their drama, and indeed, their actions remain starkly similar. Replace a Chand with a Shah, a Khan with an Owaisi, and it could well be playback time!

Ah, those early lessons in history! Conflict, cooperation, conciliation ... then some more conflict.

By the way, who was that lecturer who recommended Thapar, Habib, Chandra and brought into our classroom the dynamics of a railway station? Natasha Raina Kanwar. Seldom short of words. Never low on humour. May her tribe grow or least avoid extinction!

BABUR NAMA

The other day, during the course of a casual conversation at the India International Centre in New Delhi, an LGBT activist mentioned the name of Babur, the founder of the Mughal Dynasty, in defence of homosexual relations in the country. I had heard that earlier too from a prominent author. This time I decided to do the best thing possible to clear the mystery around Babur, a man with multiple wives, many offspring, could he be homosexual or bisexual? And promptly went to a library to read Annette Beveridge's work on him. However, Beveridge's translation of the *Babur Nama* is a voluminous exercise with some 300,000 words. It requires time and patience to read through. I had neither. So I did the next best thing. I picked up a copy of Dilip Hiro's *Babur Nama* (2006), which is kind of an abridged version. I came back not just with the answer to my question but a more rounded view of Babur. The founder of the Mughal Dynasty rose in my esteem. He could read, he could write, he could love, he could lust. And could he fight!

At one level, it lifted the lid off Babur's love for young boys. Babur wrote candidly in his memoirs—he was at ease with his mother tongue Turkish as also Persian, the language of intellectual discourse at that time. By his own admission, he was infatuated with Baburi, a teenage boy, on seeing whom Babur composed a couple of couplets. 'Nor power to stay was mine, nor strength to part; I became what you made of me, oh thief of my heart'. Indeed Babur pined for the love of Baburi even after he had acquired several wives and sired many children. And composed poems for him, often admitting to being left speechless in front of him.

That probably explains the unbounded enthusiasm of many to use his name in their argument against Section 377. Babur is not the only one quoted, merely the most conspicuous. However, a reading of *Babur Nama* proved a useful exercise in many other ways. It is such a beautifully written account of the era, its nobles, and its people. It is both lucid and illuminating. And the Mughal emperor, the butt of some ridicule and lots of unprovoked criticism during the Babri Masjid controversy, covers himself with grace. Such is his mastery over the written word that at one time he admonishes his son, Humayun, for being too verbose in his letters. 'Although your letter can be read if every sort of pains be taken, yet it cannot be quite understood because of that obscure wording of yours. In future, write without elaboration. Use plain, clear words', he says. It could as well have been a note for a modern-day editor to his team of reporters!

The brevity of expression is endearing and led me on to discover the Mughal founder anew. And as I discovered, he was not quite a Mughal! He, in fact, held the Mughals in low esteem, reserving similar scorn for the Uzbeks. 'Mischief and devastation must always be expected from the Mughal horde', he observes. If those bent on denying India's Mughal past had read Babur's views on them, they would have been perplexed—the founder of the royal dynasty being critical of his own men! Incidentally, his mother was a Chughtai Mughal while his father belonged to the lineage of Timur. Babur happily called himself Timuri Turk and if he had his way, he would have called his dynasty Timuri, not Mughal. The surprises do not end here. For all his hatred of the Uzbeks, who often kept him at bay, modern Uzbekistan has a museum dedicated to him at his birthplace of Andijan. Even a public square is named after him! Why go all the way to Uzbekistan to discover paradoxes surrounding Babur? Don't we call him the founder of the Mughal Dynasty?

The ironies continue as I discover more facets of Babur's personality through Hiro's book that was released a little under a decade ago. Hiro calls him a man of piety and principle, a man who had transcribed the holy Quran. Yet the same man used to host parties where wine flowed like water. And he consulted astrologers too—both the actions are prohibited in Islam. And was frank about his love for Baburi, again contrary to Islamic injunctions against homosexuality. The Quran talks of a prophet, Lut, who was sent to a community where men were often guilty of sodomy. Babur was far more than a skilled warrior and a shrewd strategist. He was a poet, a lover, a connoisseur of wine. And a man who did not think it less than macho to express love for his son. In fact, he was a doting father who is said to have prayed to God to transfer his son Humayun's illness to him and save him! Yet he was also the man whose first wife, Ayisha Sultan Begum, left him following the death of their month-old daughter, Fakhru Nisa, born three years after their marriage. In an age when emperors could choose any girl their eyes rested on, it was a rare case of a woman walking out on a man, the same man who was to later give the status of women of the harem to two of his Circassian slaves gifted to him by Tahmasp Shah Safavi of Persia.

So what does one make of Babur? A learned scholar of Islam? A pious man regular with his five daily prayers? A talented and honest historian? A debauched man given to a life of pleasure? A man who loved to hunt with his friend? And was brave enough not only to cry after a loss on a battlefield but also to pen it down for posterity? Or, maybe, an emperor with some rare gifts and some very human foibles; a man who projected most beautifully the assets and rare gifts of Samarkand as also Kabul; a man who saw Agra too with the eye of an observer; and an emperor with seemingly the most modern mindset! That may just be Zahir Uddin Muhammad Babur.

GOPAL GANDHI'S *DARA SHUKOH*

Few men who read history in school remember Dara Shikoh, the philosopher-prince of Mughal India. Shah Jahan's eldest son and Aurangzeb's principal rival to the throne, he is but a fleeting figure even if an enlightened one. The spotlight is well and truly on Aurangzeb, terse, taciturn and untamed. In a world looking for convenient, even if inaccurate, summations, Dara is reduced by our historians to being a favourite son of Shah Jahan and Aurangzeb a fratricidal ruler who did not hesitate to put to the sword his own. That almost all kings in the years of yore did the same matters little. That Dara had a life before the fatal battle of Samugarh with Aurangzeb, that he had a life quite removed from that of any of his brothers is seldom pointed out. For most, Aurangzeb is a convenient villain, Dara the easy but fallible hero. To many, he reminds of the *mayoos ashiq* (defeated lover) who could not wield the sword befitting a Mughal-e-Azam; his intellectual attainment, his mastery over religious scriptures held against him. Poets and philosophers are not supposed to be skilful generals.

However, today, as our nation is helmed by those into revisionist politics, angry fringe elements now walking up to centre stage. Ironically, they seem to be mixing up with their history lessons too. It is important to take some time out, and realize what we lost when Dara lost, and what we can gain if we imbibe his spirit. With such a thought, I picked up Gopal Gandhi's *Dara Shukoh: A Play* (2010).

However, the events unfolding in the run-up to the General Elections in 2014, and the years that followed made me go back to it. Dara is relevant, even necessary today. His vast spiritual canvas, his ability to look at and appreciate faiths beyond his own set me thinking. It set in motion a series of conjectures: what if the heterodox Dara and not the more orthodox Aurangzeb had won the battle of brothers? If mid-17th century India had thrown up a different victor, would the nation have been partitioned? Didn't medieval India throw up a man who was wedded to pluralism of thought and faith much before the founding fathers of our Constitution made it a benchmark for future generations? And would Hindus and Muslims have lived here, as Sir Syed Ahmed Khan said, like the two eyes of the nation? Imagine if a Sufi had outlasted a warrior! Dervish for a shahenshah! Imagine.

The questions shall never be answered. But revisit Dara we must. More so at a time when all that he stood for is being challenged anew. Understand what he stood for, preach many of his things, and we might just end up with a nation that takes pride in its pluralist culture, a society where Hindus read both the Vedas and the Quran, the Muslims appreciate that the concept of one universal God precedes their arrival here; appreciation rather than mere tolerance of each other's culture being the hallmark. Follow this, and the need to combat the challenge thrown up by communal elements disappears. Who can argue with a man who drinks from the common nectar of Sufis and bhakti saints? A man called a dervish by Maulana Azad. In an essay, 'Sarmad Shaheed', Maulana Azad (1910) wrote about Dara:

> He always kept company with philosophers and sufis. His writings indicate that the author was a man of excellent taste. The overwhelming proof of his taste is that in pursuing his goal he lost the distinction between the temple and the mosque. The humility with which he met the Muslim divines was matched by the devotion with which he bowed his head before the Hindu saints and sadhus. Who can deny the purity of this principle?

And Gopal Gandhi, with an enviable and apt lineage for such a project, goes about demolishing many prejudices, exposing many lies. He chooses to spell him Shukoh, explaining beautifully that 'Shikoh' in Persian means 'terror' while 'Shukoh' stands for 'glory'. Gandhi's Dara is not a tragic figure, rather he is a man whose time is now. Mughal-e-Azam is long gone. The prince is here to stay. Gandhi chooses not to dwell much on a failed general—a poet is doomed to be a failure on a battlefield anyway. He stays focused on the undercurrents of the thoughts of the man who translated the Upanishads into Persian—ideas that did not endear him to the radical elements on both sides of the religious divide. A play may not necessarily be an ideal substitute for a history textbook, but hey, did not Rajkumar Hirani's *Lage Raho Munnabhai* do more for introducing Mahatma Gandhi to the bubblegum brigade than any academic book or lecture?

The best help often comes from the source least expected. A play, a film, a book or a philosopher may yet show us the way. After all, amid all the political mudslinging and a society being rapidly polarized, we could do worse than heed Dara's words. Remember what he said when his followers screamed, 'Shuja—his brother and fellow claimant to the throne—murdabad?' Dara replied, 'Let us not wish death to anyone/That is base;/All of us have God's breath in us,/In any case./We live and have our being/With his grace'. In this age, Dara deserves attention. Not that he was a man without a fault. As Vincent A. Smith (1919) pointed out in *The Oxford History of India* (excerpted also in Gandhi's *Dara Shukoh*), 'Dara's considerable natural abilities were neutralized by the violence of his temper and an intolerable arrogance of manner, which gained him hosts of enemies'. But, the Mughal prince, the darling of the cerebral Indian, could well show the nation the path to glory. Dara to Shukoh.

AKBAR AS THE NEW AGE AURANGZEB

None of us ever met Akbar. All of us though know him well. After all, he was Akbar the Great, the man who gave us a stable administration for close to 50 years—it was a no mean accomplishment considering before him North India had at least five rulers in 25 years, with wars for conquest as also succession being a frequent phenomenon. Through a mix of military prowess and acumen, Akbar brought stability at the top. Having defeated the top Rajput kings, including Rana Pratap, he brought the Rajputs virtually into the ruling class through matrimonial alliances with them. A man way ahead of his times, Akbar respected each individual's right to practise any faith. Even marriage to the emperor did not mean a change of religion for Rajput women. Of course, he sought to give the nation a glue-like concept of Deen-e-Ilahi, a new religion incorporating concepts from all religions. A contemporary of Akbar, Fr Monserrate, a Jesuit, opined that by tolerating all faiths, Akbar was dismissing all religions. He was a hero none could hate. And wasn't Akbar an able builder and a man who respected scholars, artists and poets, with the likes of Abul Fazl, Faizi and Tansen among his Nav Ratna? He was. Indeed. Akbar could do no wrong. He was a brave warrior, great administrator and a man blessed with a mind way ahead of his times.

Fortunate are we who were told these realities of shared past in our school days. It is courtesy our NCERT books that all Indians have a ready and enviable portrait of Akbar in our mind. Akbar was always held at par with the best. And an expression 'Akbar the Great' is indelibly written on our mind, much like 'Ashoka the Great'. The next generation though may not be as fortunate. Efforts are underway to project Akbar as a diminutive ruler who lost the Battle of Haldighati to Rana Pratap. In turn, Rana Pratap is being hailed as the man who inspired the revolutionaries of 1857! Not just that. All accomplishments of Akbar are being questioned in a sinister manner. If earlier students of history were told about Aurangzeb's bigotry as if he had a patent over it, the youngsters are now being taken away from the glory of Akbar. He has also been called an invader!

In early 2017, an attempt was made to rename Akbar's Fort in Ajmer as just Ajmer Fort by erasing his name from the gate of the fort. That it went against what the Gazette of India said seemed to matter little. Within no time, a new blue board was put up at the fort without a mention of Akbar. The fort, it seems, sprouted after rainfall in monsoon. Granted that the city of Ajmer and its fort predates the Mughals. Epigraphic evidence and sources, including bardic literature (as cited by well-known historian Dashrath Sharma) shows that they were probably founded by the Chahamanas (Chauhans) around the 11th century. However, the buildings within the present fort date back to Akbar's period. If we believe Abul Fazl, the structures within the fort were constructed in 1570. It remained an important fort under Jahangir who also stayed there for long periods as Prince Salim.

Not content with rewriting the Akbar ka Quila story, the Hindutva brigade got support from dubious historians to turn the good old Battle of Haldighati story on its head. Generations of students have talked of the valour of the Rajput king Rana Pratap, yet always concluded that for all his bravery, Rana Pratap lost the Battle of Haldighati to the Mughals. Importantly, Akbar is said to have stayed away from the battle himself, leaving the responsibility to Rajputs such as Man Singh. An attempt is being made by the Rajasthan government to rewrite textbooks for school students and reference books for graduation students where Rana Pratap, not Akbar, is declared the winner of Haldighati. That the claim flies in the face of historical evidence matters not a dot; it is perception rather than reality which matters. Akbar is the new age Aurangzeb—a man dubbed an invader by none other than the Uttar Pradesh Chief Minister, Yogi Adityanath. Of course, the fact that Akbar was born in Amarkot was considered superfluous to the argument.

Yogi got support from a minister at the Centre. Unveiling a statue of Rana Pratap on his 477th birth anniversary, the minister asked the historians to look again at the contribution of Rana Pratap and wondered aloud if he should not be conferred with the title of Great!

Incidentally, the term Maharana affixed to Rana means the Great Rana. Pratap's name was appended to the honorific title. Even after being defeated by the Mughals, who never humiliated him, he continued to enjoy the title.

These attempts to project Akbar in a sad state are not new. For the past four years, beginning 2014, constant efforts have been made to belittle his contribution to the country. In May 2016, a proposal was aired to rename Akbar Road in New Delhi as Maharana Pratap Road. What was said was obvious—give the Rajputs a place of honour; what was left unsaid was critical and objectionable—the greatest of Mughals had no business having a road named after him in Delhi, which was once an important component of his empire.

Incidentally, this proposal came on the heels of renaming the good old Aurangzeb Road after late President Dr A.P.J. Abdul Kalam. Many read in the rechristening of the Aurangzeb Road the reiteration of the age-old 'Good Muslim versus Bad Muslim' debate. No such nuances need be read in the case of Akbar Road, as the Indian government seems keen to undermine the contribution of Akbar towards nation building and indeed project him as the New Age Aurangzeb. We are living in a time which can be defined as 'post-history'. It does not matter what the past tells us. Whatever happened in the past is now unimportant. What matters in these times of New India is what we perceive or feel, and what and how it happened or should have happened. It is our perception which is important.

What need not be forgotten though that some Hindutva proponents have a problem with Akbar because he was a great warrior, a great builder and a great humanist too.

He does not fit in with the Muslim ruler stereotype. He is not reviled for being cruel. He is not said to have too many vices. Through not a litterateur, he favoured historians and was above considerations of religion when it came to politics. He never claimed to wage a jihad. He never addressed the local residents as kafir. He was a pragmatist who sought to take everybody along. The proponents of Hindutva hide the fact that Hakim Khan Sur was the commander of Rana Pratap. They suppress the truth that it was not only Hemu who was defeated but also the descendants of Sher Shah Suri who were vanquished by Akbar. They do not want the world to know that the Afghans and the Mughals were arch-rivals until both were finished in the 19th century. In other words, religion did not provide a bond of familiarity to peace. It was overweening ambition that decided alliances and hostilities. Attacking Akbar is part of a long drawn out exercise of 'othering' the Muslims, and thereby marching towards Hindu Rashtra. Earlier, Muslims were supposed to bear the brunt of the alleged misdeeds of Aurangzeb; today, they are supposed to feel sorry for the supposed non-achievements, imagined defeats and heightened excess of Akbar! Truth be told, Akbar is projected as the New Age Aurangzeb.

As a noted historian (Syed Ali Nadeem Rezavi) specializing in medieval India said at a seminar in Aligarh Muslim University,

> To the Hindu Mahasabha who licked the boots of the colonial masters and opposed the freedom movement, Akbar was an anathema. As for Rana Pratap being an inspiration for the revolutionaries, well, the leadership of the Revolt of 1857 was given by Nana Phadnavis and Rani Jhansi not to

the Maratha Peshwas but to Bahadur Shah Zafar; though advanced in years and not much more than a nominal ruler, in the minds of common Indians, the Mughal king was still the emperor of the country. Both Nana and the Rani were 'mujahids' who then became 'shaheed'! Where was the invocation to Rana Pratap or Shivaji?

REVISITING AURANGZEB

'I came as a stranger, and I leave as a stranger', wrote the sixth Mughal emperor Aurangzeb Alamgir in a letter to his son a little before death in 1707. On his deathbed, he lamented, 'My precious life has passed in vain'. This from a man whose empire was the most vast of all Mughals, and probably the biggest in Indian history, a man who ruled over 150 million people, an emperor whose empire was bigger and richer than any in the world. His treasury included the famous Kohinoor. Yet all he wanted was peaceful death, and be buried in a simple, open-aired tomb—in contrast to his parents Mumtaz Mahal and Shah Jahan whose last resting place, Taj Mahal, evokes awe to this day. Yet, as noted historian Audrey Truschke argues in *Aurangzeb: The Man and the Myth* (2017), 'Aurangzeb may have been content to be forgotten but the world is not ready to let him go. Aurangzeb lives as a vibrant figure in public memory in twenty first century India and Pakistan'.

Indeed, he has never gone too far away from public imagination. Ever since Independence, his reign, his alleged destruction of Hindu temples, indeed, even his alleged religiosity, have all been held up as a debt the modern-day Muslims of India must pay to be accepted as free and equal citizens. For more than 300 years after he breathed his last in 1707, Aurangzeb threatened secular

India with his deep religiosity. It was only at the height of the Babri Masjid controversy in the 1980s and early 1990s that he yielded the place of being the man most hated to his ancestor Babur, when Muslims were often addressed as '*Babur ki Aulad*' (Progeny of Babur) by some votaries of Hindutva. Otherwise, Aurangzeb has been almost alone as a vilification target, his legacy defiled, not just debated upon, the emperor pronounced guilty for the decline of the Mughals. In doing so, all his contribution to Indian society and polity has been dismissed as nothing significant.

Yet, Aurangzeb was a pious ruler, a man of honesty and integrity, someone who deserves to be judged by the moral system then prevalent across the world, not by contemporary yardsticks of democracy, human rights, etc. As Truschke (2017) writes,

He made a lasting contribution to the interpretation and exercise of legal codes and was renowned—by people of all backgrounds and religious stripes—for his justice. He was quite possibly the richest man of his day and boasted a treasury overflowing with gems, pearls, and gold, including the spectacular Kohinoor diamond.

Incidentally, so keen was Aurangzeb on being seen as a man of justice that during the war of succession he waged against his brothers, he wrote a letter (*nishan*) to Rana Raj Singh of Mewar. This letter survives in the famous *Vir Vinod* of Kaviraj Shyamladas. In the letter, Aurangzeb claims that kingship is nothing but a trust from God.

The people are khalqullah, creation of God, as the king is Zillallah, the shadow of God. He should thus deal equally with them and not discriminate on the basis of religion or sect. Kings are like pillars of God's court, and if he bends on one side, the justice of God would fail.

Yes, he did destroy temples, but equally he protected many more, gave imperial grants to Brahmins. There is a recorded instance of Rani Hadi, the widow of Jaswant Singh. During the Rathore Rebellion of 1679, she wrote to Aurangzeb offering to demolish temples herself if he bestowed *tika* on her. Aurangzeb refused. The information is contained in Waqai Ajmer. Similarly, he is harangued for restricting the celebration of Holi. What is not mentioned is he did likewise with Eid and observation of Muharram too. Forgotten is the fact that he employed more Hindus than any other Muslim ruler until that point in history. His *diwan* was a Hindu, the only instance in Mughal history when such a responsibility was vested by an emperor in a Hindu raja. And contrary to common perception, music did not die a slow death during his reign. Himself a proficient veena player, the famous book on Indian music *Raag Darpan* was composed in his reign by Faqirullah, a high ranked *mansabdar* (a member of imperial bureaucracy). And when he did employ *jizyah* (annual tax), it was to finance his military campaigns in the Deccan. For the first 21 years of his reign, no *jizyah* was levied on his Hindu subject. It was political necessity rather than religiosity that drove him to it. He was just a monarch who fought to extend or consolidate his territory. He was no proselytizer, no preacher who wanted to convert all to Islam.

Interestingly, contrary to the common perception, the Rajputs supported Aurangzeb, and not his brother Dara Shukoh in the battle for succession following the imprisonment of Shah Jahan. This is brought into light in a letter written by Prince Akbar, after he had rebelled against his father, Aurangzeb, and joined ranks with the Rathores who rebelled against Aurangzeb in 1679, that is, more than

20 years after Aurangzeb had assumed the throne. Prince Akbar and the Rathores, however, were defeated by the forces of Aurangzeb. He went to Sambhaji, Shivaji's son. He wrote to his father, 'Have you forgotten why Dara lost and you gained the throne? Dara lost the support of the Rajputs who rallied around you'. On the other hand, Dara, much hailed for his width of vision, called Mirza Raja Jai Singh a *Dakkani bandar* (Deccan monkey). Hardly a surprise then that it was Aurangzeb who was supported directly or indirectly by the likes of Mirza Raja Jai Singh, Jaswant Singh, Rana Raj Singh, Rao Dulpat Bundela and Raghu Ram, etc. Even less a surprise comes from his contemporary historian Bhimsen who never regarded Aurangzeb to be a dogmatic ruler.

However, for all his positives, such has been the hatred towards him, that New Delhi, the place he ruled for 49 years, decided to do away with any vestige of association with him in 2015 when the centrally located Aurangzeb Road was renamed Dr A.P.J. Abdul Kalam Road. Aurangzeb, the man who imprisoned his father, was treated no better by posterity. Himself accused of bigotry, Aurangzeb suffers due to widespread intolerance today.

Not all is lost though. As Truschke (2017) proved, Aurangzeb is being looked at anew, at least in academic circles. No longer is he the man who indulged only in wanton destruction. No longer is he just a patricide. Today, in scholarly debate and academic discussion, he is regarded as an emperor with great accomplishments and obvious flaws. Greys, rather than black and white, describe him better.

Truschke's work is like a necklace of the gems which have come our way over the past five years or so. In fact, it started a few years ago when widely read author–historian William Dalrymple sprang a little surprise in his introduction to *Princes and Painters in Mughal India* (2012), which he co-edited with Yuthika Sharma, by pointing out that Aurangzeb was 'a pragmatic ruler who frequently patronised Hindu institutions'. Dalrymple argued that some of his measures such as imposition of *jizyah* should be looked at from the prism of exigencies of administration rather than religion. Of course, the fact that there were no communal riots during Aurangzeb's time gave credence to the view. And no mass conversion of Hindus by Aurangzeb's warriors with a sword in one hand and the Quran in the other. Aurangzeb, the convenient bigot of history, got a new coat of paint.

Dalrymple showed that Aurangzeb's rule was 'less tyrannical than previously thought'. Incidentally, the book had paintings about the early years of Aurangzeb's reign where he is shown in confabulation with his courtiers, laying to rest all claims of him being opposed to art and culture, music or dance.

Then came Rajmohan Gandhi's *Punjab: A History from Aurangzeb to Mountbatten* (2013) where he showed both his political accomplishments and his gentle, human side.

> Diligent in religious observance, Aurangzeb was a tenacious fighter as well. The empire under Aurangzeb's long rule increased in area. New territories annexed included Little Tibet beyond Kashmir in the north, Chittagong beyond Dhaka in the east, and, in the south, the Muslim kingdoms of Golconda and Bijapur.

He hailed his simplicity too: 'of small stature, with a long nose, a round beard and an olive skin, Aurangzeb, usually wore plain white muslin' and 'applied himself assiduously to business'.

Now comes the best attempt of them all by Truschke (2016) who, incidentally, had written at length about patronage to Sanskrit during the Mughal era in *Culture of Encounters*. Sanskrit declined because of the flowering of Hindi during the reign of Aurangzeb, she reasoned, about the man who, in his early years, had read the Quran and the Hadith as also Rumi and Saadi and was exposed to Persian translations of the Ramayana and Mahabharata too. Aurangzeb even composed in Braj Bhasha!

Today, if Aurangzeb is being looked afresh in academic circles, it has not necessarily meant that Aurangzeb has got an image makeover for the common man. If he is not as loathed now, the reason comes from competition. Today, the Hindutva lobby with its revisionist history has made sure that Babur, and even Akbar, is projected as new age Aurangzeb. The original's image is cast in stone.

PART 2

Muslim Identity

BEING MUSLIM

I AM THE 'OTHER'

I AM THE 'OTHER', an ill-disguised term coined by M.S. Golwalkar to succeed expressions such as *yavana, asura* (demon) and *mlecchha*. I am the beef eating, bearded 'Other'; the man Bankim Chandra Chattopadhyay referred to in *Anandmath*. Yes, the same *Anandmath* that gave us the *pratima* (idol) of Bharat Maa, the national song 'Vande Mataram' and the subsequent '*Bharat Mata ki jai*' slogan, steeped in the hues of Hindu nationalism. He called the Muslims the 'bearded degenerates', projecting them as enemies, belittling their contribution to the Sanyasi Rebellion on which the novel was loosely based. He added through Jnanananda, the most accomplished disciple of Satyananda,

> For a long time we've been wanting to smash the nest of these weaver birds, to raze the city of these Muslim foreigners and throw it into the river—to burn the enclosure of these swine and purify Mother Earth again! Brothers that day has come! (Chattopadhyay 1882)

When *Anandmath* first found space on bookshelves in the early 1880s, the Muslims were no longer the rulers, the last of the Mughals having been vanquished over 25 years ago. The passing of political power from the hands of the Muslims to the British meant that Chattopadhyay did not have to look over his shoulder while portraying Muslims as *asuras*. Remarkably, it equated Muslims with the lowest of the Hindu caste hierarchy, an obvious statement about the disdain in which the author held them.

Interestingly, a film too was made in 1952 by Hemen Gupta. Chattopadhyay felt safe from any possible retribution. Much like Rajeshwar Singh of the Hindu outfit Dharm Jagran Manch would have felt in late 2015 when he was first emboldened enough to claim that the country would be rid of Muslims and Christians by 2021. 'We have so far ensured *"ghar wapsi"* (reconversion) of three lakh Muslims and Christians back to Hinduism', he claimed, rejoicing in climbing a molehill before a mountain of 180 million Muslims and another 27.8 million Christians!

Provocative as Singh's plans are, I am not in the least bit shocked. Rather as the 'Other' whose *janmabhoomi* and *punyabhoomi* are not one and the same, I am used to such rabble rousing. Nearly 90 years ago, a journal called *Hindu Panch* came into being with a five-fold strategy. '*Hindu Panch*'s strategy was different. It was provocative in its tone, strident in language and content, courted controversy openly, yet cleverly', writes Akshaya Mukul (2015) in *Gita Press*. Reminds you of the modern-day Singhs and Togadias? Wait, there is more to come.

What could one say of a weekly that stated its five-fold mission on the cover—Hindu Sangathan (Organization), Shuddhi Sanskar (Culture of Reconversion), Achhootddhar (Removal of Untouchability), Samaj Sudhar (Social

Reform), Hindi Prachar (Spread of Hindi) and a motto on
its cover page that openly spelt out its goal of restoring the
dignity of Hindus, saving the Hindu name, bringing Hindu
rule of India and waking up Hindus from their slumber....
Hindu Panch would focus on reports of Muslims attacking
and abducting Hindu girls and widows, carrying highly
objectionable columns like 'Choti Banam Dadhi' (Brahmin
Tuft versus Muslim Beard) where Muslims would be
derided. (Mukul 2015)

What *Hindu Panch* sought to achieve through goals such
as Hindu *sangathan* and *shuddhi sanskar* (culture of
purification/reconversion) in 1920s is sought to be done
by a Central minister such as Ram Shanker Katheria and
his appeal for Hindu *sangathan* besides various *ghar
wapsi* campaigns in Agra. His party colleague Kundanika
Sharma went one step further, equating the community
with 'demons' and 'Ravana' even as she urged her followers to 'behead ten heads for one head'. Her ideological
peer, Vishwa Hindu Parishad's Ashok Lavania emphasized, 'The revenge of the killing of one brother demands
killing of ten rakshas'. Whether Katheria or Lavania
speaks, only the name of the speaker changes, the crux
remains the same—take up arms against Muslims, who
are 'traitors' and 'demons'.

In over 90 years, nothing has changed. I continue
to be the Other, the *asura*, the *rakshas*, the demon. As
Golwalkar wrote so frankly yet heartlessly in *We or Our
Nationhood Defined* (2006),

The great patriot, the late Vithalbhai Patel, expressed his
dying wish that his remains be brought to Hindustan,
his beloved motherland. There is another picture of a so-
called 'Patriot' Maulana Mohammad Ali, (who also died
abroad) who directed his remains to be taken, not to the

land which had fostered him and his forefathers before him, but to the foreign land of Mecca. These two personalities may be taken to represent the Hindu and the Moslem mentality in our country. Love for the country being the first essential of Nationality, it scarcely need be told who is a nationalist and who a foreigner to the National life in Hindustan. This example strongly substantiates our proposition that in this country the Hindus alone are the Nation and the Moslems and others, if not actually antinational are at least outside the body of the Nation.

Greeted with invectives by Chattopadhyay, distrust by Golwalkar and regarded as an easy pick by Singh and his ilk, I am the 'Other', now called 'Akhlaq' in Dadri, 'Mazlum Ansari' or 'Imteyaz Khan' in Jharkhand or 'Dilkush', 'Ajmal' and 'Naim' in Delhi's Begumpur. I am accused of cow slaughter, of storing beef in my fridge, trading in cattle and not being ready to say *'Bharat Mata ki jai'* on a stroll in the park, as Ajmal and Naim were in Delhi. Never mind that the accusers who claim to love Swami Vivekananda and revere V.D. Savarkar did not have an idea of what they stood for. Vivekananda wanted people to take recourse to beef, biceps and the Bhagavad Gita for the salvation of India, the 3Bs. And Savarkar, that icon of Hindutva who wrote clemency letters to the British from the Andaman, wrote, in an essay titled 'Care for Cows, Do Not Worship Them', that considering the cow as divine is an insult to humankind. Continuing with Savarkar's sentiments on the cow, Jyotirmaya Sharma (2011) writes,

> He also ridicules the idea that cow dung and urine could purify the impure. He argues that in order to save a few temples, a handful of Brahmins and a few cows, orthodox Hindus allowed the Hindu nation's subjugation for centuries.... In terms of usefulness, a buffalo, a horse, a dog

and even a donkey are animals that are equally useful. Therefore, to consider the cow as holy is not only madness, but a sign of utter foolishness, concludes Savarkar.

Savarkar believed that the Muslim armies, capitalizing on the Hindu sentiments with respect to the cow, kept the animal at the forefront of their armies, thereby avoiding any direct attack by the enemy!

In the case of Savarkar's take on the cow, history has acted as a sieve, retaining little, draining out almost everything. Of course, today, when the Chief Minister of Maharashtra suggests that those who do not pronounce '*Bharat Mata ki jai*' have no right to live in India, one wonders if he has ever read Savarkar.

As for those who barged into Akhlaq's house or waylaid Mazlum or the man who mutilated and killed Afrazul, the less said the better. For everybody, from the Chief Minister to the Jharkhand killers, I am simply the 'Other'.

Today I am accused of following what Vivekananda desired for my Hindu countrymen. Ah! Lest I forget, I am the 'Other'; the 'Other', the Prime Minister deemed necessary to refer to in his conversation with the Saudi king; the 'Other' called Cheraman Perumal who is believed to have met Prophet Mohammed and converted to Islam and helped establish India's first masjid in Kerala during the prophet's time. I have been here for almost 1,400 years. Yet, I am the 'Other'.

THE OTHER AS THE NEW NORMAL

We live in the age of the Other. Rather in the age of distancing the Other. Hating the Other. Attacking, maiming and even killing the Other is the new normal. A society that rose as one when Nirbhaya was gang-raped in Delhi has no time for tears for Afrazul's widow. Nirbhaya died a gory death; she was assaulted multiple times by men driven by hate and lust. It was almost barbaric. Afrazul's death was not normal either. On 6 December 2017, coinciding with the 25th anniversary of the demolition of the Babri Masjid, Afrazul, a migrant worker from Malda in West Bengal, was called on pretext of work by Shambhulal Regar. Once there, he was attacked with a pickaxe. Then as he screamed for help, he was set on fire. The body was recognized by his son-in-law who almost fainted on seeing the charred remains. This happened barely a kilometre from a police station. While Shambhulal murdered Afrazul, his 14-year-old nephew made a video which soon went viral. Many boasted about the new vigour of Hindutva forces; others threatened a repeat. Disconcertingly, hundreds joined hands to pool in more than ₹3 lakh for the wife of Shambhulal who was arrested by the police, long after the crime had been committed.

A good section of our society was appalled though. Some words of disgust were shared in private. Then everybody went back to work. No candle marches, no dharnas, nothing. Killing a Muslim was the new normal. Much like it was with Pehlu Khan in Alwar, Junaid in Mathura, Mazlum Ansari in Jharkhand. A few feeble noises, a discussion or two in rarefied confines of an auditorium. That is all. It reminded one of Martin Niemoller's 'First they came for the Socialists...'. I dread when they go for others.

But it is not about lynching, killing, burning alone. These are tragic incidents which get across to the larger society, thanks largely to social media. It is about being killed every night on television, about being put through the crucible every evening. Every night on television,

Muslims are the new villains. The hashtags on English and Hindi channels with barely an honourable exception or two are shamelessly anti-Muslim. The panellists, often even anchors, are anti-Muslim too. There have been cases when spokesmen of the ruling party have abused Muslim clerics on air, even threatened to finish off the community in 15 minutes. That they continue to be seen on television after such rants is a proof of official blessings to their deep-seated prejudice against Muslims. Interestingly, the channels' attempt to strike a balance by getting a representative of the community to appear on the show gives a further chance to show Muslims in a more negative light. People such as Taslima Nasreen and Javed Akhtar, self-declared atheists, are called to talk of Muslims and Islam. That they would not have read even the Quran, leave alone authentic Hadiths, is considered no disqualification. Just their Muslim names are sufficient. Occasionally, there is Tarek Fateh, a person who cannot enter his land of birth, but feels free to give sermons to Indian Muslims. But a Muslim is supposed to feel sorry, hang his head in shame for every instance of Triple Talaq and every time ISIS bombs the innocent in some part of the world. It is as if they themselves instigated these happenings. No such questions are asked of every Hindu who appears on television every time an Akhlaq, an Afrazul is lynched to death. Then it is just the deed of a few loony characters, at worst, local goons or stray case of political violence. Imagine, for a second, in Rajsamund or Dadri, if the tables were turned. That Akhlaq and some Muslims had killed a Hindu on suspicion of storing pork in fridge! Or Shambhulal had been hacked and burnt alive by Afrazul! The difference in reaction would have said it all.

For proof, just look around you, how questioning a Muslim's patriotism is the new normal. In Kasganj, on 26 January 2018, Muslims were hoisting the national flag, exhibiting pride in their nation. Yet, an unauthorized bike rally led by some Hindutva activists created trouble. The bikers asked the community to unfurl saffron flag and after Jana Gana Mana, recite Vande Mataram. It reminded one of the fate of a policeman in Maharashtra who was forced to carry a saffron flag across the town, and say 'Jai Bhawani'. In the Kasganj scuffle, a Hindu boy was killed and a hundred shops of the minority community were set afire. And close to 80 boys from the community were picked up for questioning. Hoisting the Tricolour or not, singing the national anthem or not, it is no longer good enough. A community seems to have a monopoly over nationalism, however warped its ideas, however question-able its credentials. This further distancing of the Other is the new normal too. And the community already boxed in, lives in perpetual state of fear.

It is all in stark contrast to our freedom struggle. That was the time when the modern-day self-appointed nationalists were all helping the British, leaking crucial information on where was a particular national leader at what time; an ace Hindutva votary even pledged to work for the perpetuation of the British rule if he were to be released from prison in the Andaman Islands. Indeed, in word and action, these men considered Muslims and Christians their prime enemies, the British later. At such a time, it was Abid Husain 'Safrani' who coined the slogan of 'Jai Hind' while the words 'Inquilab Zindabad' came from the pen of Maulana Hasrat Mohani. Even *Angrezo Bharat Chhoro*' was a call given by Yusef Meher Ali. Not to forget

Suraiya Tayyabji who designed our Tricolour, the way we know and love it. Today, it is their succeeding generations who are assaulted on the roads of India, harangued on television shows, and frequently asked to go to Pakistan. And the society does not protest—'#NotInMyName' campaign being the sole exception—not much more than a whimper anyway. How ungrateful can a nation be! How forgetful of its history, how unapologetic for the killing of fellow Indians!

Today, when a Muslim talks of a shared past, of times when Hindus and Muslims fought shoulder to shoulder against the British, the times when Swami Shradhanand, otherwise a votary of conversion, preached from the steps of the historic Jama Masjid in Delhi, times when the Muslim priestly class gave calls to the community to desist from cow slaughter on Eid as a mark of respect for the majority community sentiments, of the times when Sir Syed Ahmed Khan considered the two major communities as the two eyes of the nation, he is considered a weakling, someone harking back to the past to cover his own inadequacies of the present. Even a reminder to the words and action of Mufti Abdul Bari Nomani, who went to Sankat Mochan temple in Banaras to empathize with the purohit following serial blasts in the city in 2006, cut no ice. As has been the experience of Kafeel Khan, the Gorakhpur doctor who saved the lives of hundreds of infants in the city in 2017, or Salim Shaikh, the bus driver who saved the lives of scores of Hindu pilgrims in Amarnath the same year. Khan was instead held responsible for children's death (corruption charges were dropped against him). A Gujarati newspaper falsely but deliberately gave credit to the son of the owner of the bus for saving lives! It was probably too much for it to take that a Muslim man saved the lives of Hindu pilgrims. Whether he saves lives, or he hails India, in modern-day India, a Muslim cannot be a winner. Worse, he is dubbed a 'Khangrezi' in constant online abuse. Being a Muslim and Congress supporter is to invite serious online abuse. That very Muslim upholds the tradition, the values of our nation, the principles enshrined in our Constitution matters not a bit. In public perception, Muslims are the Other, kind of roadblocks on the path of development, the anti-nationals who take the focus away from economic advancement of the nation. Indeed, in 2018, in the battle of perception, Muslims are rank losers, the new popular villains, just like what noted filmmaker Sanjay Leela Bhansali so painstakingly attempted to project Alauddin Khilji. What Bhansali was doing was only technically an attack at a Muslim monarch, albeit a non-practising one. What he exhibited was his bigotry, his deep dislike, even hostility towards Muslims. Much like many other Indians today. From television newsrooms to Rajsamund killers, to those asking the community to migrate to Pakistan, they are all the same; it's just the tone, the tenor varies. Polarization is sadly the new success mantra.

THE FIRST MUSLIM

A little more than two years ago when I first laid my hands on Lesley Hazleton's *The First Muslim* (2013), I could not put it down. I distinctly remember sitting at the dining table with the book, narrating the story of Prophet Muhammad, occupying my mind space as also that on the table. The glass, the plate and all else could wait. I knew about the Prophet from the beginning of my life, had read about him in elementary books of theology, not to forget a few hagiographies sought to be palmed off as biographies. Lesley's book was different. She projected him not as a superhero with a halo around him but as a normal human being, something the Quran too emphasizes more than once. In fact when his enemies of the day wanted a prophet to be a magician, an angel or at least a rich man with a garden and wealth, they were rebuked by the Almighty in the Quran—the emphasis all along being on the prophet being a normal human being who earned his living, went to market, ate, rested, slept, etc. Lesley, to her eternal credit, put him against the socio-economic backdrop of the day and sought to make sense of his actions accordingly. For instance, his call against female infanticide in a society where the male child was treasured, the females often buried alive.

Without any hues of divine enlightenment, Lesley, a Jew settled in Seattle, talked of the Prophet as a boy who had very unusual and trying circumstances. A boy who had lost his father before he was born, he lost his mother when he was all of six. Brought up by his grandfather, his was a remarkable rise from the edges of the society to a reasonably well off and trusted business agent by the time he was getting into middle age. Except that all this paled when compared to what transpired on Mount Hira when he was 40, the moment he got the first revelation. It is here that Lesley rises above various biographers and puts Muhammad's reaction—he was shaken to the bone—in a dispassionate manner, casting aside various accounts of mythical peace and bliss. It is also the point that the role of his first wife, Khadija, comes into play. It is the reason too why I picked up the book again. First time round, I read her to know the first Muslim—the Quran instructs, 'Muhammad say, "I am the first Muslim"'. This time I picked up the book to know more about Khadija, the woman who stood by him when he needed her, the wife who trusted him, lent him her shoulder. Hers is an unusual story which comes through as Lesley seeks to complete the picture of the life and times of the prophet.

Not enough has been written about Khadija, but whatever Lesley has written projects her as a woman of unusual merit. It also puts in place the sundry maulanas of the subcontinent who are against the idea of a woman having her own identity, her own will. The reality is quite different. Khadija was an extremely successful businesswoman who had been married twice. She was a financially independent woman who hired Muhammad as her business manager. It was 'an unusual marriage. She was older than he, and, while accounts vary as to exactly how much older, most settle on age forty for her, twenty-five for him. Not that this was what made the marriage unusual'.

It was not a marriage of convenience either. For 24 years, the two were in a monogamous relationship until she passed away and 'long after her death, he would hold her up as far superior to any of his later wives'. It was love pure and simple. As Lesley (2013) puts it, 'What made the marriage unusual, then, was not the age difference but its closeness, especially given the difference in social status between husband and wife. And the fact that it was she who proposed to him'.

She is described as a 'determined' and 'intelligent' woman, traits not often used to describe women those days. The two of them had four daughters and a son, Qasim, who did not survive until his second birthday.

Here too Khadija sought to mitigate the Prophet's sorrow through Zayd, a slave boy she had given him as a marriage gift. The Prophet treated him more like a son though.

Lesley draws a graphic picture of the revelation of the first verses. Following the revelation, the Prophet came from the mountain, his robe torn, his arms and legs scratched. It was then that Khadija comforted him.

> She held him, cradled him as the night sky began to grow pale in the east with the reassuring prospect of the day. Slowly, haltingly, the words he had perhaps felt more than heard began to find physical shape in his mouth. Even as he still shook in Khadija's arms, Muhammad found his voice, and the first revelation of the Quran formed into words that another human being could hear.... What had been breathed into him up on the mountain was now breathed out, to take its place in the world. They had been man and wife for fifteen years, but she had never heard him speak with such beauty before. His speech was unusually terse and restrained.... Yet even as the words entered her mind, she was aware of how extraordinary they were. Not just for the man she loved, but for her whole world. Whatever this was, she instantly grasped one thing: it was the end of the quiet, almost modest life they had lived until now. Nothing would ever be the same again. Another woman would have thought it unfair, perhaps.... She would have tried to protect herself as much as him by denying the validity of what had happened.... Instead, Khadija reacted as though this was what she had been half-expecting all along—as though she had seen in Muhammad what he had barely glimpsed in himself.... And once he told her everything that had happened, her calm conviction was reinforced. 'By him in whose hand is my soul', she said, 'I hope that you may be the prophet of this people'. She held him until sunrise, feeling his muscles relax as the shuddering fear subsided. (Hazleton 2013)

This is a description with a clear focus on the Prophet's wife that set me thinking. I wanted to read more about her, know her better. Almost in desperation, I called up my niece settled in Seattle to meet Lesley Hazleton. And tried to read whatever I could on this remarkable woman. Soon, I discovered, Khadija traded goods through the major commercial centres of that time, from Mecca to Syria and to Yemen. Her business was larger than all of the Quraysh trades combined. Twice widowed herself, she gave her earnings to the poor and the orphans. And then of course, she was the first person to believe in the revelation sent to the Prophet. All along, she retained her identity, her name, even after her husband became the leader of the times. She was always Khadija bint Khuwaylid, never Khadija Muhammad. Yet she has remained in the background, never really centre stage, as various biographers have written about the last messenger. Not easy, but Lesley Hazleton's book has made sure I want to know about Khadija, the woman, her man and her times.

EXTRAORDINARY TALES OF MUSLIM WOMEN

Love sells. The furtive kind sells better. Many summers ago when life was about affirmation and acquiescence, Ismat Chughtai came up with *Lihaaf* (The Quilt). And lo, the world was shaken out of its slumber. We were not living in times of acquiescence, after all! The fiercely independent author had done the unmentionable—she had talked of women who loved their own, of furtive touches under a quilt and of moments of stolen pleasure. Muslim society was outraged. Years later, it turned out that the larger society shared the sentiments. The proof came when Deepa Mehta's *Fire*, starring the redoubtable Shabana Azmi and the then upcoming Nandita Das, hit silver screens across the country. Cinema halls at many places had to thwart dharnas; at others, the film's posters were smeared with black ink. The show went on. But it almost didn't. It was almost too much for the society to accept two women seeking solace in each other.

Times, they have changed. Quietly, with barely a ripple. Some five years ago, I came across Nighat M. Gandhi's book, *Alternative Realities* (Gandhi 2013), which talks of 'love in the lives of Muslim women'. In the decades gone by, it would have been a head-turner; for many, it would have been worthy of a sermon. Not so today despite the fact that it is not just the usual love stories that Gandhi talks of—boy meets girl, they fall in love, their parents object and ultimately love conquers all. That kind of love is for escapist cinema. For Gandhi, love is a four-letter word. Forbidden love is more tempting, more tantalizing. She disdains the conventional, and is hooked to the extraordinary tales of ordinary Muslim women in the Indian subcontinent. These women love across the barriers of religion, region, caste and even mock at gender stereotypes. Some are happy to be second wives of married men, some cannot understand why they cannot have a same-sex husband or wife.

For reasons easy to understand and harder to appreciate, she chooses to highlight the story of Nisho, who considers herself a woman in love with a man, except that she is not quite a woman. Yet she is in love with a man, seven–eight years older to her, a man who professes love but who cannot marry her. In the chapter *Rakhee Sawant of Sind*, Gandhi quotes Nisho:

> Who hasn't been in love? At least once in their lifetime? ... People think only a man and a woman can make a couple.... But, the truth is, anybody can fall in love with anybody. A man can fall in love with a man, a woman can fall in love with a woman. But society doesn't accept such love.

It is a story of alternative love, the one destined to be doomed in a society where those born different are regarded as either deviants, or worse, hijras. As Nisho laments, 'There comes a time even in the life of a hijra, when she wants to settle down'.

Then, there is the more engaging story of Firdaus, a feminist who can walk out of a loveless marriage but cannot give up on love, with or without marriage. Here Gandhi begins by quoting from Maulana Ashraf Ali Thanvi's widely read *Behashti Zevar*, where he advises that women should not be taught to write! Firdaus, obviously, thankfully too, would have none of it and happily talks of how her mother burnt all books at home following the imprisonment of the noted poet Faiz Ahmed Faiz, holding literature to be the refuge of the escapist. The collection of Firdaus's father was burnt too. Firdaus, though, hid hers. Years later, when her first novel was published, her father advised her: 'Keep writing. You'll save yourself a lot of suffering'.

For a while, the fate of Firdaus reminded me of our own Salma, the talented Tamil writer who had to withdraw from school when she reached puberty; had her books and magazines burnt or sold as waste paper and initially, had to write under a pseudonym—she was born Rokkiah—to avoid recognition. It was a classic case of what Oscar Wilde said about a classic artist: Reveal art and conceal the artist. Salma, more appropriately, Rokkiah, though could not remain concealed for long. She went on to carve out her own niche.

So too would Firdaus, Nisho and others featured in this book. The author weaves personal stories of women in villages, towns and cities of the subcontinent. Word by word, she demolishes many silences, gets rid of many stereotypes. Like Chughtai many summers ago, she removes the veil of silence covering Muslim women's sexuality and quietly hands over a heart-warming message with stories of how these women overcome the restrictions placed on their freedom. For instance, a woman like Ghazala, who prefers the life of a second wife, or Nusrat and QT who believe theirs is a normal marriage, although they are both women! She does not confine herself to women on the margins of society. She widens her canvas by talking of Mahmuda, Bangladesh's first woman ambassador who still grieves for her first husband who was picked up by the Pakistan army during the 1971 war, never to return. Mahmuda married again, only to be caught in a loveless marriage. Completely different is the story of a Gujarati Muslim poet who sacrifices her love for a Gujarati Brahman man in the wake of the 2002 Gujarat hate violence.

At the beginning of the journey, the author explores her own unconventional story as a woman who dared to make choices that pitted her against her family and cultures. And in doing so, the distance in time and place help her locate it better. All of this adds up to tell us, ever so quietly, that times are a changing. Alternative realities might be just that, but they are real. Not every generation gets a Chughtai; for the moment, Gandhi will do fine as a modern-day raconteur.

NOT EASY BEING A MUSLIM

It is not easy being a Muslim in India, it never has been, especially being a secular one. Back in my school days in 1980s, Sharjah in the UAE hosted what turned out to be *the* match, the one where Javed Miandad, that incorrigibly abrasive cricketer, hit the famous six off the last ball of the hapless Chetan Sharma to win a match India had no business to lose. All through the day, like millions of youngsters, I had cheered India on every ball. Colour television was still a novelty, and we had bought one just a little before the tournament to watch the fun from the desert. As India outclassed Pakistan for the better part of the match, I often found myself jumping up and down in front of the television, my hands turned red because of the loud and consistent clapping whenever an Indian batsman hit a boundary or a bowler took a wicket to break a crucial partnership. It was heady stuff. Until that incorrigibly abrasive cricketer ruined it all.

On 18 April 1986, Miandad's six hurt. The worst came the next morning in school as I was asked by one of my classmates from the Walled City of Delhi, if I had been distributing *laddus* following Pakistan's come-from-behind victory? Too hurt, too shocked, I could not muster up any words and consoled myself into believing that he hailed from a lunatic fringe. My agony was far from over. The fringe again occupied centre stage in my life a few years later in a prestigious college of Delhi University. This time, India had defeated Pakistan in a match it seemed doomed to lose. The next day, a classmate, hailing from the more upmarket Siri Fort area of the city, asked me if I had been mourning. '*Toone to kal khana bhi nahi khaya hoga*' (You must not have even eaten your food yesterday), he mocked. His words still ring in my ears. I could not win any which way. India lost. I lost. India won. I still lost.

These thoughts came back to my mind when I started reading Anees Salim's powerful work, *Vanity Bagh* (2013), a book where he talks freely and passionately about mini Pakistans in the country, those pockets of Muslim domi-nance where many believe the loyalties of the residents in case of Indo-Pak cricket matches lay elsewhere. Anees writes with a rare mix of humour and gravity. He does not hold his punches; he goes for the jugular. What he writes makes many feel uncomfortable; what he writes must be written. With such a direct approach and an extremely sen-sitive subject, he easily grabbed my attention. And, indeed, of so many others, considering he also won The Hindu Prize for Best Fiction (2013). The first time around, I read the book in a hurry, almost like a river in the mountains not ready to wait too long. The joy was all in the movement of the moment. I came back to it recently. This time I read with patience, care and rapt attention, almost like a river in the plains, tranquil, silent but profound. *Vanity Bagh* seemed to have more qualities for admiration.

The book stays on my shelf. I go back to it every now and then. I read it when I find myself silently cheering Misbah-ul-Haq as he tries valiantly to rescue Pakistan in umpteen matches. One day, a little more than a couple of years ago, I pushed myself away from work for a few

133

minutes to catch up on the score of an Indo-Pak match. As luck would have it, I had barely watched three balls that an Indian batsman got out followed by a longish commercial break. As I retraced my steps towards my office, I heard a photojournalist comment, '*Miyan bhai toh out ho gaya ... ab aap kahan rukenge?*' (Miyan Bhai has got out ... now what will you do here?) Something twisted inside me. But words failed me again. Yet again, a dirty look was all I could give him. And went back to reading Anees Salim that night. How many mini Pakistans and Pakistanis exist in the minds of my countrymen!

At night, I read a few pages of the book for the *n*th time and closed the book. For how long could I fight my demons through someone else's words, however powerful they might be? I asked myself many questions that night: Why is it that in any crucial cricket match, or at the time of a controversy about, say, a Taslima Nasreen seeking asylum here or an M.F. Husain painting Bharat Mata in his own way, I am required to speak up, I am supposed to have an opinion? Why should I have to prove my patriotism to those who had never undertaken a similar test? And many of them, it must be said, have owed their allegiance to organizations that have not respected the Tricolour or regarded our Constitution with the dignity it deserves. Why should I always be expected to have politically correct opinions? And pray why cannot I live my life quietly, unobtrusively without any doubting Thomases knocking at my door, the way those lunatic elements did at the height of the Babri Masjid–Ram Janmabhoomi controversy, shouting '*Musalman ke do hi sthaan, Pakistan ya qabrastan*'.

Back then, I took recourse to a book by Girilal Jain to understand the challenge in front of me. His *The Hindu*

Phenomenon (1994) helped clear a few cobwebs. Then came a book by M.N. Srinivas, making me wonder, why can't I live my life like a little stream that joins the mainstream yet manages to retain its identity? Like Mr Moorthy next door or Mr Singh down the lane, why can't I wear trousers to work and come back home to slip into pyjamas, like they don a *mundu* (a garment worn around the waist) or a dhoti at home? Why can't I enjoy a cricket match for the fare it provides and for once cheer a good shot or a good ball without the fear of being tagged a traitor? Why can't I enjoy the simple joys of life? Why can't I just be an Indian?

There are no easy answers there. I tried to find some though, in the essays by Irfan Ahmad and Tanweer Fazal which form a crucial part of the book, *Being Muslim in South Asia* (Jeffery and Sen, 2014). But as Ahmad and Fazal will appreciate, it is not easy being a Muslim in India. It was not easy when Indira Gandhi ruled. It did not become easier during the reign of Narasimha Rao. It certainly is not easier today.

MUSLIMS IN INDIAN CITIES

'Call me Shaikh, not Shubham' ran a headline in the Kashmir Monitor (2016). Intrigued, I started reading the story of 21-year-old Ansar Ahmed Shaikh, who, defying steep odds, had cleared the civil services examination and was all set to get into IAS. Shaikh, hailing from Jalna's Shedgaon village in Maharashtra, had a story more gripping than his success tale to reveal. Until his selection for the civil services, Shaikh lived a life of absolute anonymity—in many ways, an uncomfortably double life.

In Pune's Fergusson College, where he studied political science, he was Ansar Shaikh. Only a few knew that his father was an auto-rickshaw driver, and that his two sisters were married by the age of 15. His brother worked in a garage and financed young Shaikh's academic dreams. But there was another facet of his life which remained largely unknown. As he looked around for a house in Pune, he realized most doors were shut on Muslims. All of his Hindu batchmates got accommodation, but Shaikh was refused. Until Shaikh decided to introduce himself as Shubham to his to-be landlord! Then, he got a room on rent. Day time, he was Shaikh, by dusk, at home, for his landlord and neighbours, he was Shubham; helped, of course, by the fact that he was not obviously a Muslim. He sported no beard, no skullcap. But it was Shaikh's reaction when he first heard of his selection for bureaucracy that was revealing. 'Call me Ansar Shaikh, not Shubham. Now, I do not have to hide my identity', he put an end to his double life with a finality. With the selection, he had reached the upper echelons of our society, where religious identity is not always paramount.

Shaikh's incident brought back memories of my own experience of looking for a house around 2004 in Noida, a cosmopolitan township to the east of Delhi. After looking for an accommodation matching my budget and needs, I settled on a second floor flat in an upmarket sector. All was agreed upon with the landlord and the real estate agent who asked me to give advance money within 24 hours. It is when I reached the pre-decided spot to handover the cash that things started unravelling. After having kept me waiting for more than a couple of hours, they finally showed up with an apology, not for being very late but for their inability to sell the house to me. But why, I insisted on knowing. They had agreed less than 24 hours earlier. After a lot of dilly-dallying, the owner conceded, '*Aap log maas-machchi khate ho na*' (You eat meat and fish). 'But, what's your problem? You are selling the house. You are not going to be living here', I said. 'But still...', he said, his words tapering off. 'Still what', I demanded to know. The real estate agent whose office had a lofty name Kargil and Tiger Hill Properties—an obvious throwback to Kargil war with Pakistan—chipped in, '*Aap samajh jao na ... aap Mohammedan ho na*' (You please understand ... you are Muslim). He reminded me that I was a Muslim. And hence by some inscrutable logic, disqualified from buying the house!

Shaikh's experience is fairly common, except that not many change their name for the purpose of renting a room. And my experience is not so unusual either in modern India's urban living spaces. Supposedly cosmopolitan, almost every city lives in ghettoes; there are pockets of Bengalis and South Indians just conveniently dubbed as Madrasis in Delhi just as there are pockets of UP *bhaiyas* in Mumbai and those of Madrasis too. And there are clusters of Muslims. Everybody lives in the same city but occupies different geographical and mind space.

Amid all this, I was reminded of a book I last read in 2012. Called *Muslims in Indian Cities: Trajectories of Marginalisation*, it is edited by Laurent Gayer and Christophe Jaffrelot (2012). The work is remarkable for its clarity of thought and the doubtless ability to go beyond the surface. At first glance, it is yet another take on marginalization of Muslims in Indian cities. But there is more to it. Gayer and Jaffrelot look out, they look within too, in the process they discover the keys to ghettoization that has dogged Muslims in India. I remember in the wake of Mohammed Kaif's match winning knock in the NatWest trophy in the summer of 2002, overeager media had gone to town about how a Muslim had played a crucial role in a victory at a game of cricket—the religion of the masses. Of course, one had pointed out that it was not Kaif or Zaheer Khan the cricketers who stood as guarantees of India's secularism, but a Kaif the carpenter. Would the society open its doors to Kaif the carpenter, as easily? Would a Zaheer with an MNC job under his belt, get a house on rent in Mumbai or New Delhi? The answers were not exactly easy to find until Jaffrelot and his co-editor put everything to rest with clinching arguments. They analyse in an instructive manner and refuse to paint all Muslims with one stroke. From Delhi's Abul Fazl Enclave, a self-help almost exclusively Muslim colony developed by a local real estate developer Abul Fazl Farooqi—'They (Hindus) call it Next to Pakistan here', Faznullah, brother of Farooqi is quoted as saying—to Bhopal's Muslim elite who, after the trauma of Partition withdrew into a shell, 'besieged in the Old City', the authors track various trajectories of marginalization. In Delhi, it was a desire to find economic opportunities in Old Delhi after the Walled City reached a saturation point that drove the Muslims to a place such as Abul Fazl Enclave; in Bhopal, it was the opposite. The community retreated inwards to the Old City, as the last resort, as Bhopal marched forward without the traditional elite. In Mumbai's Shivaji Nagar, it was always a cloistered existence, ignorance of the world outside, fear of the police inside, a throwback to the days following the Babri Masjid demolition in 1992.

Noting the decline of the Muslims in North India in socio-economic and political terms, they explain that the Muslim elite never recovered from the loss of power they experienced in the 18th and 19th centuries. Then they point to the absence of business-oriented traditions in the community. Pointing to the Bohras and Khojas, they feel they have never been fully integrated with the community, always like a little stream within the bigger stream. Quite different has been the deliberate marginalization of the Muslims by the state, they say in the conclusion.

While Nehru tried to endow them with all the attributes of a fully-fledged citizenship, the Hindu nationalists, who ruled over North India, never implemented the policies that had been designed by the government such as the promotion of Urdu. The impact of discrimination by the state is well reflected in the minimal presence of Muslims among the salary earners of the public sector and within the civil services. Since the early 1980s, the percentage of Muslims among the successful candidates in the civil services examination has oscillated between 1.2 and 1.17 per cent. (*It has since risen to a little under 3 per cent*). And in 2000, the percentage of Muslims among central government employees varied from 5.12 per cent in the least qualified positions to only 1.61 per cent in the highest posts. (Gayer and Jaffrelot 2012)

Yes, the impact of discrimination is not faced only in the percentage of Muslims in government service but at the ground level when an Ansar Shaikh has to become a Shubham to get accommodation, when Kaif, a carpenter, fails to get a room on rent in Ahmedabad beyond the Old City. Results? The community draws inwards, towards their own.

MUSLIMS OF DELHI AND JAMMU

I have always been an outsider. I spent a fair bit of my early days in Lajpat Nagar, a colony of Hindu and Sikh refugees from Lahore and Peshawar. Our family, with my Mufti father, was the lone Muslim family, wherever one looked or listened in the area. Many years earlier, my father, against all advice, had opted to leave a safe job in Lahore and shift back to his '*desh*' Hindustan, his '*watan*' Rampur, with not much more than his education to recommend him. This at a time when trainloads of Hindus and Sikhs were coming to India, leaving the newly formed state of Pakistan behind, and lakhs of Muslims were taking the train to Pakistan from Delhi. All this merely to find himself in a society of exclusion and unstated apartheid. The leaders of the Congress, Jan Sangh and other denominations would hold *sabhas* in Lajpat Nagar, Paharganj, Karol Bagh, etc. and assure the refugees that their 'dharma', '*sabhyata*' (civilization), their '*samman*' (respect) and 'sanskriti' (culture) were safe in Hindustan. Almost nobody ever thought that amid the audience, amid the families uprooted could be a Muslim family too, a family that too needed its 'dharma', '*sabhyata*' and '*samman*' to be safeguarded. I could neither long for Lahore or Rampur nor celebrate the Independence of our nation. In my own land, I was nobody's baby.

This was largely because it was unthinkable for many at that time that a Mufti could leave Pakistan and its promised Islamic republic for secular Hindustan. The sense of displacement and dejection went much deeper. As a little boy, I played cricket with boys my age from the neighbourhood, and often spent afternoons in their home playing carom during summer vacations. We were all friends, or so I thought, and happily ate and drank with them. Without my innocent mind realizing it, I was all along treated as the 'Other', an 'outsider'. Thus, a friend's mother would serve food in a *steel ki thali* to him but reserve a plastic tray with some floral print or cartoons on it for me. Initially I thought I was given special treatment; it was only a little later that I realized all the other boys from the neighbourhood who came to my friend's place would eat from the same *steel ki thali*, no special plastic trays for them! It took me only a bit longer to realize that most of the time I was the one at my friends' place, not many came to mine. And those who did, hardly ever stuck around at the time of lunch or dinner. For them all, I was an 'outsider', an impure *mlecchha*.

Many years later, as a young adult in Noida, I made friends with a guy whose father was in the defence forces. We often exchanged books and notes in our college days. The pattern repeated itself: My friend would come to my house, study for a while with me, refuse to have any food on some flimsy excuse and go home. Experience had made me wiser. I had a frank chat with him, and drew a line. It did not help that Babri Masjid–Ram Janmabhoomi protests hit the streets around the same time, and every other evening, Vishwa Hindu Parishad workers would hold a 'peaceful' march for the construction of the Ram temple in Ayodhya with slogans like '*Musalman ke do hi sthaan, Pakistan ya qabrastan*'. I had never been to Pakistan, and had no idea how a *qabra* (grave) looked like from inside. I watched bemused. It was the same in 1947 and 1992. Generations had come and gone, my father too had passed away. For the world around me, I was the 'Other', an 'outsider' who opted to live in a 'cosmopolitan' part of Delhi and Noida, yet an 'outsider'. Thus when perchance I got to know of a book through Facebook, I could not resist asking for a copy of it.

Penned by Zafar Choudhary, it is called *Kashmir Conflict and Muslims of Jammu* (2015). The title grabbed me. For years, I had heard of the plight of Kashmiri Pandits; for years, I was told of the triangular politics of Jammu and Kashmir with a Muslim Valley, Buddhist Ladakh and Hindu Jammu. The simplistic division often rankled me, but I found little in the media or literature that went beyond the stereotype until I saw Choudhary's book. A few pages into the book, I realized my enthusiasm for it was not misplaced.

In the foreword, Wajahat Habibullah reiterates what I had felt for long that Muslims of Jammu have not been given the attention they deserved. Highlighting the fact that they were distinct from the Muslims of the Valley, he writes,

> Choudhary's is an important work which will, I hope, help in addressing the impressions of Muslims of Jammu division that they are taken for granted, that the government of India, and the world, seeking to bring to final resolution the conflicts that have plagued the state of J&K over the last century, seek primarily to determine simply the views of different sections of the community residents in Kashmir. (Habibullah 2015)

A little later, Habibullah admits he too was guilty of the same once. 'In my own book, *My Kashmir: The Dying of the Light*, I have dealt with the policies of the Government of J&K, often glossing over the aspirations of Jammu's Muslims in favour of those of Kashmir'. Choudhary himself concedes that the story of Jammu Muslims is probably more painful than that of others. 'What makes the story of Jammu more painful is that ... the loss and pain of Jammu makes just a passing reference to the political discourse on Kashmir conflict'.

For him too, Jammu Muslims were like the 'other', often glossed over at the time of debate and dialogue, indeed even at the time of elections. Just like those politicians of the 1950s and 1960s in Delhi who unabashedly sought the votes of the Hindu and Sikh refugees, but never spared a passing thought for the Muslims. Indeed the Muslims of Jammu, not exactly at peace with the Muslims of the Valley, not trusted much by the Hindus of Jammu, are often in a no-win situation. As Choudhary (2015) writes,

> In a particular democratic set-up the Muslims of Jammu feel isolated on both counts—first, within Jammu as being Muslims who the majority community of the region sees as essential part of a Muslim hegemony biased against them, and second, as residents of Jammu province who are seen by the valley as people outside the definition of 'Kashmiri Nationalism'.

Although it seems a peculiar case of a state majority being in a minority in a district, it was not always this way.

> In the historical Jammu—the province that existed between 1846 and 1947—Muslims were the majority religion invariably comprising two-thirds of the total population. 1941 census confirmed Muslim population in Jammu province at a little over 60 per cent. Six decades later, the situation is half the reverse—Muslims making a little over 30 per cent of region's total population.

It is a story with a lot of heartache, and in many ways similar to the story of Muslims elsewhere in the country.

> The story of the Muslims of Jammu province in the state of Jammu and Kashmir is not entirely different from rest of the Indian Muslims primarily on three account—first, the Muslims of Jammu went through exactly the same or even more horrible patterns of division and communal violence on the eve of partition of India; second, being contiguous to the post-partition larger Indian reality, the Muslims of Jammu have passed through a social, economic and political stress similar to the Muslims in rest of north India; and third, despite being domiciles of India's only Muslim majority state, the Muslims of Jammu province are a minority for the reasons anchored in geography and history of this province.

I do not agree with a lot of what Choudhary writes, but his writing does depict his pain, the pulse of Jammu Muslims, the perpetual 'Others' in any dialogue on the state. And in many ways, he strikes a chord.

JAMAAT AND RELIGION

JAMIAT ULAMA-E-HIND

The situation is worse than 1947. At that time only Punjab
and Bengal were affected. Now, it is the entire country.
Everybody is living in fear. We all have to close ranks to
safeguard our Constitution. Across all demarcations we
have to fight the Fascist forces and make sure that the
nation we pass on to the posterity is better than the India
we inherited from our forefathers. The challenge is steep.
The regressive forces have taken the country back by a
hundred years. If we do not unite today, the consequences
will be terrible for the country.

THESE WORDS OF ARSHAD MADANI, President, Jamiat Ulama-e-
Hind, set me thinking. Yes, we are all concerned about the
march of disruptive forces, but Madani's concern seems
deeper. In March 2016, he was instrumental in bringing
people of different faiths to a common platform. The
result was a day-long conclave attended by around 45,000
people in Delhi. Significantly, there were Dalit, Christian
and Sikh leaders. Their presence being a give-away about

Jamiat's plan to bring to a common platform all the disaffected sections, irrespective of their religion.

According to Madani,

> We need to make sure that this coming together of forces wedded to our pluralist culture takes a cohesive shape. We need to sustain the resistance. What is at stake today is more grave than the post-Partition riots. This time the challenge is not confined to one or two parts of the country. It is an undeclared Emergency. (Author's interview with Arshad Madani)

Further, adding a tinge of sadness, Madani said,

> Today, we are being questioned on nationalism by those who do not have a track record of patriotism, by people who did not fight for the Independence of the country, by people who even sided with the British. If anybody has the least right to talk of nationalism today, it is these forces. People sent letters of clemency to the British. Today such people are being hailed as nation builders. Our role in the freedom struggle is well known to need reiteration. We took on Muslim communalism in the past; we are ready to take on the majority communalism today. We are ready to fight the RSS.

When Madani talks of the freedom struggle, he is actually on a sound wicket. The Jamiat Ulama-e-Hind did indeed play a crucial role in the freedom struggle, constantly opposing the separatist moves of the Muslim League and helping to counter the threat posed by the Hindu Mahasabha and the RSS. What's more, since it was from the beginning a body of intellectuals, its word carried greater weight with the common man, and also helped in Jamiat enrolling more and more members. When the

Jamiat founders talked of the Quran permitting Hindus and Muslims to live together, it took the wind out of the campaign for a Muslim state of Pakistan. Founded in 1919, the Jamiat counts Maulana Hussain Ahmad Madani, Maulana Mehmood Hasan Deobandi, Mufti Kifayatullah Dehlavi and Maulana Abdul Bari Firangi Mehli among its earliest leaders of note. All leaders urged the Muslims and Hindus to fight for the Independence of the country, and saw no conflict between Islam and love for the motherland. Pertinently, Jamiat was founded when the freedom struggle had begun to involve the common Indian. It also happened to be the time when seeds of communalism were also sowed. There was Hindu Mahasabha that aimed to a Hindu Rashtra. There was the Muslim League which a couple of decades later was to be the voice for Pakistan. At that time, though the League was happy to walk with the Congress for united India. Jamiat's leaders never divorced nation from religion. For instance, the commitment to Indian nationalism of Hussain Ahmad Madani was the outcome of his interpretation of Islam as a religion of freedom and equality, of justice, of cooperation with and respect for all mankind. He was interned in Malta for four years between 1916 and 1920. Not just a religious leader, he was a fine author who unhesitatingly wrote about composite nationalism, our shared past and scoffed at the idea of two-nation theory. The fact that he wrote in Urdu meant his word carried to the masses.

Then there was Maulana Mahmoodul Hasan, said to be the first student at the seminary, who was part of the nationalist government-in-exile set up in 1915 in Kabul which was headed by Raja Mahendra Pratap and had

Maulana Barkatullah as a foreign minister, in what is known as the Silk Letter Conspiracy.

In fact, so well entrenched was Madani with his nationalist thought process that he questioned Mohammed Iqbal's two-nation theory. And at the same time, he demolished the arguments of the Hindutva leaders who believed that only those whose birthplace and sacred land lay in India could form a cohesive nation state. 'In the current age, nations are based on homelands, not religion', he said in a statement in 1937. Madani firmly believed that despite being culturally, linguistically and religiously different, people professing different religions residing in the territorial boundaries of India were one nation. 'Any effort to divide them on the basis of caste, colour, creed, culture and religion was a ploy by the British rulers to perpetuate their hegemony'.

Madani's opposition to the two-nation theory made him equidistant to both the League and the Mahasabha. With the Jamiat winning over more and more people, his words dispelled any doubts in the minds of some Muslims about living and working with non-Muslims as part of a pluralist nation. This was in contrast to what Iqbal believed in. To Madani, living in a multi-faith society in no way came in the way of practising and propagating Islam. A scholar of Islam, he quoted often from the Quran to prove that the book addressed entire humanity and not just Muslims.

Madani even claimed that Prophet Mohammed (PBUH) also practised composite nationalism in Medina. If the prophet could do it, why cannot we, he often asked. 'The people of India as Indians, as a nation united (despite religious and cultural diversity) should become one solid nation and should wage war against the alien power that has usurped their natural rights'.

Although forgotten today, the Jamiat took every possible measure to see that India should remain united. First, it opposed Jinnah, then it opposed the Congress when the latter reluctantly agreed to the two-nation formula. The Jamiat took lead in ideologically challenging the scheme of Pakistan by producing mass literature in Urdu in order to educate common Muslims against its pitfalls. This was written in a polemical style and countered arguments, both religious and political, put forward by Muslim League in favour of a separate homeland for Muslims. When Jinnah harped on Hindus and Muslims having two different religious philosophies and social customs, the Jamiat responded,

> Muslims co-exist with Hindus since they settled in India. Till Muslims stay in India they have to live together with Hindus. They co-exist in markets, houses, railways, tramways, buses and lorries, in steamers and at stations. They are found together in colleges, post offices, police stations, in courts and councils.... Is there a place in India where they do not meet? If you are a landlord, is not it a fact that your cultivators are Hindus or vice-versa?

In the no-holds-barred campaign, the Muslim League often raised the bogey of a Hindu nation. And Jamiat thundered, 'The slogans of Muslim India and Hindu India are being raised to divide people of India so that the British rule continues', and pointed out instances when the prophet entered into agreements with non-Muslims and even waged wars in association with them. The Jamiat members got pledges from Muslims that they would not use foreign cloth and were ready to be arrested for espousing the cause of territorial nationhood. Finally, when the Congress agreed to the creation of Pakistan, Jamiat's Hifzur Rahman Seoharvi refused to agree. His words are reproduced by Shamsul Islam:

> With all respect to our leaders I would like to state that the result of the Partition of India will be far more dangerous than the complications and pressure of situations which are being presented to support Partition of India. If today the scheme of Partition of India is accepted at the Congress platform, it would mean that we are rubbing off with our own hands whole of our history and our beliefs and pronouncements. We are surrendering to two-nation theory.

Today, the angst of Arshad Madani and his colleagues is understandable. What is disconcerting is the marginalization of the Jamiat from the body politic of the nation. The notes of history are being repeated. In the past, Jinnah was allowed to raise his voice. Today, there are so many foot soldiers who masquerade as Muslim leaders. And Jamiat stays in the shadows. Under the circumstances, its newfound energy in building an umbrella of secular forces is a step in the right direction. If the Jamiat could point out the dangers of Partition before Independence, it can certainly alert the nation to the dangers of rampant Hindutva today.

A MUSLIM LEADER AGAINST PARTITION

What if ... It fuels wistfulness, even ushers in nostalgia, and is far from an ideal premise for history to unfold. Yet this is the sentiment that came rushing back to my mind again and again as I read the story of Allah Baksh, the

Premier of Sind who fought two battles at the same time: As the chief of the Ittehad Party, he sought to overthrow the British; at the same time, he sought to mobilize Indian Muslims against the exclusionist politics of the Muslim League. What if Allah Baksh and not M.A. Jinnah had held sway? What if his words had been heeded by more Muslims?

It so happened that the call of the Congress to all Indians to unite to force the British to quit India in 1942 stirred Allah Baksh. He was not a Congressman but could barely control himself when Winston Churchill made derogatory references about the Indian freedom struggle. In protest, he renounced the titles conferred on him by the British Government. In a letter to Viceroy Linlithgow, he wrote,

> I beg to inform Your Excellency that I have decided to renounce both the honours I hold from the British Government as I feel I cannot consistently with my views and conviction retain them any longer.... India has been struggling for the national freedom for a long time past. Upon the outbreak of the present war, it was hoped that under the very principles and ideology, in defence of which Allies were waging a titanic conflict, India would be made free and participate in the world struggle as a free country.... The latest speech delivered by Winston Churchill in the House of Commons has caused the greatest disappointment to all men of goodwill who wish to see rendered to India justice which is long due to her. (Islam 2015)

Allah Baksh was soon dismissed by the Governor, providing a rare instance of a Premier being dismissed for returning his awards! The Governor's action was criticized in both India and Britain. But the die was cast. Allah

Baksh paid the price for raising his voice against the British. It was not to be his loss alone but that of Sind, indeed, of India in those precious days in the run-up to Independence.

Disappointing as his dismissal was, what happened in the immediate aftermath was an eye-opener. On the one hand, it led to an increase in the membership of the Muslim League, and, on the other, it showed a picture of two communal outfits clinging to each other for their political gain. As so impressively explained by Shamsul Islam in his book *Muslims Against Partition of India* (2015), Allah Baksh's government was succeeded by a coalition of the Hindu Mahasabha and the Muslim League! If any proof was required that the two parties fed off each other, and in many ways were a mirror reflection of each other, Sind provided it.

It is not known generally that after the dismissal of Allah Baksh government in 1942, the British Governor appointed a coalition of Muslim League and the Hindu Mahasabha which was led by V.D. Savarkar at that time to form new government in Sind. In fact, the Muslim League and the Hindu Mahasabha ran coalition governments in Bengal and NWFP also in the same period. In Sind one would see the open ganging up of the British rulers, the Muslims League and the Hindu Mahasabha in achieving the political liquidation of Allah Baksh and his kind of anti-communal politics.

Returning his awards. Dismissal of his government. Fate had more in store for Allah Baksh. A year after his government was sent packing by the Governor, Allah Baksh was murdered on the outskirts of Shikarpur in Sind when he was returning to his house in a tonga. It was on his death that his real worth came to the fore. While people across all religions and castes mourned, there was a piece which appeared in *The Hindustan Times* where his transcendental popularity was highlighted. The paper described him as one of the

> finest of Sindhis, one of the truest of Musalmans, one of the noblest sons of India who loved his peasants for he loved the land and he used to wear khaddar even in the twenties, for he loved the poor. Both the Hindus and Muslims looked up to him as a leader.... He had an all-India mind and in the midst of division and strife pinned his faith on an independent united India.

Although he was only 42 when he passed away, Allah Baksh brought up the alternative to the Muslim League's divisive agenda. He was as much opposed to the League's separatist demands as he was to the Hindu Mahasabha's constant urging towards Hindu Rashtra. A few years before he passed away, Allah Baksh had organized the All-India Independent Muslim Conference in April 1940 in Delhi. The conference was attended by 1,400 delegates from bodies such as Jamiat Ulema, Khudai Khidmatgar, All India Muslim Parliamentary Board, Jamiat Ahl-e-Hadith and All India Momin Conference. With more than 50,000 Muslim in attendance, the conference opposed the divisive agenda of the Muslim League. Allah Baksh, criticizing the two-nation theory, said,

> As Indian nationals, Muslims and Hindus and others inhabit the land and share every inch of the motherland and all its material and cultural treasures alike. Even in the realm of literature one finds common classics like Heer Ranjha and Sassi Pannu, written by Muslim poets,

equally and proudly shared by Hindus, Muslims and Sikhs in the Punjab and in Sind ... the country as an indivisible whole and as one federated and composite unit belongs to all the inhabitants of the country alike and is as much the inalienable and imprescriptible heritage of Indian Muslims as of other Indians. No segregated or isolated regions, but the whole of India is the homeland of all the Indian Muslims and no Hindu or Muslim ... has the right to deprive them of one inch of this homeland.

At the Conference the community's have-nots spoke out against the idea of Pakistan. And a vast number of students pursuing theology showed up, lending their shoulder to the cause of a united nation. The most remarkable thing though was a rally from the grand old Jama Masjid in Delhi. Interestingly, for Allah Baksh the word 'independent' for his Conference did not mean independence from India, but a conference independent of the communal designs of the Muslim League!

After his government's dismissal, Allah Baksh utilized the time to counter the separatist tendencies of communal organizations and could not imagine an independent nation where Muslims would opt for Pakistan while Hindus stayed in India. To this end, it was highlighted that only a little more than every fourth Muslim had voting rights—peasant, traders and shopkeepers were kept out of the loop. Thus, the decision to ask for a separate state for Muslims was piloted not by a majority but a minority of Muslims. It was in the other 75 per cent Muslim population that Allah Baksh laid his hopes on.

Unfortunately, he fell victim at a time when he was most needed. No wonder, Saifuddin Kitchlew, a patriotic Muslim leader who finds mention in school textbooks too, said,

At this critical period of the freedom movement in the country the death of a man like Mr Allah Baksh is a thundering blow to the forces of nationalism. Mr Allah Baksh was a thorough going nationalist. Mr Allah Baksh is dead but his work will remain. (Islam 2015)

Indeed, his was a voice for the soul of India. Although based in Sind, he was not just a regional satrap. As Islam (2015) notes in his book,

Allah Baksh needed to be eliminated because he was able to muster massive support from common Muslims throughout India against the scheme of Pakistan. Moreover, Allah Baksh as a great secularist with massive support in Sind and opposed to the formation of Pakistan could prove to be the greatest stumbling block in the physical formation of Pakistan as without Sind, the 'Islamic State' in the west of the country could not have materialised. His ideas against religious nationalism were a cause of serious concern for Muslim League. Only his murder could silence him. [It did.]

Allah Baksh's passing away sounded the death-knell of inclusive politics in Sind. It gave the Muslim League a lifeline in the state. It gave the Hindu Mahasabha a chance to form the government. It meant that the India of Gandhi's dreams lost out to sectarian forces. Only if Allah Baksh had been allowed to live a few years more ...

JAMAAT-E-ISLAMI HIND

There were bearded maulanas with more salt than pepper around their chin and sideburns. There were boys in college or straight out of it, their beards, not as luxuriant but also untouched by a strand of white. With them stood a handful of Sikh activists, some clean-shaven Christian and Dalit representatives too. They had all gathered at Jantar Mantar in New Delhi as part of Jamaat-e-Islami Hind's initiative to bring the minorities and the Dalits under a common umbrella. The Jantar Mantar protest in 2015, close on the heels of the murder of Akhlaq in Dadri on mere suspicion of storing beef in his fridge, and the killing of Chimma, a 90-year-old Dalit man in Uttar Pradesh's Hamirpur district for daring to visit a temple reserved for upper caste Hindus, was an effort to forge common cause with the oppressed, the deprived, the denied. Working within the framework of the Indian constitution, the Jamaat's aim was to form a pressure group of sorts which could force the government to take remedial action, in this case, punitive action against those involved in the killing in Dadri and Hamirpur.

The reasonably well-attended protest, which was addressed, among others, by Jamaat's Secretary General, Salim Engineer, set me thinking of how far the Jamaat had come since its foundation in 1941 by Syed Abul Ala Mawdudi, who believed in striving for establishment of Allah's kingdom on earth, and the more recent overtures of the Jamaat towards secular forces, complemented with its espousal of the secular fabric of the country whereby all religions are treated alike, and the state is duty bound not to discriminate between one religion and another. Incidentally, Mawdudi had a clear demarcation between Islamic state and the 'other', the Jahiliyat—modern day democracy, West and communism, etc. He believed that a true believer, that is, one who had faith in the first pillar of Islam, *kalima, La Ilaha Illahlahu Muhammadur Rasulullah* (There is no God but Allah and Prophet

Muhammad is His Messenger), was duty bound to strive to establish God's suzerainty on earth. A country which did not have an Islamic order was *Dar ul-Kufr* (house/ land of disbelief). The mission of a Muslim then was to transform India into *Dar ul-Islam* (house/land of Islam). In his reasoning, secular democracy stood in total contrast to what Islam stood for, and was therefore haram or forbidden.

The Jamaat, for the first 14 years or so after Independence, had actively worked against participating in General Elections, holding that they brought in their wake manmade laws; a Muslim believes in the sovereignty of Allah, and *taghut* (idols) of democracy fostered a polytheist way of life, as opposed to Islamic concept of one universal God. The choice for a believer was simple but never easy: The Jamaat held that if rebellion against anti-God or secular state was a crime, then rebellion against God was a sin.

Mankind's faith was completed with the revelation of the Quran. Hence, it was inappropriate to compare a complete way of life with what was, at best, incomplete system, he argued.

Mawdudi, of course, opposed legislative bodies because they worked under secular manmade laws rather than the Quran. Its members took pledge to uphold the Constitution rather than the Quran or Shariah. He forbade Jamaat's early members from being enrolled in the Army or judiciary, the former because it killed in the path of non-God, and the latter because it was based on secular laws. Working in banks too was out of question as the banks worked on interest, something clearly forbidden by the Quran through surah Baqarah and Al-Imran. Dealing in interest meant being at war with the Almighty and His messenger. Pertinently, Mawdudi was not inclined towards social ties with *fasiq* (transgressors).

The Jamaat, as one could make out from its Jantar Mantar protest, had come a long way and away from Mawdudi's ideology. The change was neither sudden nor well thought out.

Mawdudi himself, after he had opted to go to Pakistan after Partition, refused to swear by the constitution of that country until the members of the legislative assembly took an oath upholding the sovereignty of the one and only God, Allah. Incidentally, this was in stark contrast to his early days in public life when he penned biographies of Mahatma Gandhi and Madan Mohan Malaviya, regarding the latter as a model worthy of emulation not just by Hindus but by Muslims as well, and took part in the Khilafat agitation as also Mahatma Gandhi's Satyagrahas. His association with other freedom fighters, however, was not to last a lifetime as Mawdudi was soon disgruntled with the Congress for its soft yet constant use of Hindu symbols in the freedom struggle. Unable to come to terms with the vicissitudes of a pluralist society and polity, he turned an Islamist, studying long to find out the reason for the decline of the Islamic world in comparison to the West. Yet, even after he had founded the Jamaat-e-Islami, Mawdudi did not make the cut with the orthodox sections of the Muslim society. Deoband cleric Manzoor Nomani, for instance, cut short his association with Mawdudi's Jamaat because he kept his beard short—less than a fist long—and his convent-educated wife did not observe purdah. The purists failed to align with him, the liberal sections kept at an arm's length. Yet Mawdudi succeeded in raising a body that at least in principle stood for a united ummah with one common leader, the Khalifah. It was in clear contrast to Jamiat Ulama-e-Hind which saw no conflict between Islam and pluralist democracy and incessantly took part in the freedom struggle.

Indeed Mawdudi was a man of formidable intellect. For all the criticism, he scored all the points in the early years. For instance, his organization was the first to give membership to women. Unlike modern-day Panchayat elections where one often finds wives and daughters of politicians as dummy candidates, the Jamaat considered them as individuals. Today, it runs the country's largest madrasa for women. Equally importantly, before agreeing to take men as members, the Jamaat in its verification about the candidate's merit never failed to speak to the wife, arguing that nobody knew a man better than his wife.

Yet, it has not always been smooth sailing for Jamaat, as the changing contours exhibited at the Jantar Mantar protest prove. An early challenge came after the founder migrated to Pakistan. Before Independence, the Jamaat under Mawdudi had declared its goal to be the establishment of Hukumat-e-Ilahiya or Allah's kingdom. He considered secular democracy to be haram because it replaced Allah's sovereignty with human supremacy. Yet after Mawdudi went to Pakistan, secular democracy came to have a deep impact on the Jamaat.

It was soon discovered that a majority of Indian Muslims, including intellectuals and the less educated masses, were not opposed to multihued society and polity. Guaranteed their right to worship, practise and propagate their faith, they wanted to compete for their rights in the secular sphere within the framework of the polity. This dissonance between the Muslim *awaam* (public) and the Jamaat's ideology forced the organization to move away from its earlier position of fusion of religion and the state. Incredibly, the Jamaat, soon after 1947, was in favour of a Hindu Rashtra ahead of a secular democracy, arguing that a religious state would make it possible for the Jamaat to bring about an Islamic state, if a Hindu Rashtra could be founded, why not an Islamic state, the Jamaat visioned. For that purpose, it had issued *dawat* or invitation to prominent leaders such as Pandit Jawaharlal Nehru, Rajendra Prasad, Govind Ballabh Pant, etc., the idea being not to change the hands that run the system but to change the system. That *dawat* was, of course, not accepted. But the Jamaat soon understood the common Muslim's pulse—the common man was happy to live in a multi-religious society, and the Jamaat could ill afford to be singing a solo song.

This prompted the body to open its doors and windows to people of other faiths. The 'Other' of Mawdudi became kind of one, as the Jamaat sought out allies in its attempt to impact the polity and society. The Jamaat could not operate in a social vacuum. At the turn of the century, the Jamaat, quite clearly rattled by the upsurge of the Hindutva forces, raised its voice in favour of secular candidates, unwittingly becoming a part of the system it had once criticized for being manmade as opposed to divine. The anti-God debate no longer held sway. What was considered haram in the 1950s (participating in elections, contesting in them, working as legislators, etc.) was now regarded halal, even if not explicitly so. If the system had to be changed, it had to be changed from within, not through an overhaul.

The recent actions of the Jamaat inviting representative bodies of the minorities, Dalits, Scheduled Castes and Tribes, etc., to protest, from a common platform, the killing of a Dalit man in Hamirpur and the lynching of Akhlaq in Dadri are fine examples. The Jamaat, in its new avatar, was happy to use the tools of the system to further its cause—it involved holding Eid milan get-together with media, inviting journalists and activists to address its younger members on developing issues, etc. The Jamaat of 1941, running on political theology, was opposed to non-Muslim bodies; the Jamaat of 2018 was ready to embrace them. If, as Mohammed Iqbal said, 'the storm of the West made Muslim, Muslim', the gentle breeze of Azaad Hind made Jamaat more accommodative.

An interesting change in recent times has been to offer membership to new individuals based on their aptitude, knowledge and commitment to deen. It is a far cry from the years gone by when anybody had to put in a number of years with the Jamaat before being considered for being a *rukn*, a member. Many toiled for decades to earn the membership in the past; today it comes much easier. Not that there is no heartburn about it among the rank and file of the body with many holding that the membership has to be earned through a sustained dedication to Jamaat's principles. Entry into the Jamaat is easier, exist should be likewise, they contend.

That is fine. But what are the principles of the Jamaat in modern India? Does it still even attempt to establish Allah's kingdom? Or has it gone miles away from the ideology of its founding father? Or maybe, it has just reconciled to secular democracy wherein the Jamaat, like other socio-religious bodies, is allowed to practise and propagate its faith, and hope that one day, just one day in the distant future, India will turn into an abode of Islam through a constant but peaceful churning. The Jamaat with far fewer members in villages—most consider it a largely urban body—continues to make social strides, working within the system devised by Dr B.R. Ambedkar. The recent noises on the issue of intolerance, blood donation drive, taking the girl child to school and awakening the citizens to the drought that visited Bundelkhand, Karnataka and Maharashtra, all reiterate that matters of faith go beyond daily rituals. It completes an interesting circle for Jamaat, a body that invoked the Quran before Independence and now works as per the rights and responsibilities granted by the Constitution, the holy book of secular India.

So which way is the Jamaat going, the Mawdudi way or the way allowed in a pluralist democracy? No easy answers but a clue could be found in the Jantar Mantar wind.

TABLIGHI JAMAAT

It took *Understand the Quran*, a simple book in easy-to-understand English to split the faithful down the middle. Abdur Raheem's book, claiming to help you understand half the words of the Quran in less than a day—the holy book has around 78,000 words in the Arabic original—set off a storm that went a little beyond the tea cup.

Abdur Raheem, a noted Islamic scholar, was visiting Delhi in October 2015 from Hyderabad for a few days and had just finished his lecture post Friday prayers at New Delhi Jama Masjid wherein he taught the faithful the meaning of Surah Fateha, the opening chapter of the Quran. 'If you know the meaning of every word of this surah, you know around 4,500 words of the holy book', he said. So impressed were his students, among them top bureaucrats of Lok Sabha and Rajya Sabha, engineers, professors, bankers and journalists that they decided that the lecture must be held at various mosques across the city. That first step, full of enthusiasm and well meaning, was also a foray to a long hidden schism in the world of the faithful. Most mosques, in and around Delhi, were, as it turned out, in the control of Tablighi Jamaat, the organization founded by Muhammed Ilyas Kandhlawi in 1927. Tabligh, which was founded to counter attempts to convert Muslims in Mewat region in pre-Independence time, is today an organization that works at the grassroots level. It is now said to be the largest Islamic jamaat across the world. Back then when it was founded, Ilyas believed that the way ahead was to look within. He focussed on cleansing from within before attempting to cleanse the world. The route to *falah* (success) lay through coming back to Islamic pillars, including five daily prayers and fasting in the month of Ramadan. Once it was taken care of, Muslims, he argued, could hope for God's mercy which, in turn, would translate into a triumph of the faithful in this life as well as afterlife.

Today, from early morning to late evening, its volunteers go from door to door, inviting the believers to join the prayers in the local masjid. Although students and middle-class men are also invited, the main targets are the unlettered, economically impoverished young men, who in many cases, would not have read the Quran—very much like the Meos, many of whom did not know the *kalima*, and hardly anybody had read the Quran when Ilyas stepped on the scene—and may not know how to say their prayers too. Today, the organization that claims to maintain no records of its volunteers and has no website has lakhs of such men preaching a version of Islam that is steeped in rituals. The body concentrates on five daily prayers and fasting in the month of Ramadan. It is considered sufficient to read the Quran in Arabic without understanding the language—it is something that attracts a lot of criticism from scholars who believe that the holy book should be understood in the mother tongue and then implemented in everyday life rather than just be read for favours from the Almighty. The Tabligh is unconcerned about the affairs of the world, not for it the dreams of the Caliphate. Or even taking the message of the Prophet to non-Muslims. It seems sufficient to read, and listen to, Fazail-e-Amal (Virtues of Deeds), a compilation of Hadith and other anecdotes, not all of them considered authentic, after Fajr (dawn) prayers. Indeed, after Fajr and Asar prayers, the more devoted of Tabligh members—their give-away signs being a fist-long beard, clean-shaven upper lip and pyjamas that end above the ankles—spring to action, asking the men who come to offer prayers in masjids to stay on for a '*deen ki baat*' (talk about faith). The talk is usually just a reading from Fazail-e-Amal (compiled by Muhammad Zakariya Kandhlawi and earlier called Tablighi Nisaab), never is there is a *tafsir*, a commentary of the Quran. The approach of individual reformation derives from the thoughts of Ilyas who felt that Muslims had to go back to the basic principles of Islam, and to observe the instructions in their personal lives strictly. Once the personal lives were taken care of, other aspects shall improve too, which in turn will earn the pleasure of Allah who would grant them *falah*. This apolitical approach has helped the Tabligh grow world-wide as not many have felt threatened with their pursuit of 'heaven above, grave below'.

As Ilyas himself believed, political power would be granted as a blessing by Allah after Muslims follow the dictates of the faith. They were not to pursue it. The immediate task for them was to imbibe the teachings in their personal lives. Importantly, unlike some of the modern-day practitioners, Ilyas himself did not find any contradiction in the approach of various Islamic bodies, and believed there was space for all. It is something lost on many of his followers.

Understandably the Tabligh volunteers with their perfect-your-rituals approach seldom encounter problems with visa when they travel across the world, ranging from Indonesia to the United States, from South Africa to the United Kingdom; their silence on political affairs often construed as their implicit acceptance. Importantly, at the time of Emergency when the then Prime Minister Indira Gandhi came down with a heavy hand on religious bodies, and banned Jamaat-e-Islami Hind, Tablighi Jamaat was not touched.

Interestingly, they believe in giving *dawah* (invita- tion) through a tour ranging from three to forty days, four months and finally a year. All along, the *dawah* is for prayer, never to understand the Quran. Nor are any consultations held to establish institutes of Islamic excellence. And volunteers are not recruited through 'bait', the Islamic pledge to lead life according to the spirit of the Quran and the example set up by Prophet Muhammed (PBUH). The opponents hold that Tabligh's actions are against the letter and spirit of faith. They argue that the

Prophet never sent a party to other cities and townships to spread the word for the first 18 years after revelation. His first approach was through a letter to the Iranian king and patriarch of Caucasus. Never once did he send any party of men to convert, to instruct men on rituals. And he always emphasized knowledge, something about which Tabligh is practically unconcerned. They point out that the organization is not clear on fundamentals of *riba* (interest) and jihad. The need to have clean earning, free of interest is not inculcated among the volunteers nor is the concept of jihad being a way to control your desires first. This, the opponents argue, comes from an understanding of the Quran.

So, when some students of Abdur Raheem broached the proposal of holding a Quran class in the masjid wherein the believers could understand the Quran and learn to implement its teachings in everyday life, it was met with tactics that ranged from a polite no to a more persistent negation of the effort to finally a belligerent disapproval backed by threats of violence. 'The Quran should be read and explained by the *ulema*', is their persistent cry. Abdur Raheem, and his batch of achievers, obviously did not count as intellectuals in the eyes of the Tabligh members. And holding the class in the masjid meant the devotees would begin to understand the Quran, which in turn, would bring more responsibility on them. The faithful believe that Allah, on the Day of Judgement, will question you on the basis of your knowledge and intellectual attainment. So, more knowledge translates to greater responsibility for its implementation. Hence, the Tabligh members would rather say their prayers without understanding them, read the Quran without understanding its meaning, never read the meaning for fear of going astray—'only an *alim* can guide to the right meaning' is their oft-repeated statement. Hence, the easier option is do not, under any circumstances, allow any Quran class in the masjids, do not allow any congregation where the faithful discuss the different surahs of the Quran nor do try to understand *tafsir* (interpretation). Abdur Raheem had to beat a retreat. Like countless others before him.

Do they cheat the Lord or do they short-change themselves? Well, to each his own.

SUFISM: IS IT ISLAM?

The World Sufi Forum's congregation of *ulema* (Islamic scholars) from 20 countries across the world, including those from strife-torn Egypt, Syria and Iraq, besides delegates from Morocco, Bangladesh and Pakistan, would have passed off with barely a ripple in the media but for the presence of Prime Minister Narendra Modi on the opening day in March 2016. Modi, in a meeting with Muslim clerics, seemed an irresistible proposition! Was it a heartening support to the pluralist ethos of the country by the Prime Minister? Were the Muslims' worst fears allayed by the single gesture of Modi, the man who famously refused to wear a skullcap offered by a Muslim cleric in Gujarat as part of Sadbhavana fast? Modi had changed as the PM, they felt; even as Modi, in his address to the august gathering of Muslim intellectuals, talked of the beautiful names of Allah, quoting from Surah A'raf of the Quran. 'When we think of the 99 names of Allah, none stands for force and violence, and that the first two names denote compassionate and merciful. Allah is

Rahman and Raheem. Sufism is the voice of peace, co-existence, compassion and equality; a call to universal brotherhood', he said, adding, 'Sufism became the face of Islam in India, even as it remained deeply rooted in the Holy Quran, and Hadiith'.

There had been occasions in the past when Indian Prime Ministers had associated with Sufi priests of Nizamuddin dargah in New Delhi as also those from Ajmer and other towns. Indira Gandhi used to send a chador to be offered at the Chishti shrine in Ajmer. Her son, Rajiv, and later daughter-in-law, Sonia Gandhi, kept the tradition alive. But this was the first time, a PM had addressed a meeting of the clerics and intellectuals organized by the All India Ulema and Mashaikh Board, the apex body of dargahs and Sufis. The meet, although, raised a few questions with no easy answers on the anvil.

Once the platitudes were out of the way, it became clear that the Modi government was keen to find an alternative to the Islam preached from the corridors of Deoband. Without ruffling too many feathers, quietly gone was the usual courtesy extended to clerics from Jamiat Ulema, and to a lesser extent those from Jamaat-e-Islami Hind and Tablighi Jamaat. These bodies, according to the emerging thought process, presented a more conservative face of Islam. Easily forgotten was Jamiat's role in the freedom struggle, and Jamaat's social outreach programme and its ability to step in at the time of crisis. The Sufis, it was felt, were steeped in the shared traditions with the Bhakti movement. They presented a wall against radicalization of the youth at a time when the ISIS threat loomed large on the doors of the subcontinent. The Sufis presented a counter to fanaticism, extremism and violence with their message of peace and universal brotherhood. Pertinently, Modi called Sufism the best contribution of Islam to the country. Willy-nilly, Sufism had become a tool in the hands of politicians for an image makeover amid constant reports of assaults on the minorities in the name of cow slaughter, *ghar wapsi*, etc. The support for Sufi stream stemmed not from a genuine reflection of what Sufism stood for, but was a damage control exercise by the government after many incidents of intolerance and an attempt to tell the international community that everything was fine with the minorities in India.

As widely respected and renowned imams chose to stay away from the meet, it became clear there was some heart burning, a degree of turmoil within the community on the issue of Sufi Islam. Some called it downright distortion of Islam which at the core is about belief in One God and leaves no space for image worship; others felt it appealed to the common Indians brought up on notions of idol worship. Lighting a diya at a dargah was akin to lighting a lamp at a temple. Hence, on the one hand it brought communities together, on the other it appealed to sections of the majority community. Others found a parallel between *mata ki chunri* and offering a chador at a dargah. Either way, it seemed a win-win situation for the proponents of Sufism in the country. After all, Nizamuddin Auliya, Moinuddin Chishti, Baba Farid and Bakhtiyar Kaki are respected beyond the boundaries of India. In fact, it is not unusual for visiting dignitaries, including Presidents and Prime Ministers of Pakistan, to pay obeisance at either Nizamuddin dargah or Ajmer when they touch down.

Modi's patronage to Sufis, reminded many of what Muhammad Iqbal had said nearly a century earlier. The man, whose works are still read out in Muslim gatherings and morning prayers in schools in pre-dominantly Muslim areas, had little love for this stream of Islam. In both Shikwa and Jawab-e-Shikwa, he was scathing in his criticism of Sufi practices. He had little time for mysticism of Sufis, a practice that went against the grain of Islam. Islam, he argued, gave importance to this world as also the next—this life being a preparation for the next. Neglecting this life altogether was not in consonance with the spirit of faith. Also, the commercialization of worship, as many dargahs tended to do, did not go down well with him. In fact, as pointed out by noted translator Mustansir Dalvi (2012) in *Taking Issue and Allah's Answer*, Iqbal 'disapproved of "shrine worship" and such rituals as the kissing of the graves and covering them with offerings of flowers and chadors. Such practices were, to Iqbal, far removed from the fundamental tenets of Islam, almost turning into idolatory'. Indeed Dalvi said, 'With fame and wealth that comes from the trade of tombs, what can prevent you cashing in on gods made of stone?' Interestingly, while he disapproved of Indianized version of Sufism, and held it partly responsible for the decline of Muslims as a power in India, he was more accommodative of Arab Sufism and its innate connection with mysticism. He urged the Muslims, like the Jamaat-e-Islami and other Muslim bodies, to return to the Quran, the Shariah and the love for Prophet Muhammad as first practices.

If Iqbal penned his thoughts at the beginning of the last century, the end of the century saw author Shahid Chaudhary being more vocal about Sufism not being a branch of Islam. In his much talked about work *Sufism is Not Islam: A Comparative Study* (1998), he argued that '*ruh*' (soul) in Islam is associated with the revelation of the Divine through His angel, not human beings.

> On the basis of Divine guidance and on his capacity to acquire knowledge, man can develop his *nafs* (personality or self).... In Sufism the words '*ruh*' and '*nafs*' have been given entirely different meanings. The '*ruh*' or the rational soul is considered to be a part of the Divine Soul (*Ruh-e-Ilahi*) and therefore its essence is potentially good and pure, whereas the '*nafs*' or animal soul is associated with material or carnal desires. So, when a Sufi realises his '*ruh*' is being obstructed by his '*nafs*' in his journey to the Divine, he declares war on '*nafs*'. This struggle generates restlessness, heat, fury and goes on till he effaces the '*nafs*' and becomes one with God. Thus, Sufism, according to Junayd of Baghdad, is that God should make thee die (*fana*) away from thyself, and make thee live in Him (*baqa*). It is at this stage that a Sufi, like Mansur Al Hallaj cries, *An'al Haqq* (I am God, the Creative Truth, or in the Vedantic term—*aham Brahmasmi*).

With Chaudhary drawing stark similarities between Sufism and Vedanta philosophy, it is easier to understand why Sufism is often better appreciated than other strains of Islam in the subcontinent. As J.S. Grewal (1991) observed in his essay 'The Sufi Beliefs and Attitudes in India', carried in *Sufism: Inter-Religious Understanding*,

> Probably, the best way of understanding Sufism is to look upon it as a parallel interpretation of Islam as a religion. The Sufis emphasised the omnipresence and the immanence of God, as against the Ulamma's emphasis on God's omnipotence and transcendence. Whereas the essential relationship between man and God, in the conception of the Ulamma, was that of a servant or a slave with his master, the essential relationship between man

and God for the Sufis consisted in the relationship of love. Consequently, the supreme aim of life for the Sufis was not to gain paradise but to attain to union with God. Notwithstanding the formal recognition and respect given to the Prophet, the essential importance of the pir underlined in actual practice.... In the writings of the Indian Shaikhs, it is preferable to visit the pir's *khanqah* than to go on pilgrimage to Mecca. In actual practice, a large number of people had started visiting even the *mazaars* of the Shaikhs before the end of the 15th Century.

With the pir or murshid being regarded so highly, it is easy to understand the objection of other practitioners of Islam who brook nothing ahead of the Prophet in their love for him.

Coming back to the World Sufi Forum, while some exulted at the Prime Minister quoting the names of Allah, to the discerning, it became clear that the attempt to emphasize the Sufi strains in Indian Islam was a tactic to divide the faithful. If in the past, some Tabligh members had been recipients of government patronage, now it seemed to be the turn of the Sufis. But Islam is just Islam, whatever sect or sub-sect one adheres to within the parameters of the Quran and Hadith. Sufis, Shias or Sunnis. They are all relatively modern-day terms which echo what a BJP leader has been advising for years. The leader concerned is on record saying that the party must highlight the divisions within Indian Muslims to prevent consolidation of anti-BJP vote. The political leaders, clearly, will have to do more than just refer to the 99 names of Allah in speech. Some action on the teachings of Rahman or Raheem would do well for a beginning.

ASLAM PARVAIZ: ONE-MAN MOVEMENT

In a community where millions follow Tablighi Jamaat which emphasizes rituals, recitation of the Quran, Fazail-e-Amal and little else, there is an Islamic preacher who keeps no beard, is happy to be seen in his formal trousers, shirt and tie, speaks English and all along urges his audience to understand the Quran, think, ponder, introspect. First read, then understand, then implement is his advice. He is conversant with the Vedas too. Crucially, he *understands* the Quran, as opposed to those who have memorized it but do not understand it as they do not know Arabic and have not deemed it necessary to read a translation of its meaning. It is an anomaly that confronts a vast majority of Muslims in the subcontinent. It is a lacuna that suave speaker Mohammed Aslam Parvaiz is striving tirelessly to address, reminding the faithful to treat the Quran as a guide book or users' manual. Just as one reads the manual before operating a new gadget, it is imperative to understand the Quran to live life to the fullest, he pleads with his audiences. He is meeting with success too; his annual Quran conference every winter in New Delhi attracts impressive footfall, and, youngsters, in particular, cannot have enough of his blend of science and religion, English and Hindi, Urdu and Arabic. It seems he mirrors their aspirations. In his persona, they find a role model. Upwardly mobile young men and women identify with Parvaiz more than any Islamic body. He makes a bridge with the new generation that thousands of bearded maulanas with knowledge of Hadith on their fingertips failed to build.

It did not start that way though. Parvaiz was brought up in the lanes of Old Delhi and groomed in a typical, conservative Muslim family. In other words, he was taught to recite the Quran, say his five daily prayers and observe fast in the month of Ramadan. It is the kind of upbringing that would have won him good boy brownie points but little else as an adult. Parvaiz was not taught the meaning of the Quran and seldom encouraged to ask questions about faith. Then one day he read an Urdu translation by Abul Ala Mawdudi. It opened the window of his mind. He read other translations. And soon realized that every translator interpreted the verses according to his understanding, his wisdom. So to understand the Quran, translations were the first step for him, learning Arabic the next.

He started with the original language, analysed the root words, compiled all root based meaning and then analysed which part of it would be relevant and hence developed understanding of the Quran. He soon realized that what he had been following in the name of Islam was hardly Islam. But understanding and practising Islam as gleaned from the Quran changed his life. 'It is difficult to explain how different my life had become once I understood the Quran. I am a more peaceful person who has learned to serve humanity', he happily recounts. He has now made it the mission of his life. He wishes, plans and works to motivate people to read the Quran with translation. Not a believer in bifurcation of knowledge into worldly and religious, he has worked tirelessly for 25 years to unite these streams of knowledge to propagate education where knowledge is not divided and which is always connected to Almighty to develop a humane personality. His talks are almost always backed up by a free distribution of the meaning of the Quran in multiple languages—English, Hindi and Urdu.

Interestingly, his Science background helps—Parvaiz, a student of the subject, who was the Principal of Delhi University's Zakir Husain college and is now the Vice-Chancellor of Maulana Azad National Urdu University, Hyderabad, has been editing an Urdu journal called *Science* for more than 20 years. With science, he would connect to the Creator in a better way. Unlike many others who feel that science and religion have mutually exclusive paths, Parvaiz believes that science is but a means to understand the Almighty. He started teaching his students by mixing both the verses, textual and universal. As he did so, he redefined the role of an Islamic preacher in India; it went beyond his dress and language. His entire approach was miles removed from the way other preachers look at Islam. For him, Islam was not confined to five daily prayers and the like but an ideology which needs to be followed in every sphere of life.

As he set out to express his understanding of the faith, it inevitably brought him into conflict with those who could not make out the difference between Islamic and Arab culture. Parvaiz had his hands full as he tried to remind the faithful that the Prophet was a messenger for entire humanity and not just the Arabs. The Prophet cannot, and should not, be projected as a representative of one culture. This separation of Islamic and Arab brought Parvaiz into confrontation with those members of the community who alleged that his talks were never about the traditions of the Prophet, his Hadith. It is an impression he still lives with, although every now and then he tries to clear the air. He reminds the faithful that the Quran tells us that the

Prophet delivered exactly what was revealed to him with utmost honesty and sincerity.

> He dare not mix it with any other thing lest he is also warned that he will not be spared and he would face the consequences ('*And convey [to the world] whatever has been revealed to you of your Sustainer's writ; there is none who can alter His words, and you shall not find any refuge besides Him*'; from surah Al-Kahf: 27). If we claim that we are Muslim we must practice what the Quran tells us. If a Hadith elaborates a particular verse explaining it differently, I take it as a word of the Prophet but if we have something which is beyond the letter and spirit of the Quran and may be even against the teaching of the Quran I will never take it as a Hadith because the Holy Prophet will never say or practice anything which is not in the Quran. (Author's interview with Aslam Parvaiz)

While his independent ideology and unconventional ways have endeared him to the educated segment, conservative sections are harder to please. And the fact that he has not taken a pledge at the hand of a scholar makes the rift wider still; Islam emphasizes that pledge, a bait at the hands of a scholar. Parvaiz stays unperturbed, confident that it is character rather than the appearance which matters in the long run. A beard is no guarantee of piety and vice versa.

Yet, for all the adulation and fan following, his is a one-man movement. He agrees that it is a different course that he has charted but insists that it is the only option available.

> To me this is the only course. Because if you understand and follow Quran then no other course is left to you, neither are you expected to follow something else. If one approaches the Quran with a clean slate without

preconceived notions of religion or region or any other dogmas, then to him/her Quran appears a very simple and understandable book which can be conveniently practiced. If one goes through the Quran, one can easily pick up that the emphasis is on grooming the character of the person, developing good traits and habits so that he becomes a real human being, the most evolved and developed living creature on this planet. It never emphasizes how you look, rather it instructs to remain modest and without any exhibitionism, extravagance and show off. Islam is all about practicing the Quran, but, it has been reduced to a set of rituals or practices focusing on five daily prayers, fasting for 30 days, paying the Zakat and visiting Saudi Arabia for the pilgrimage. Why these things have failed to produce the real Muslim personality and character should be our concern.

The answer, he claims, comes from a lack of understanding of the Quran which, asks the readers that why don't they ponder upon the verses, are their hearts (minds) locked?

When Quran asks each and every reader to ponder upon its verses, it in fact encourages one to understand, interpret and analyse the divine guidance with one's own understanding. And that makes it easy for everyone to follow and practice it because what he/she is practicing is his/her own understanding and something to which he finds an organic linkage. It is not something which is thrust upon someone and he/she is asked to just follow it because it is an order from someone. (based loosely on Surah Muhammad verse 24)

With such a mindset, it is scarcely a surprise that Parvaiz follow no Jamaat, no Islamic organization. But, as things have turned out, with his solo lecture programmes, he has started a jamaat uniquely his own. Today, he is happy to share his thoughts with people of different faiths, sects and sub-sects. Yet again, his only guideline comes from the Quran. 'And (as far) those who strive hard for us, we will most certainly guide them in Our ways; and Allah is most surely with the doers of good'. The verses from surah Al-Ankabut provide succour to Parvaiz when the going gets tough.

JIHAD AND IJTIHAD

The first word revealed to the Prophet by angel Gabriel was *Iqra* (read). It emphasized the importance of reading, of attaining knowledge in Islam. No doors barred, no windows closed, if *ilm* (knowledge) was available anywhere, it had to be assimilated and spread. It is under the light of the first revealed verse of the Quran that many faithful quote a tradition of the Prophet whereby he is said to have asked them to gain knowledge even if they had to go to China, a place considered far off on those early medieval times. Importantly, China was neither a Muslim nation nor a centre of Islamic learning. It was well advanced in the field of science. And the Prophet is still said to have asked the believers to go to China to acquire knowledge. Yet, in an irony, Muslims seem to have divided the world of knowledge into two halves—sacred and secular. Under this seemingly watertight demarcation, a person who pursues Islamic studies is often kept at a distance from the world of science, mathematics and literature. Similarly, a person pursuing modern secular subjects such as physics, chemistry and mathematics, etc., is well removed the world of Quran and Hadiths. It is this dichotomy which is at the root of the trouble in the Muslim world: The cleric does not understand new emerging challenges in everyday life, the common man has no grooming in Islamic tradition. And when the two talk, which is not often, they talk at cross purposes. Little wonder, the Islamic civilization which at one time showed the way to the rest of the world in terms of geometry, medicine and astronomy is deeply embroiled in *jahliyat* or ignorance today. Curiously, it is the Age of Jahliyat that the coming of the Prophet is supposed to have ended. C.F. Andrews puts it beautifully when he says that one of the principles

> which finds its place in the Quran is that knowledge is to be sought by Musalmans. In accordance with this principle it has become an established fact of history that progress and enlightenment have resulted, when Muhammadan culture has come into close contact with an intellectual environment other than its own. (based loosely on Surah Taha verse 114)

Today, the spirit of inquiry seems to have gone out of the life of the faithful. Any attempt to ask questions within the community is often brushed aside by maulanas saying, '*Mazhab mein sawaal nahin karte* [Do not question religion]. It is a matter of belief'. Yes, faith is all about belief but the Quran encourages a man to think, ponder, inquire, explore and learn. But today when a child asks his Islamic teacher, how would he be raised up after death because Islam has no concept of *saat janam* (seven lives, which is primarily the concept of rebirth) and the like, the teacher is seldom likely to entertain such a question. The attempt is always to brush the things under the carpet. The policy being ask no uneasy questions, expect no answers.

In fact, the holy book has a surah called Furqan which loosely translates into criterion of right and wrong. And yes, it answers a child's query too about rebirth after death. 'Does man think that we cannot assemble his bones together? Yes! We are able to put together the very tips of his fingers perfectly', says the Quran. Of course, few clerics will tell you this. Never mind if this revelation came more than 1,400 years ago and it was only in 1880 that fingerprinting became a scientific method of identification following research by Sir Francis Golt, who pointed out that no two persons could have the same fingerprints.

It is the same spirit of inquiry, of interrogation, of asking and assimilating that is lacking in today's Muslims in the subcontinent. Hence, the discussion, both in Muslim and non-Muslim circles, is often abut jihad rather than ijtihad. That the common man is brought up on a staple diet of jihad being an act of violence, of forcible conversion, matters. For centuries, a stereotype of an Islamist with the Quran in one hand and sword in the other has been repeated. And the believers have done little to counter the impression about jihad. Few have said that jihad is essentially a peaceful agitation with the self, gaining control over oneself. Fight with the enemy outside comes later. It is the jihad with the self during peaceful times that is more important. The real jihad was defined by the Prophet himself when he said after his return from a battle, 'We return from the lesser jihad to the greater jihad, the more difficult and crucial effort to conquer the forces of evil in oneself and in one's own society in all the details of daily life'.

And what about ijtihad? Well, both are at the core of Islam. While Jihad is oft misunderstood, ijtihad has been forgotten altogether. Attempting to provide clarity is S. Irfan Habib's *Jihad or Ijtihad: Religious Orthodoxy and Modern Science in Contemporary Islam* (2013), a cogently argued book. Ijtihad is independent and rational thinking. The gradual disappearance of ijtihad was initially confined to legal matters but later expanded to include other areas as well. By the nineteenth century, particularly after the colonization, scholars felt that the lack of ijtihad had led to intellectual stagnation. The poet–philosopher Muhammed Iqbal, for instance, saw ijtihad as the catalyst for Islam's intellectual resurgence, whereas the Grand Mufti of Egypt, Muhammad Abduh, considered it a break from traditional scholarship. Today, even a proponent of Islamic science, Ziauddin Sardar, concedes that with the disappearance of ijtihad, science in Islam has become a matter of history.

Of course, as Habib writes, some of the earliest progress in the field of science started from the Muslim world. Yet it is the Muslim countries today that languish in the field.

> While Europe was still stuck in the Dark Ages, scientists in the Islamic world were translating Aristotle, and making huge strides in astronomy, mathematics and philosophy. Two thousand years later, the idea of 'scientific progress' seems to be locked in a hopeless war with Islam. (Habib 2013)

This unseemly struggle stems from a lack of understanding and interpretation of the Quran which nowhere insists on the literal interpretation of the text; rather, it constantly stresses the need for intelligence in deciphering the 'sign' or 'message' of God. Muslims are not to abdicate their reason but to look at the world attentively and with curiosity. 'It was this attitude that later enabled Muslims to build a fine tradition of natural science which has never been seen as large a danger to religion as in Christianity', reminds Habib.

Science though remains an enigma for the Muslim world—a world peopled by many who are too arrogant to seek knowledge from others, and often too conceited to admit their limitations. These feelings, of arrogance, conceit and lack of a spirit of generosity, have led to a situation where the faithful lag behind rest of the world and do not even realize or admit it. Incidentally, Islam is all about a world free of arrogance, conceit and tyranny. This so-called Islamic position is un-Islamic as it lacks Islamic humility, which is the very cornerstone of Quranic philosophy as well as central to the Prophet's own conduct. As Habib (2013) writes in his book,

> The Quranic term for humility is *khushu*. The opposite of humility is arrogance (*kibr*). The Quran speaks of Satan (Iblis) as the arrogant one who refused to obey God's command to show humility towards His creatures. In other words, one may consider the absence of humility tantamount to arrogance, which is not an angelic but a satanic attribute.... Further, the Quran states that arrogance leads to tyranny (*zulm*).

Absence of *khushu and* presence of *kibr* and *zulm*. These are some of the attributes one can hardly associate with the community today. Sign enough that many Muslims know little about Islam. Under the circumstances, is it a surprise that they are not able to clear the air on something as fundamental as jihad? And that ijtihad is all but a forgotten virtue.

FATWA ON TERRORISM

As a boy, I often got angry on reading the newspaper in the morning. Often the provocation lay in our cricket team's inability to win a certain match against Pakistan. The coverage of the 1978 Pakistan tour of the team led by Bishan Singh Bedi and the loss at the hands of the genius of Imran Khan agitated my young mind for days on end. As did frequent headlines such as 'Amritraj goes down fighting' or 'Krishnan gallant in defeat'. Why could Vijay Amritraj not go up fighting, or why could Ramesh Krishnan not be gallant in victory? Why did Indians have to lose, I asked to no one in particular.

Occasionally though, there were more serious issues which occupied my young impressionable mind. For instance, whenever Imam Bukhari pronounced a fatwa on any sociopolitical issue that occupied the Muslim community—which itself was a huge exaggeration considering the imam's vision of Muslims was limited to those staying near the historic Jama Masjid built by Mughal Emperor Shah Jahan. Of course, he talked in terms of 'ummah', and the newspapers faithfully reproduced his words in daily reports. Nobody bothered to find out if a man staying in the Walled City of Ahmedabad or Old Hyderabad had even heard of the imam, leave alone his fatwa. To a hungry-for-headlines media, he gave quotable quotes. Often, in the run-up to elections, our newspapers wrote about the so-called fatwa in favour of the Congress or Janata Party as the case may be, or later the Bahujan Samaj Party, the Samajwadi Party, etc. Pray, he has even been known to have recommended the BJP after 2002!

Often, in the 1970s, I rushed to my father for his views on the fatwa supposedly pronounced before the *khutba* of Friday prayers. A *mufti* by qualification, my father would drive away my fears saying, *'Yeh sab kam ilm waalon ki baatein hain* [These are the things of people with little knowledge]. The imam was not qualified to issue the fatwa. He had no scholarly credentials'. His pronouncement of the alleged fatwa was akin to those quacks practising in jhuggi clusters as medical professionals. The quacks get by on luck, the imam on his political acumen.

Those days when *kam ilm* (little knowledge) reigned spilled over to my youth and beyond. In fact, more misnomers were added. For instance, the term Islamic terrorism. Again, I fumed when I first heard the term a little under two decades ago. Terrorism did not have a religion when the United States destroyed Vietnam or when Japan was bombed. It didn't have one when Mahatma Gandhi was assassinated. Or when Afghanistan and later Iraq were destroyed. Why associate a religion's name with acts of terror, I often asked in my social circle. Many nodded in agreement, yet the terms continued to gain currency even after a distinguished author such as Dilip Hiro openly found fault with the usage, and even sought to provide alternatives. Unfortunately, when he spoke a few years ago at Sapru House in New Delhi, few turned up to listen.

Recently, I found an answer, an answer stemming not from shared faith or viewpoint but from men whose width of vision far exceeded that of lesser mortals. The answer came not from an Islamic scholar alone but from two others following their own faiths in the book appropriately named *Fatwa on Terrorism and Suicide Bombings* by Dr Muhammad Tahir-ul-Qadri (2010) with a foreword by Professor John Esposito and introduction by our own Sudheendra Kulkarni.

Now Dr Tahir, hailed by those given to the moment as Pakistan's Anna Hazare, is a scholar whose words command attention wherever he goes. When he came to New Delhi three years ago, there was not an empty seat in the auditorium and no space for parking on the road leading to the India International Centre. He spoke; we all listened. And now I read. What a wonderful book, easy to read, simple to comprehend! He does not hold back; he goes for the jugular whether talking of suicide bombers or the so-called Islamic terrorists, demolishing the arguments of those gone astray with direct and indirect references to the Quran and Hadith. It is an elucidation that forced Kulkarni to go all the way to Canada to meet Dr Tahir at his modest but hospitable home.

Without naming the Islamic state terrorists now wreaking havoc on the faithful in West Asia, he talks of the unlawfulness of violence against Muslims. Reproducing an oft-quoted verse from the Quran, 'Whoever kills a person (unjustly), except as a punishment for murder or (as prescribed for bloodshed, robbery and spreading disorder in the land), it is as if he killed all of humanity', he writes, 'Islam not only outlaws the mass killing of Muslims but the whole of humanity, without any discrimination on the basis of caste, colour, race or religion'. With such simple words, he pronounces his verdict on suicide bombing, something which was defended by some scholars in the case of Israel's aggression in Palestine. Then in a move which will ring a bell with those who have had a soft corner for terrorists of any denomination, he states, 'Becoming an accomplice to terrorists is also a crime'. Here he reminds us that Prophet Muhammad 'categorically forbade people to provide help material support to terrorists. He ordered to isolate them and deny them any numerical strength, financial assistance and moral support'.

A little later, Dr Tahir takes on those who attack mosques—and such activities are known to happen frequently these days—and reminds them of the verses of the holy book wherein such people as those who forbid the remembrance of Allah's name are called 'unjust'. On similar lines, not only does he condemn suicide bombers but also their leaders. Importantly, he does not get into a verbal slugfest. Nor does he stoop to one man's word against another. He uses his vast knowledge of hadith, Sunnah and Islamic history to drive home the point in an irrefutable manner.

Little wonder, his words got Esposito to dig up a Gallup World Poll, the largest and most systematic poll of Muslims of 35 Muslim countries. According to the poll, of a majority of respondents who were asked in an open-ended question to explain their views on 9/11, those who condemned terrorism cited religious as well as humanitarian reasons. By contrast, not a single respondent who condoned the attacks used the Quran or Islam as justification. Instead, they relied on political rationalizations such as the United States as an imperialist power, and so on. Similarly, Kulkarni writes that the US war on terror is counter-productive and the death of the innocent in the drone attacks cannot be defended.

He goes on to talk of legal commands about protecting non-Muslims in an Islamic state, writing, 'neither violence nor compulsion in religion vis-à-vis non-Muslims is permitted in Islam'. Kulkarni recalls the speech M.A. Jinnah gave about the future of Pakistan on 14 August 1947—that is, Jinnah's equivalent of Nehru's 'Tryst with Destiny' speech. Jinnah is reported by Kulkarni to have said,

> The tolerance and goodwill that great Emperor Akbar showed to all the non-Muslims is not of recent origin. It dates back thirteen centuries ago when our Prophet not only by words but by deeds treated the Jews and Christians, after he had conquered them, with the utmost tolerance and regard and respect for their faith and beliefs. The whole history of Muslims, wherever they ruled, is replete with those humane and great principles which should be followed and practised by us.

That Pakistan, unfortunately, could not always follow up Jinnah's words with action is another matter.

The noted BJP leader came back enlightened after his Canada trip a few years ago. I got a ray of similar enlightenment reading the book, *Fatwa on Terrorism and Suicide Bombings*. Now, if the imams, the Bukharis and indeed a good section of the media could read it as well, the days of *kam ilm* could well be over.

ISLAM AND PRACTICES

TRIPLE TALAQ AND *KHULA*

SINCE 1986 WHEN THE SHAH BANO CASE HIT THE HEADLINES, no issue has occupied the mind of India's largest minority as Triple Talaq or Talaq-e-Biddat (innovated form of divorce). Much before the Supreme Court passed its judgement in the Shayara Bano versus the Union of India and others in August 2017, the community was discussing instant *talaq* at various sociopolitical fora. The urban–rural divide was clearly visible to anybody blessed with a perceptive mind. While Muslims in cosmopolitan India were largely against Triple Talaq, a way of ending a marriage under which a husband can pronounce the word *talaq* thrice and put an end to years of matrimony. This way of instant, on the spot divorce rules out all attempt at reconciliation, negotiation or even a rethink. Simply put, it is like a bullet which has left the gun.

Those opposed to Triple Talaq argued that this is a unilateral way of ending marriage. 'Marriage itself is an understanding between a man and a woman with clear demands and conditions, accompanied by two witnesses.

How can it then end without the wife having a say', they often ask. Rightly so. The opponents of Triple Talaq derive their strength from the Quran which clearly emphasizes a process of reconciliation and arbitration before any marriage is dissolved. In fact, as told through Surah Nisa of the Quran, a squabbling couple is supposed to seek help to bring their life to an even keel. At the first sign of trouble, the husband and wife are supposed to talk to each other in private. This attempt to thrash out their issues should not be shared with anybody. Every word of the spouse is a treasure to be protected by both of them. If, however, despite their best attempts, the situation does not improve, the man is still not to pronounce divorce. The attempt at exploration of conciliation avenues has to continue. At this stage, arbiters have to be brought in from both families, one from the wife's family, the other from the husband's family. The arbiters are then required to attempt to smoothen out the differences, and bring the couple together. Their role is not confined to a one-off sitting with the couple. Rather they are to talk to them for up to three months to attain domestic harmony. It is only when the arbiters too fail to bring the husband and wife to the same page that the husband is allowed to pronounce divorce.

At this stage also, he is expected to give only one divorce, *talaq-e-ahsan*. After the man pronounces single divorce, the wife continues to stay with him during her three-month long *iddat* (waiting) period. During this time, the spouses are asked to stay under the same roof to give them a chance to get rid of their differences. As the wife is in *iddat*, the husband is supposed to look after her needs as he usually does, that is, provide food, clothing and shelter. Importantly, during this phase, the husband can annul the divorce through word or action. If any physical intimacy is established between the couple, the divorce is automatically dissolved.

If, however, the three month waiting period expires, and the husband does not take back the divorce, it is considered complete divorce. The couple get yet another chance to atone for any wrongdoing. They can marry each other with a fresh *nikah* and *mahr*.

The process is repeated in the instance of second divorce too. It is only when the husband pronounces divorce for the third time, that is, divorce pronounced with a gap of one menstrual cycle, during the woman's clean period during which no sexual relations are established, that the divorce is final, irrevocable. Now both the man and the woman are independent, and can choose a fresh marital partner, if they so desire.

At this stage, there is a little asterisk put by our society. While the Quran through Surah Baqarah gives a woman complete right to do with herself what she may choose to do, some clerics, however, give it a patriarchal twist by innovating the concept of *halala*. The Quran allows the divorced woman to marry again. Or stay single. In case she marries again, and somehow things do not work out with the new spouse, and he divorces her, she performs *iddat* as the wife of the second husband. Once this waiting period is over, she is yet again a free woman with earlier rights. At this stage, she may choose to marry a third man. Or instead of going for a new marital arrangement, she might opt to go back to her first husband with a fresh *nikah*, if he too is agreeable. This gives the woman a choice; it is not compulsory for her to go back to her first husband. But yes, she is eligible and permitted, or *halal* for him.

Unfortunately, in sections of Indian society, this right of a woman to go to her first husband after a failed second marriage, including the death of the second husband, is made a mockery. Some clerics feel that after a woman has been divorced thrice over by her husband, the only way she can go back to him is by performing *halala*. That is, marry another man, consummate that marriage, then get a divorce from him. After this, she performs *iddat* of the second husband before being eligible to marry her first man again. In this system, some maulanas suggest a short-term marriage. The divorced woman marries a man with a tacit condition of immediate divorce, at times within hours of consummation of marriage, at others within 3–7 days. It is an arrangement that gets no support from the Quran. The Quran gives the woman the right to go back to her husband even after three divorces in case her second husband either divorces her or dies. Nowhere is a short-term husband mentioned. Also, there is a Hadith under which the Prophet is supposed to have cursed those who perform *halala*, and those who get it performed, that is, both the original and short-term husbands.

Both instant *talaq* and *halala*, unsupported by the Quran, are rigorously opposed by many educated Muslims, particularly those in big cities.

In small towns and villages of India, however, things are quite the opposite. Here, the common man often lays much stock by what the maulanas decree. Thus Triple Talaq is accepted as a means of ending marriage with a single pronouncement of the word *talaq* followed by multiple expressions in a single sitting. Those in favour of Triple Talaq draw solace from a ruling of Caliph Hazrat Umar who is said to have allowed it in certain circumstances. While that is true, it is only partial truth. While allowing men to divorce women through instant *talaq* method, he also announced punitive measures against men. They were given lashes in public. But the punishment part is forgotten, as those who wish to empower men remember only a part of the caliph's ruling. Importantly, they forget too that the Prophet too was confronted with similar cases. Once, a man came to him, to admit that he had divorced his wife. The Prophet asked him, if he had done so at a single sitting. When the man said yes, the Prophet allowed him to treat it as only a single revocable divorce and resume cohabitation with his wife. No fresh *nikah* needed, no *halala*, nothing.

Incidentally, it is against Triple Talaq that women have often raised their voice in the subcontinent. Both Pakistan and Bangladesh did away with it many decades ago. It took the Supreme Court ruling under Chief Justice J.S. Khehar for Triple Talaq to be set aside in August 2017 in India.

The five Bench judge, through a split 3:2 verdict set aside Triple Talaq, thereby invalidating it. Interestingly, the five judges hailed from five different faiths, there being one Sikh, a Muslim, a Christian, Parsi and a Hindu practitioner, thus underlining India's plurality. The Constitution Bench comprising besides Chief Justice J.S. Khehar, Justices Kurian Joseph, Rohinton Fali Nariman, Uday Umesh Lalit and S. Abdul Nazeer, invalidated Triple Talaq while hearing five writ petitioners filed by Muslim women who were all victims of Triple Talaq. To the lead petition of Shayara Bano were clubbed the petitions of Ishrat Jahan, Afreen Rehman, Atiya Sabri and Gulshan Parveen. The women were all divorced through instant *talaq*—Bano received the *talaqnama* (divorce papers) through post, Rehman's father received it on behalf of his daughter. Jahan was given divorce over phone from

Dubai while *talaqnama* on a ₹10 stamp paper was sent to the Rampur residence of Parveen by her husband through his lawyer. Sabri's *talaqnama* arrived by speed post at her brother's residence. In short, all women were victims of unilateral divorce, a final separation which explored no chance of reconciliation. It was this way of ending marriage that was set aside by the Supreme Court.

Interestingly, while a large section of the Muslim community had gone into an aggressive mode following the Shah Bano judgement in 1986, the community expressed great restraint, confining itself to a few discussions on the merits and demerits of the judgement in 2017. Nowhere did Muslim women come out on the streets to protest the judgement, nowhere did men launch a dharna against the decision. Everything was accepted with a blend of grace and sobriety. While this reaction showed the community to be much more mature than in the past, at least a part of the quiet acceptance of the verdict stemmed from the fact that the honourable Supreme Court in its judgement had quoted extensively from the Quran. In fact, the judgement of the Chief Justice itself ran into 272 pages where he quoted from the Quran as also Hadith. Other judges too were appreciative of the concerns. Importantly, the judges only set aside Triple Talaq, refraining from sitting in judgement on *halala* and polygamy as sought by the petitioners. They set that for a future, undecided date.

The judgement was interpreted in various ways. While most women activists hailed it as a step towards gender justice though the judgement did not talk in terms of gender parity, the representatives of Muslim bodies, surprisingly, hailed the judgement for giving paramountcy to personal laws. The politicians too interpreted it to suit their political convenience. Everybody had something to cheer in the judgement of Shayara Bano and four other women petitioners—all except the women themselves. For them, the court had set aside Triple Talaq, but refrained from giving a direct word on the state of their marriage, whether it subsisted or not. It too was taken that as the divorce had been annulled, the marriage continued. But the Quran gives a three-month period for any *talaq* to be taken back after a single pronouncement which is what the Triple Talaq pronouncement amounted to after the Supreme Court verdict. In this case, all the women had been divorced much longer. So, were they actually finally divorced despite the court's judgement? Also, if Triple Talaq was taken as only a single pronouncement of divorce, the marriage continued. But as the waiting period was long since over, the women needed a fresh *nikah* to go back to their husband. There was no guarantee that a husband who had been dragged to court by his wife would accept her following the verdict.

So, the judgement left many points to ponder too.

The Supreme Court refrained from commenting on *halala* and polygamy, the two practices though stand at two ends of the spectrum when it comes to religious sanction. The Quran nowhere sanctions short-term marriage with a pre-decided date of divorce, thereby annulling the practice of *halala* the way it operates in India. In fact, the Quran lays a lot of stock by marriage and encourages a couple to make all attempts at making the marriage work. It even asks the spouses to overlook the flaws in the partner and concentrate on the good aspects of his/her personality. While Triple Talaq negates all attempts at reconciliation, *halala* makes it worse. A woman who has been divorced in a fit of anger by her husband, is often told by some maulanas that now she is haram (prohibited) for him. And the only way of going back to him is to have a fresh *nikah* with another man, obtain divorce, perform *iddat*, then go to her earlier husband with a fresh *nikah*.

This arrangement, while is often described as a punishment for the man for his anger, is actually a punishment for the woman for the man's anger. Since it is almost impossible to procure a short-term husband for marriage, often the clerics offer their services in secret. A *nikah* is performed after Isha prayers in the evening. The marriage is consummated the same night. Next day, the woman is divorced. This kind of marriage mocks at the concept of *nikah* in Islam. It degrades the women. And is totally against the letter and spirit of the Quran. The Quran upholds the dignity of women, gives them a chance to choose their partner even after divorce, if they so desire. This concept of *halala* finds no support from any verse, any chapter of the Quran.

While *halala* has zero support from the scriptures, the situation is totally different when it comes to polygamy. The Quran, just as it permits a woman to marry a second or a third or fourth time, allows a man to have *nikah* with more than a single woman. A man is allowed to have up to four wives, although he is strongly urged to be satisfied with just one. The Quran asks men to do justice with their wives, treat them at par. And upon their inability to treat all wives equally, men are told to marry just one woman. But nowhere does it rule against multiple marriage.

Two verses from Surah An-Nisa state,

And if you fear that you might not treat the orphans justly, then marry the women that seem good to you: two, or three, or four. If you fear that you will not be able to treat them justly, then marry (only) one, or marry from among those whom your right hands possess. This will make it more likely that you will avoid injustice. (Surah Al-Nisa, Verse 3)

You will not be able to treat your wives with absolute justice, not even when you keenly desire to do so. It suffices (in order to follow the Law of Allah that) you incline not wholly to one, leaving the other in suspense. If you act rightly and remain God-fearing, surely Allah is All-Forgiving, All-Compassionate. (Verse 129, Surah Al-Nisa)

The book put a limit to four wives at a time when men in the Arab world were known to have multiple spouses, at times running into hundreds. Similarly, the Quran put the limit of divorces at three as at that time many men had reduced the concept of divorce to a plaything, divorcing women one day, taking them back after a few days. Then repeating the course, leaving the women on tenterhooks. It was humiliating and emotionally distressing for women. The Quran safeguarded women's life and dignity through both *talaq* and permission for polygamy. Also, an avenue against polygamy is available for women. Instead of leaving things in the hands of men, they are allowed to have a clause inserted into the *nikahnama* that the husband will not take another wife. Or if he were to do so, it would be within her rights to cancel her marriage.

WOMEN'S RIGHT TO DIVORCE

Talking of a woman's right to end marriage, brings us to *khula*. It is a Muslim woman's right to opt out of marriage. In simple terms, it is a woman's equivalent of the man's right to *talaq*. In many ways, *khula* is more powerful. When a man pronounces divorce through the Quran-approved method, it takes three months for the divorce to be completed. He either has to pronounce one divorce, *talaq-e-ahsan*, then wait for the three menstrual cycles of his wife to be completed without the divorce being annulled through word or deed. Or he has to pronounce divorce after each monthly cycle, as in the case of *talaq-e-hasan*.

The woman's right to divorce is much simpler. If a woman wants to end wedlock, she just has to opt for *khula*. It is her inalienable right to divorce. The moment a woman expresses her wish to obtain *khula*, the man cannot say no. Even the *qazi* cannot ask her to take back her decision or reconsider it. If the man delays in acceptance, the *qazi* has to prevail upon him to accept *khula* and release the woman from his *nikah*. Once *khula* is pronounced, either through spoken word or in writing, the woman walks out of the husband's house immediately, thus safeguarding her modesty from the man who is now a stranger to her. Thus, it can all be completed in a matter of minutes.

In case a woman is not paid her *mahr* till then, she is advised against pressing for it, as she is the one opting out of marriage. But the man too is told not to ask for the gifts he may have given her in earlier days.

While the media is largely silent on *khula*, and politicians don't spare a breath to talk of a Muslim woman's right to divorce, the *khula* cases are increasing across the country. In sundry madrasas of Delhi, more and more women bring up cases of *khula*. In Bihar too, the situation is similar where Imarat Shariah in Patna gets 10 times the number of *khula* cases in comparison to Triple Talaq. In the South too, in Darul Qazas, or qazi courts, more divorces are initiated by women than men.

Incidentally, Muslim women enjoy many other ways of ending an unhappy marriage besides *khula*. One of them being *faskh* or judicial divorce. If a husband fails in his conjugal responsibilities or does not give any maintenance or accuses the wife of moral turpitude, she can obtain divorce through *faskh*. Similarly, a woman can end marriage through *talaq-e-tafweez* (delegated divorce). For this, a condition has to be stipulated in the *nikahnama* that the man vests his right to divorce in the woman. Of course, there is the option of divorce by mutual consent too. Called *mubarat*, it is a way of ending unhappy marriages on an amicable note, much like our courts often suggest warring spouses to do.

With all these rights, one wonders, just where is the helpless, hapless Muslim woman, living under constant fear of instant divorce? The answer may well be in the prejudice of the society as also in its patriarchal ways. While often women are not aware of their rights, the fact remains that only half a per cent of Muslim women ever have a divorce, Triple Talaq, *talaq-e-ahsan*, *talaq-e-hasan* and other forms included.

A WOMAN LEADS FRIDAY PRAYERS

The last Friday of January 2018 arrived like any other Friday for the faithful across India. Muezzins got busy with cleaning the mosques, the carpets hung out on Thursday evening were placed back inside the prayer hall. The overhead water tanks were filled to the brim to accommodate the *namazis* (devotees). And extra *safs* (rows) of jute mats were neatly lined one after the other. At some places, even the roads leading to the mosque were freshly swept and a layer of a germicide sprinkled on the drains. The microphones were double-checked for clarity and volume. All bases covered, the community prepared for the weekly sermon followed by prayer. In fact, even those people who did not go to the mosque on a daily basis took time out for Friday congregation. Imams too prepared their talk, based on the Quran. At most of the mosques, the imams confined themselves to Arabic text, and, in a few mosques, notably in Hyderabad and Chennai, the imams made sure that they read out the translation in local language. In the bigger mosques, the imams guided the devotees on contemporary affairs in the life of the community.

All was fair and normal. Until there came a piece of news from the otherwise quiet township of Mallapuram in Kerala—the place had etched its place in the annals of the faithful. Courtesy, a woman who stepped in where no woman had dared in the past, a woman who not only decided to step into men's shoes but also decided she would do things her own way. Against all convention, Jamida led Friday prayers for men and women in Quran Sunnat Society in Kerala. This was a brave action that attracted a lot of criticism, not just from men but also women. Millions accused her of not knowing Islamic history. Thousands imputed political motives, arguing the deed caused com- motion in the life of the faithful, taking the attention away from other issues. Just a handful stood by her.

Jamida led the Friday prayers, replete with a sermon. There were a few things remarkably different from what other imams were doing at the same time. To begin with, Jamida was a woman. Then the devotees included both men and women. Almost all men were bare headed. Not all women abided by the exact degree of hijab. Jamida herself though was covered from head to foot. The differences were not limited to the mixed gathering, significant as it was. It may be pertinent to recall that most mosques open their doors only to men for Friday prayers. Only a handful of mosques, maintained by Ahl-e-Hadith followers, and members of Jamaat-e-Islami allow women to offer prayers, their sections clearly marked and removed from the prying eyes of men. It was not so at Jamida's jamaat. Significant as this difference was, it was soon reduced to a footnote. The real difference came in the prayer. Yes, Jamida, like all imams read verses from the Quran as she led the prayers as an imam, but the prayer was shorter than usual. While Islam permits, even desires shorter prayers when the congregation is large—this is done keeping in mind old and sick people who may not be able to take the rigours of a longer prayer—Jamida took another route to shorter prayers. While across the country the faithful did two prostrations in every *rakat* (cycle) and four prostrations across two *rakats*, those standing in prayer behind Jamida did only one prostration in a *rakat*; in all, only two prostrations across two *rakaats* (cycles) of Friday prayers. This action of having only one prostration in a *rakat* was unprecedented in Islamic history anywhere across the world. Further, in every *rakat*, Jamida, when she came up from the bowing position, did not say *Sami Allahuleman Hamida*, as is the norm. Instead, she said *Allah-o-Akbar*. This action too was not reported from anywhere across the world. Not also from many women who routinely lead prayers of fellow women.

Not even from Amina Wadud, the American imam who was the first woman in contemporary world to lead mixed gender prayers. While the devotees behind Wadud included both men and women in a common row, Wadud, herself stuck to the Prophet's way of leading the prayer, reciting the verses given for the purpose with all the attendant submission and prostration to Almighty. It may be recalled, Wadud's action in 2005 had caused an uproar in the world of the faithful, with many openly criticizing her and accusing her of spreading mischief in the matters of faith. Among those who questioned her action was noted writer Kamala Das, who had by then embraced Islam. She openly pointed out that the reason why a woman cannot lead men in prayer has nothing to do with discrimination, but all to do with men's conditioning. 'A man can get aroused on seeing a woman's behind', she said.

Jamida's case was more unique. Not only did she lead men and women in Friday prayers, she also chose a new way of offering prayers, something nobody had seen at any mosque anywhere. She defended her manner by claiming that she regarded the Quran as the touchstone of all her action. She claimed that nowhere does the Quran ask the devotees to do two prostrations per cycle. Further, she stated that when she said *Allah-o-Akbar* while standing up from a bowing position, she did so as the words *Sami Allahuleman Hamida* are not from the Quran. 'All my actions are based on the Quran. I don't go by Hadith as men have interpolated many things according to their understanding while not a word of the Quran has been changed since it was revealed to Prophet Muhammad'.

Her action was greeted with a social outrage. Not just conservative sections but also the progressives were shaken. While hardly anybody had a problem with a woman offering Friday prayers, many had an issue with a woman leading the prayers for men. They pointed out that such a thing had never occurred in Islamic history anywhere, including the time of the Prophet. At that time, many women used to frequent the mosque for daily *salaat* (prayer). Women were not prohibited from going to a mosque. And the Prophet is reported to have said, 'The best prayer for a man is in the first *saf* (row). The best prayer for a woman was in the last *saf*. What it implied was both, that women were permitted by the Prophet to frequent the mosques, and they did so with his knowledge. Also, that there was segregation on the basis of gender inside the mosque—men prayed with men, women did likewise with women. In the case of both Wadud earlier and now Jamida, this division was done away with. When Jamida claimed that she did not do a thing in the prayer that went against the word of the Quran, it was pointed out that the Quran asks the faithful to establish prayers not offer prayers. Which obviously implies prayers offered in a congregation, but it did not give the methodology of prayer. The Quran outlines the way of preparing for prayers, the method of ablution, etc., but nowhere does the Quran give the method of the prayer as such, like when to hold hands across the stomach or chest, when to go in submission, when to offer prostration. All these actions came to the faithful through the example of the Prophet. It is an example which has been followed for more than 1,400 years across the world, with not a word of dilution, no action deleted or added. Many believers, obviously shaken and enraged, pointed out that it is everybody's duty to follow the example of the Prophet as no action of his was contrary to the Quran. He, in fact, lived the message of the Quran through his actions. When Jamida stood in prayer, that very gesture of hers, derived from the practice of the Prophet, not a verse from the Quran.

Jamida remained unfazed in the face of opposition, pledging to lead special *taraveeh* prayers in Ramadan. It is something she has done in the past too. As for Friday prayers, she is not likely to find popular approval anytime soon, all her claims of following the Quran notwithstanding. What her action did prove was that the winds of dialogue and debate even dissent are blowing across the Muslim world. And the world of the men with skullcaps may not remain secluded for long. Jamida's action had its flaws, but what she achieved is to force men to go back to the scriptures independent of local tradition.

MUSLIM WOMEN AND MASJID

Seventy-six-year-old Ikhlasi Begum was understandably nervous as she prepared to offer her first Eid prayers. A quick lukewarm water bath was followed by new clothes, specially stitched for the occasion. She applied attar too, telling her granddaughters that it was a Sunnah, a practice of the Prophet. The girls had had henna applied to their little hands on *chand raat* (the night of the new moon). All the way to Jama Masjid, some 20 kilometres from her place, Begum repeated the verses she was supposed to say before and after the prayer. Not that she did not know her prayer. She had offered it five times a day on her personal *ja-namaz* (prayer mat) in the privacy of her room ever since she could remember. After thousands of prayers offered in seclusion, it was for the first time she was heading to a masjid to offer Eid prayers with her sisters in faith. Her heart throbbed with anticipation. She was anxious to listen to the imam's *khutba* sitting inside the masjid for the first time. For decades, she had heard the *khutba* while cooking in her kitchen. For the first time, she imagined herself standing in a *saf* with other women for the two *rakahs* of namaz. With her were two granddaughters aged 10 and 7. She did not want them to lag behind.

For over 30 years Begum had spent her life in a two-room house on the edge of a madrasa. Her husband, a scholar of Islam, had translated *Sahih Muslim*, a book of authentic hadith into Urdu. He used to give daily sermon after the Fajr namaz (prayer at dawn) at the historic Fatehpuri Masjid in Old Delhi. Every day, Begum got him ready for the masjid before the crack of dawn. Never did he get late for his talk. Never did Begum fail in her duty. Never did it strike her that she could actually go out with him for the prayer. All along, she offered her own namaz on a *takht* (wooden cot) at home. Every afternoon she would read the Quran too in the Arabic original. Every day, she would draw satisfaction that she had read another chapter of the holy book. That she did not know the language merely meant she never understood what the book conveyed. She just read. Like countless other women, and men. It went on for many years. Her husband passed away. Kids grew up. It was then somebody told her to read the Urdu translation of the meaning of the Quran. 'The Quran is a book for the living, not the dead. It tells you how to lead your life', he stated, 'find out the solutions of your problems through the book. Do not depend on the maulanas'. Begum's way of reading the holy book underwent a change. Instead of reading the Arabic original cover to cover, she would read the Arabic verse followed by its Urdu translation. With each passing day, she felt more complete. Still one day when her son told her the meaning of azaan, the call for prayer, she was surprised. 'When the muezzin says *"Haiyya alas salah, haiyya alal falah,"* he calls to prayer, to success. He calls everybody, not just men', he explained. Begum nodded. Her decision to head to the masjid was taken then. It was at New Delhi's Jama Masjid, she realized that women had attended the special Eid prayers for many years. And Jamaat-e-Islami's headquarters, popularly called Markaz, attracted women in hundreds to Eid prayers. 'Women are merely exempted, not prohibited from prayer in masjid', the words rang in her mind. She went back from the masjid tired for the exertion but visibly happy. It was to be her first and last Eid namaz by jamaat—prayer by congregation—as the wheel of life completed a full circle a few months later.

For years, before Begum, women had been offering their Friday prayers, even the special *taraweeh* prayers where the Quran would be recited aloud across the month of Ramadan at Markaz and elsewhere. Some came from the immediate vicinity of the masjid, many from as much as 20 kilometres away.

Around the time Begum had started to understand the Quran by reading the translation of its meaning, noted author Anees Jung had studied the place of Islam in the life of women in India. She invested her study with rare sensitivity, being careful enough to clear a few cobwebs. For instance, women's right to pray in a masjid. 'Women were never barred from going to the mosque. They were, only exempted as they had household chores. When they go to Haj or Umra they go and pray in the mosque', she gathered.

Thus, when the media went to town with the plea of Zakia Soman, co-founder of Bharatiya Muslim Mahila Andolan, it surprised many. Soman approached the Supreme Court to provide Muslim women with the right to worship in mosques, and enter the Haji Ali Dargah in Mumbai. The need to take constitutional recourse for something denied neither by Shariah nor the law of the land raised more than a few eyebrows. 'Women already have the right to pray in a masjid, though their best prayer is at home', reasoned a member of All India Muslim Personal Board, adding, 'there is no question of opposing the plea. Women offer namaz at the Prophet's mosque, Masjid-e-Nabvi. How can anybody deny them access to masjids here?' The point is, in India, women can offer prayers inside mosques, although admittedly few have provisions for them. There is a big Ahl-e-Hadith masjid in Jogabai, Delhi, where a complete floor is reserved for women to attend Friday prayers. In fact, many members of the Ahl-e-Hadith sect want more women to come to masjid, as it is essential for a feeling of unity and cama-raderie. 'On Friday, there are special sermons to guide the faithful. If women won't be allowed to attend Friday prayers, how are they going to gain from the sermons', they reason.

Noble as the words are, more than infrequently there have been violations, with many of the clerics actually believing that masjids are out of bounds for women. While some have talked in terms of physical impurity during menstruation, when women are not supposed to pray anyway, others feel it would lead to uncalled for hassles. In an all-men's mosque, one floor without any partition suffices. Also one ablution place and indeed one rest room.

With the entry of women, the entire dynamics change, they reason. It is an exclusion that rankles.

As stated by Asra Nomani, a noted author and activist,

> The interpretation of Islamic law, or Shariah, in India doesn't protect the right of women to enter mosques in India. From Tamil Nadu to Uttar Pradesh, I have personally visited mosques in which women are barred, banned and denied permission to enter mosques. This policy is not only a betrayal of the tradition, or sunnah, of Islam in the seventh century, when women freely entered the mosque of the prophet Muhammad, in Medina, but it is a violation of the ethos of equal rights enshrined in the Constitution of India's secular democracy. (Author's interview with Asra Nomani)

It is a betrayal of Islamic tradition that denied Begum, and millions others, her right to pray in a masjid. She was never barred, just that the menfolk never informed her of the right. It was just understood that men would go to a mosque, women would go to some inner chamber of the house for prayer. For decades, Begum lived under the shadow of a masjid and madrasa; for decades, she never once participated in a community prayer. Every Eid, husband and kids would deck up in new clothes and head for prayers in the masjid. Begum would confine herself to preparing Eid delicacies. That is until it all changed when she read the translation of the meaning of the Quran.

> Wherever men are mentioned, women too are mentioned. The Quran often refers to 'believing men' and 'believing women' in the same sentence. They get the same reward for fasting, for Hajj, for a deed of charity.

Why then should women not be given their rightful place in the masjid? Indeed, it is time to reclaim the lost space. In every mosque, in every *mohalla*, and not just in Jama Masjid or Markaz.

NIGHT OF THE NEW MOON

Through with almost a month of fasting in Ramadan, the heart longs for Eid, that wonderful festival which brings with it *seviyan* (vermicelli), *sheer* and *kheer* (desserts). The newspapers never tire of photographs of little boys locked in a hug, saying 'Eid Mubarak' at the historic Jama Masjid. Else, they come up with pictures with a nice interplay of shine and shade showing the faithful bowed in devotion at Feroz Shah Kotla. But talk of Eid and all its celebrations, and I think of a book which I read more than a couple of decades ago. It is a book that has stayed with me down the years. It is a book that comes to mind on the eve of Eid too, as I see young men and women climb to the terraces of their apartments and houses to catch a glimpse of the new moon, the moon that would mean an end to fasting and usher in revelry.

Aptly called *Night of the New Moon* (1993), Anees Jung's book stays with me after all these long years. I have greyed; the pages of the book have yellowed. It smells nice. Reads nice too.

Anees talks of the new moon more in the context of the eve of Ramadan when people look for the moon with an air of devotion, knowing that the new moon will usher in a month of fasting, the month when the Holy Quran began to be revealed, the month with *Laylat al-Qadr*, a night equivalent to a thousand nights. As she writes,

As a child I climbed the highest terrace of our house to sight the new moon. Would it rise or would its crescent curve evade our eyes? It was a night of waiting, of not knowing, of wondering. When it wanly appeared it was hailed as a great sign from heaven. From the glittering minarets of mosques the grave mullahs would announce that the moon had been sighted. The old cannons in my childhood city would boom. (Jung 1993)

Yet when the new moon was sighted after 30 days, the feelings would be completely different. This time, people would anticipate its arrival on a cloudless sky, giggling girls would rush to say salaam to their grandparents, and young men would step out to announce to the world that the Eid moon had been sighted. But that too is more of a memory now.

As Anees (1993) writes, 'Today I sight the new moon in Delhi's smog-filled skies. High terraces open to the heavens are a thing of the past ... Eid no longer means a celebration that marks the long wait'.

Although she talks with passion and detached reason about the night of the new moon, Anees's book is much more than that. In fact, it is a portrait of Muslim women across the country, from Bhopal, the city of the Begums, to Hyderabad the city of Ameena, the girl who refused to be married off to an old Arab, to the towns of Kerala, and of course Delhi and Lucknow. With each snapshot, she opens a new world to the readers. Although written more than a couple of decades ago, some of the words retain their relevance. For instance when she talks of Najma Heptullah, Minister in the Modi government for a few years, then the Deputy Chairperson of the Rajya Sabha. Najma gives an insight into her childhood, the days when her grandmother, sister of Maulana Azad, was an inspector of schools during the reign of Sultan Jehan Begum. 'For a woman to be educated in Bhopal was not an exception but the rule....Women were never barred from the mosque, only exempted'. This rings a bell today as women across the country seek to have their own space in mosques, arguing vociferously with maulanas. Interestingly, neither the Shariah nor the Constitution prevents them from entering a masjid or even saying their prayers there. Even a prominent Islamic body such as the Jamaat-e-Islami Hind reserves a special section for women at their headquarters in Southeast Delhi, as do masjids of the Ahl-e-Hadith sect. Some semi-literate maulanas, of course, are a different matter!

Then at the other extreme, Anees presents a 9-year-old in Bombay, visiting a famous shrine. Asked what would she pray for, the little girl replies, 'a black satin burqa'. For her, the burqa was not a garb that locked her out of the world, but a gift. Yes, the same 'gift' which many countries seek to deny any girl. It is in sharp contrast too to the women in Delhi who gathered to protest against the Muslim Women's Bill. They dropped their veil, not the privacy it implied.

Somewhere in between comes Saleha, a teacher in a convent school, who wears no burqa and drives her own car. And is content looking after her widowed mother and aged aunt. She does not fear Allah. And is determined not to read the Quran on anybody's death, as is the custom in Muslim families. 'How can the dead man get benediction if I read the Quran? Isn't the Quran more a book of conduct that tells you how to live life?' Unwittingly, in this simple query, she sums up what many intellectuals within the community have been trying to drive into the minds of middle-class men and women who treat the holy book as a source of benediction. That is all.

The best, though, comes from the Begum in Bhopal. She had adjusted to a life of sharing her husband with other women. Many years removed from the age of royalty, she never stepped out of her 'golden cage'. When her husband was stripped of his title, she remained untouched by the loss. 'She had her faith', says Anees. And went about her life with her husband's co-wives and companions. After all the years of suffering, did she ever feel like crying, bursting out in front of the world? No. Begum says it all: 'One cries before Allah not in front of fellow human beings.... Never let your heart be empty of God. Only He stays. All else is *fanna*, that extinction which marks the end of all human journeys'.

So, as I write this day on what is probably the last day of Ramadan and Eid is all but here, I cannot but remember the Begum's words. 'Never let your heart be empty of God. Only He stays'. Thanks Anees, for a book that has stayed the course for so many years!

MADRASAS AND FARHAT HASHMI

It is a particularly chilly afternoon in an otherwise warm winter. Immediately after Zuhr prayers at Masjid Bhoori Bhatyari on New Delhi's Bahadur Shah Zafar Marg, I find myself surrounded by boys not more than 13 and not much less than 9. All of them are clad in a white kurta–pyjama; some have the traditional white skullcap on their head. Only a few can afford to wear a jacket or a sweater to ward off the cold. All stand barefoot on the cold marble floor, looking at me with inquisitive eyes, some avoid direct eye contact, preferring to look at each other instead. They are all from different districts of Bihar and Uttar Pradesh, and have come to the Capital to study at the madrasa. The madrasa is combined with the masjid—same premises, same staff and all. During prayers, the boys occupy the left side of the rows, the menfolk from nearby offices stand on the right. Prayers over, the men head to their work places, the boys get down to revising the lessons they were taught in the morning. The boys have a couple of sessions of study every day. They read the Quran, listen to Hadith, learn Urdu, some Arabic as well, they claim. Do they then understand Arabic beyond the Quran, I ask. The youngsters have no clue. Some computers? Well, no. Arithmetic? No. For a year or two, they learn to read the Quran, some manage to memorize it as well, joining the ranks of millions of hafizs across the world. Their ability to remember every word of the Quran is laudable considering they do not understand a word of it. Every year, in the month of Shabaan, the boys are given their certificates, the hafizs felicitated. For an evening, it is a different world. The masjid is lit up, flower petals ordered, a goat or two slaughtered for a special feast. And some faithful among the regular *namazis* even give cash prizes besides a suit. The suit is nothing but a fresh kurta–pyjama set. At times, a skullcap is added. Almost nobody ever thinks of gifting them slippers. Most students throughout their stay at the madrasa use plastic sandals—some have not had a new pair for a long time. As a result, often their heels touch the ground as they walk, in turn inviting admonition of the ustad in the madrasa for not being able to keep their feet clean. Incidentally, the boys, all hailing from poor families, some without even electricity at home, clean the madrasa themselves. They sweep the floor, fill the overhead tank and make their own bed. The 'bed' is a glorified word for what is essentially just a worn-out rug spread on the floor. There is a pillow too, only thing is, it was probably last washed a couple of years ago.

Some two weeks before the month of Ramadan, they step out to face the world, knowing not how to read simple English or Hindi, or how to switch on a computer, or send or receive an email. They have the certificate and the blessings of Madrasa Rasheedia with them besides their meagre belongings. The boys, most on the brink of teen-age, follow the footprints of their seniors; the madrasa has been churning out hafizs every year for decades.

Someday step out of Madrasa Rasheedia, walk not more than a kilometre to your left and watch how a few steps can change the world. Located on the first floor of a lane off Sir Syed Ahmed Road near the now closed Golcha Cinema, there is a centre to learn the Glorious Quran by Tajweed, a way of learning under which one understands the meaning of each expression along with its root word. Usually, there is a working professional who doubles up as a Quranic scholar by night to teach the students at the Al-Hudaya centre. The students themselves are almost all working men—some bankers, others call centres employees—and others still pursuing courses such as business management and company secretary. The teacher acts as a messenger here; he basically repeats what he has learnt at a similar class a couple of years ago. That teacher in turn had learnt the same way. The chain goes all the way to Farhat Hashmi, a name so often heard among the faithful in cities and towns across North and West India that it is difficult to believe that she has never set foot in any of the classes anywhere! Yet her words guide the faithful, her spirit breaks many a gender barrier in a world where men still occupy pre-eminent position.

Hailing from Pakistan and based in Canada, Hashmi devised a course through her lectures where one reads and understands every word of the Quran. It might sound simple, but it is actually revolutionary when one considers that almost all madrasas across the country teach the youngsters to read or even to memorize the Quran without understanding any of it.

So when Hashmi says, 'when you read "*Alhamdulillahi rabbil aalameen*," you are saying, "all praise and thanks belong to Allah, the master of the universe,"' it rings a bell. The faithful repeat this line at least 17 times a day if they say their basic prayers, yet most do not know the meaning. Not those who read the Quran at home under the guidance of a local maulana, nor those whose parents admitted them to a madrasa near their place. In Hashmi's class, they repeat the words and their meanings like children in nursery class. Most enjoy it; nobody minds it.

But it was not all smooth sailing for Hashmi and her students. When the first class was held in Mumbai, and soon after in Delhi, the faithful were only critical. Only women were allowed to attend the classes. With a view to get more students, pre-teen children were allowed to accompany their mothers, the kids to be accommodated in a separate playroom. The attendance was thin and irregular. Most men did not allow their wives to attend the classes. '*Aurat ka matlab hota hai chhupane wali cheez* [Women mean something to be kept in secret]. Best for a woman to study at home', was an oft-heard refrain. Some women broke the barrier, prevailing upon their husbands or father to allow them to study only on weekends. Soon though, most husbands realized that when women attended weekend classes, they ended up doing baby-sitting at home or idling away the hours they would like to spend with the family. Thus came into being two-hour lectures in the afternoons or early evenings exclusively for women. Importantly, the women would get a CD or a pen-drive of the lecture. They would play it at home to revise; the husbands, who had probably never been taught the meaning of the Quran, became interested. And soon joined the ranks.

Where qualified maulanas from places as distinguished as Darul Uloom Deoband or Nadwatul Ulama failed to get the common Indian Muslim to know the meaning of the Quran, a foreign woman succeeded. What's more, she spurred many of her ilk.

Indeed, it is her students today who take the classes in places as far removed as Lucknow and Jaipur, Bhopal and Delhi. In the Al-Hudaya centre in Delhi, while many men show interest to learn, most do not seem to mind that the course was devised by a woman in a community where even Maulana Mawdudi once expressed reservations about women being at the helm of affairs.

Every evening, as public school educated men, young and not so young, go back home after learning to read and understand five verses of the holy book, they are accosted by self-styled maulanas. Regularly, they are advised against attending the class as it could lead them 'astray', or at least to join the maulanas in their regular walks and meeting to invite the faithful to offer five daily prayers in a congregation in masjid. The students hear them out, move on. And come back the next day to learn the meaning of five more verses. Occasionally, they play Farhat Hashmi's CDs in their car on their way back home.

A woman has transcended many a limitation in the world of the believers.

CONVERSION AND RECONVERSION

In these surcharged days, there is so much discussion on conversion and reconversion, *ghar wapsi* (returning home) and *shuddhi* (purification). At one level, my mind goes back to Dayanand Saraswati; at another, to Dilip Singh Judeo, the BJP leader who much before the current batch of *sakshis*, *sadhvis* and *sadhus* had undertaken prolonged *ghar wapsi* exercise in Jashpur, Madhya Pradesh. His focus was on tribals whom he brought into the fold of Hinduism through a series of rituals that involved washing their feet. The media was not outraged; it merely reported the events as they took place. Of course, the sight of a political leader washing the feet of the poor made for a pretty picture. The tribals were considered easy targets though. Atal Bihari Vajpayee was the Prime Minister then and not many thought Judeo had his blessings in the whole exercise. This time the aspiration is higher; hence, Agra and Aligarh have been sought to be used as laboratories of Hindutva. There is talk of *ghar wapsi* once again, the underlying belief being that all Indians were born Hindu and people, down the centuries, converted due to inducement or coercion. This is exactly what Balraj Madhok did in the 1960s. As did Deendayal Upadhyay around the same time, and V.D. Savarkar much earlier. The RSS Sarsanghchalak Mohan Bhagwat while inviting the minorities to join the RSS, back in 2009, said, 'the Muslims of India were Hindus in the past. They have only changed their way of worship, and if they accept this fact there will be no clashes'. While the argument makes a mockery of human spirit of inquiry and exploration, it also reduces human beings to sheep, not reasoning thinking beings. Much earlier, Madhok (1969) said it in as many words. 'Christians and Muslims living in India are also Hindus', he wrote in his book, *Indian Nationalism*.

The talk set me thinking. Muslims too believe everybody is born one and the aim of life is to complete the journey from being a Muslim to a *momin*—one following Islam as a religion to one following it as a way of life. The Christians too believe that faith provides a way of life. And Christian missionaries have in the past often sought to better the lot of the dispossessed and the deprived by providing education, giving access to better opportunities in life, and promising an egalitarian society without the prejudice of caste. Once Vivekananda is reported to have said, 'Why amongst the poor of India so many are Mohammedans? It is nonsense to say that they were converted by the sword. It was to gain liberty from zamindars and priests'. In fact, over the years, the opponents of *ghar wapsi* programmes have wondered aloud about where the fresh converts would be placed in caste hierarchy in the Hindu society where one's station in life is determined by the caste in which one is born.

All these heated discussions led me to Deborah Baker's book all over again. This one too is about conversion, not the kind the media highlights with usually the poor and uneducated crossing from one faith to another without understanding either, but about an American woman who left her free society with all the attendant material benefits for a fathomless life in an alien country where nobody spoke her language, nobody dressed up like her. Yet, she felt like one of them.

The story that Baker recounts in *The Convert: A Tale of Exile and Extremism* (2011) is a well-known one of how Margaret Marcus, an American Jew, became Maryam Jameelah. Through the letters Margaret/Maryam exchanged with her parents and adoptive father, Sayyid Abul Ala Mawdudi, Baker talks of Margaret's early years with all the love of her family, her troubled youth, her sympathy for displaced Palestinians after the formation of Israel and her decision to leave the United States, and spend the rest of her life in Pakistan, initially at the home of Mawdudi.

The book opens on a most pertinent note to our times with Baker reproducing the letter Mawdudi wrote to Maryam—yes, he addresses her by her new name— wherein he cautions her about the vast changes in culture and the way of life in the two countries and religions.

> As you must know, our way of life and social conditions are vastly different from those in America. We lack many facilities and amenities that Americans take for granted. Therefore, the first months here will certainly prove fatigu- ing and taxing upon your nerves. Unless you have patience and are resolutely determined to mould your life according to ours ... you might find it extremely difficult to reconcile yourself to our ways. (Baker 2011)

He then goes on to offer his family's hospitality to her, and requests her to introduce him to her parents. The following despatch from Margaret's father bears out his concern for her welfare yet a willingness to let her sail out for her dreams, her contentment. Interestingly, as Baker highlights a little later, 'Self-taught, untraveled, and unlearned in any foreign language, Margaret Marcus had sacrificed the supposed freedoms and privileges of a Western lifestyle to live in upright exile in Pakistan', adding, 'the choice she lays out for her readers is stark and familiar: a life lived by the sacred laws laid out in the Holy Quran or one blackened by hell-bent secular materialism'.

Not unsurprisingly, Baker had not heard of either Mawdudi or Maryam when she went to the archives division of the New York Public Library where she stumbled upon the family portrait of the girl who was to revolutionize the way the West would interact with the Islamic world. The transformation of Margaret to Maryam was gradual, she noticed.

I noticed that as Margaret Marcus grew older, the photographs became less forgiving. Awkwardness radiated from her. Trussed in fancy dresses, she stood apart from her respectable-looking parents and lipsticked sister, gamely smiling and looking as if she wanted to disappear. By mid-twenties, she began wearing a scarf to cover her hair. Finally, a news photo taken soon after her arrival in Pakistan showed her in a burqa posed standing in front of a sunlit door, only her hands and feet visible.... It was a photograph of a woman, who, after a lifetime of hiding, now wanted to be seen. It was a photograph of someone who would only be herself beneath a pitch-dark burqa. Twenty-eight years into her life, Margaret Marcus had been transformed. Through this veil Maryam Jameelah saw the world and her place in it with absolute clarity. (Baker 2011)

Will Margaret's journey to being Maryam classify as *ghar wapsi*? Or will it fall into the category of conversion through inducement? Probably neither. It is simply the result of a human exploration of life beyond the immediate.

NOT BEING THE OTHER

NOOR ZAHEER'S HERESY ON HEARSAY

NOOR ZAHEER IS A COMPULSIVE FICTION WRITER. Her reputation, limited as it is, has been built around the success of *My God Is a Woman*. She should have stuck to fiction. Here, she steps into the domain of society, religion, clerics and scriptures and ends up tying herself in knots.

Cannot accuse her of hypocrisy though. Right from the title of the book, *Denied by Allah* (2015), which forced a Muslim cleric invited for the book release ceremony in New Delhi in April 2015 to refrain from lending a helping hand, to the contents, Noor goes around with the intention to provoke. She succeeds. In the author's note itself, Noor says,

> This book is not an attempt to reinterpret the Quran, find inner, deeper meanings, or to prove that the original text gives equal rights to the woman. This is an attempt to show the contradictions within Quran, the way they have been highlighted and interpreted to give an edge to patriarchy, the manner in which tribal customs have been made out to be the actual Islam and the woman has been relegated to the position of being a non-entity.

She subsequently proves herself to be a wonderful bundle of contradictions, a virtual non-entity as far as matters of faith and society go. The verses she quotes later in the book come back to disprove her avowed intention!

Truth to tell, Noor is consistent in her follies. She hides behind no fig leaf—oh, that word stemming from faith! In the author's note she writes,

> The Quran relegated women to a secondary position, right from where it describes the formation of the universe and the creation of Adam and Eve. It accuses Eve as the cause of the original sin and the reason for Adam being thrown out of paradise....

A simple reading of Surah al-Baqarah at the beginning of the Quran would have enlightened her. Agreed, it is the longest chapter of the Quran but even a cursory reading would have ensured that she won't mix up her Bible and the Quran. She takes a passage from the Bible and seeks to pass it on as from the Quran! Disrespectful and dishonest. By the way, the Quran talks of Adam and Eve through Verses 30–39 of Surah al-Baqarah in the second chapter. Through Verse 35, we are told 'And we said: "O Adam! You and your wife live in the Garden. And eat of the plentiful things in there (wherever and whenever) you want. But do not approach this tree, or you will run into harm and transgression"'. The next verse says,

> Then Satan did make them slip from the (Garden) and get them out of the state (of joy) which they had been. We said: Get down, you all (people) with hostility between yourselves, on the earth; (that) will be your living place and your means of livelihood—For a time.

Importantly, the word used is 'they', not 'she', unlike what Noor would have us believe.

But who is to suggest that to the author who has never read/understood the scripture in the original and concedes, 'I have relied in [her expression] the translations of the Quran by Syed Yusuf Ali and M Marmaduke Pickthall'. Sorry, but isn't it a little like trying to understand Rabindranath Tagore through the pen of Gulzar?

Her declared cause for this book has been the alleged maltreatment of Muslim women at the hands of insensitive husbands, often unlettered, temperamental and drunkards. Yet she goes on to launch a diatribe not against such men, or indeed the maulavis who facilitate the ignoble actions of such men, but against the scriptures. The anomalies do not end there. Almost throughout the book, she quotes verses from the Quran which project women in a very positive light, yet insists that the scripture is unfair to them. For instance, writing about Triple Talaq, she quotes from three different verses of the Quran, all correct in letter and spirit. She reproduces the opening verses of Surah Talaq wherein men are allowed to divorce women at fixed intervals and instructed to keep them during the duration from one pronouncement to another, thus giving reconciliation a chance. It tells, in other words, that *talaq* has to be pronounced at the passing of a menstrual cycle, an inability or unwillingness to do so for the second or third time nullifies the earlier pronouncement.

Amazingly, after such clear promulgation, it strikes Noor not that it is the society, not the book to blame. In doing so, she harms the cause of women. Talking of *halala*, like a commercial Hindi film director, she shows women as helpless beings, weak and vulnerable with no powers of thinking or reasoning. Indeed, in her case studies, they hardly come across as human beings. For *halala* cases, Noor heaps all the blame on scriptures whereby, according to her, the woman has to marry another man to marry her husband again after divorce. According to her, the scriptures punish her for the fault of the man who might have divorced her in a fit of rage. On the contrary, they strengthen her making sure she takes no hasty decision to go back to him. Noor answers no obvious questions. Why would a woman want to re-join an abusive husband? For kids, for social or economic society? Well, the man gets two chances to reform. If he commits the deed for the third time, does he really deserve her consideration? Isn't he responsible for the maintenance for a fixed period, even giving money in case a baby has to be suckled?

For *halala*, a woman has to agree to marry another man, she is no dumb doll. Without her consent, the marriage does not take place. She has to fix her *mehr*, loosely termed as dower. Pray, why would a woman fix her *mehr*, find another man and give her consent to marital tie-up only to ask him to break it after the nuptial night? There is no provision of temporary marriage in Islam. But so obsessed is Noor with *halala* that she imagines a *halala* centre in Belgium, quoting Sultan Shaheen! Now when was Shaheen an authority on jurisprudence? It would have done a world of good had she read or consulted noted legal expert Tahir Mahmood on the subject. Mahmood is of the opinion that the Islamic law provides an option for a woman who has been divorced thrice—irrevocable divorce—by her husband to marry him again if after she has married another man and failed to find comfort with him, leading to divorce. This second marriage is called *halala* or something that removes a legal obstruction. *Halala*, unlike what Noor suggests, was meant for exceptional instances, and it is simply outrageous to regard it as a device to humiliate women.

Of course, the scene at the ground-level could be quite removed where uneducated or poor women may not know their rights, maulanas may not have read the *tafsir* or commentary of the holy book, and men may be both ignorant and ill tempered. But does that explain the assault on the book closest to a believer's heart?

Noor could have done better had she read Surah An-Nur in the Quran. Talking of modesty, Verse 30 advises men to keep their gaze lower. Only the following verse advises women accordingly. Right through, men and women are addressed together; an act of sin or piety is the same for both genders. Quite removed from the UAE case, she quotes where three men were not charged with promiscuity/rape for outraging the modesty of a woman. Again the problem lay with the patriarchal set-up, not the laws; the Quran instructs lashing in such cases. She finds women relegated to an inferior position in the Quran yet the quoted verses prove otherwise. Does it strike her that in Islam no woman is expected to change her name following marriage and she can even walk out of it without giving any reason whatsoever? The prophet's wives retained their maiden names. And a woman enjoys three times the rights of the man over her children.

These nuances would not have struck her mind. In the season of Islam bashing, she adds to the din. Full of contradictions and anomalies, low on facts, *Denied by Allah* is a book that denies readers the right to complete picture. And Noor denies herself the right to read and assimilate, ponder and introspect.

OF PEACE AND WAR

Life, at times, does not allow you the luxury—or is it necessity?—of reading, soaking in a book before going on to the next. One day in the summer of 2016, I received a copy of Tarek Fatah's book *The Tragic Illusion of an Islamic State* (2011). Now Fatah, as most would recall, is a known baiter of the Muslim community, reserving special vitriol for Pakistan, but no less scathing of Saudi Arabia, Iran and imams across the world. A Pakistani born to an Indian-origin father in Karachi, Fatah has assiduously courted controversy, now taking aggressive shots at Islamic clerics for their stance on homosexuality, now urging Muslims in Canada not to send their kids to mosques for the fear of indoctrination, but also simultaneously denouncing Israel and its policies in Palestine, and Bush's handling of the Iraq issue post 9/11. In short, he defies easy definitions. Of late, with his 'quote-on-demand' ways, he has become quite a regular face on Indian television. His views though endear him not. A couple of days after I started reading Fatah's book, I received a couple of books penned by Maulana Wahiduddin Khan, as soft-spoken a man as one can come across. Also a proponent of enduring peace who never tires of reminding Muslims—and the world—that Islam stands for peace, he is an intellectual who believes that jihad begins not with fighting the enemy in battle but overcoming your own *nafs*. This does not necessarily mean that everybody within the community or the larger polity happily soaks in what he says. Indeed, he was at the receiving end of criticism from some quarters during the Babri Masjid controversy, and more recently during the scheduled visit of Salman Rushdie to the Jaipur Literature Festival. Appealing to the community

225

to engage with Rushdie, rather than demand a ban on him, his was a lonely voice. He did not shy away from debate, his preferred tool being a discussion, a dialogue. In fact, such is the distrust towards him in sections of the community that when some volunteers sought to distribute his penned copies of the meaning of the Quran at mosques across Delhi, members of various Muslim bodies objected sternly. At some places, the distribution had to be called off. At others, people were allowed to read the translation and draw their own inference on its basis. Now, when I read his books *The True Jihad* (2002) and *Islam and World Peace* (2009), I understand why. The much talked about maulana writes with the felicity which comes from a clear head and a heart that is unfettered and fearless. He abjures profundity for simplicity. Writing about jihad, he reminds the readers that it is a continuous process, not a one-off battle to glory. 'Islamic jihad is a positive and continuous process. It is at work in the entire life of a believer...It is essentially a peaceful struggle'.

> The literal meaning of jihad is 'effort' or 'struggle' the Quran speaks about a great jihad—engaging in jihad through the Quran.... Jihad, if understood correctly, is an entirely peaceful action. At the individual level, to engage in jihad is to refuse to deviate from God's path in the face of desires and inclinations of one's *nafs* and the baneful influence of the environment. At the collective level, jihad may be defined as a peaceful struggle.... Some people misunderstand jihad as the equivalent of war, or what is called *qital* in Arabic.... *Qital* is a very limited and temporary action ... jihad is a continuous process in Islam.

The maulana quotes from a hadith to buttress his argument.

To save one's faith from erosion requires a continuous jihad. Living in society one is repeatedly beset by negative feelings or emotions, such as anger, jealousy, revenge, pride, ingratitude and so on. In such a situation, one has to awaken one's consciousness and struggle against these negative tendencies. This is jihad.

Quoting Musnad Ahmad, he calls a *mujahid*—one who engages in jihad—as one who struggles with himself for the sake of Allah. Arguing that there is no space for an aggressive war in Islam, the maulana forcefully states that the Prophet himself always opted for reconciliation over confrontation or unprovoked aggression. 'Whenever the Prophet had to choose between the two courses, he would always opt for the easier course', he writes. Yet he is candid enough to say that in the contemporary world, things have not shaped up that way.

> A perusal of the Quran followed by a study of latter-day Muslim history will reveal a blatant contradiction between the two—that of principle and practice. Where recent developments ... bespeak the culture of war, the Quran, on the contrary, is imbued with the spirit of tolerance. Its culture is not that of war, but of mercy.

Similarly, in *Islam and World Peace*, he does not shy away from pointing out an oddity, the expression 'Islamic terrorism'. Stating that violence and Islam—which is derived from the word 'silm', the Arabic for salaam or peace—are contrary to each other, the Maulana writes, '"Islamic terrorism" is, in fact, as much of a misnomer as the phrase "pacific terrorism"'. These words have the potential to resonate with everybody, not just Muslims. And they help clear many a cobweb, and cure an impressionable mind of prejudice.

Now, on to Fatah. Well, Fatah's book is all about what he is known to have advocated for many years. A fair degree of anger, a much larger degree of opposition to Shariah, and an espousal of a secular State. Also a continuous proclivity to shy away from debate—he did not turn up for a debate with Imam Sheheryar Shaikh of the North American Muslim Foundation. His is the literary equivalent of the guerrilla warfare technique; fire a shot, then retreat to the confines of his chosen circles, only to come back for another passing shot. It makes for an interesting piece of celluloid, not a thought-provoking debate. Here, he reserves his ire for hadiths, as compiled after the life of Prophet Muhammad. Writes Fatah (2011), 'More than the Quran it is the hadith literature that incites radicals to fight in the name of Allah', going on to talk of Abdullah bin al-Mubarik, al-Bukhari and others. A little later though, Fatah asks a pertinent question: 'If the so-called lesser jihad is a defensive war, how do we Muslims explain the Muslim invasion of Egypt and Persia by the early caliphs?' He questions the Shariah too. 'The word "sharia" appears in the Quran only three times: one as a noun in chapter 45, and twice as a verb in chapters 5 and 48. The term sharia means "way" or "path to the water source"'. Further, quoting legal scholar L. Ali Khan, he adds, 'The Quran and Sunnah constitute the immutable Basic Code, which should be kept separate from ever-evolving interpretive law (*fiqh*)'. He admits that the Quran is one of the sources for Shariah, but insists it is only one of the many, including local Arab customs. Interestingly, rather intriguingly, Fatah dedicates his latest book to Dara Shukoh, Bacha Khan and Maulana Abul Kalam Azad—'Muslim giants of India who fought against the concept of an Islamic State'. Wonder how Azad would have reacted to it, considering his wonderful work on the meaning of the holy book contained not a line of rancour, and is widely regarded as a work of great expertise and rare insight.

So which of the two authors will find durable space on my book shelf or merit serious discussion? Well, both! Maulana Wahiduddin Khan to help bring about peace at a moment of unprovoked aggression. And Fatah? To understand how anger clouds judgement. So, it is time to stay calm and talk of peace. Just the way Khan Sahab has been advising us all.

A MOCKERY OF SATIRE

Many years ago I interviewed a Hindi author for a little over an hour in Mayapuri in southwest Delhi. We had had a pleasant discussion with the author talking animatedly of how English newspapers seem to have no space for Hindi authors, decline of poetry and the fading away of short stories. As he got up to shake hands with me at the end of the meeting, he had a look at my visiting card. Clearly surprised, he said, '*Aap Mohammedan hain?*' (Are you a Mohammedan?) 'No', I corrected him, 'I am a Muslim'. '*Ek hi baat hai. Lekin Lagte nahin ho ...*' (It's the same. But you don't look like one ...), his voice tapered off. 'No, it is not the same to be a Mohammedan and a Muslim', I protested, adding, 'Pray, do you expect every Muslim to go around with a beard and a skullcap? Or maybe, wear a sherwani and recite Urdu poetry?' Very much on the back-foot, the author only managed to add, '*Woh baat nahin. Hamare bhi Mohammedan mitr hai* (Not that, even I have Mohammedan friends), but you speak English ...'. He was clutching at straws. I took leave.

The incident stayed on the back-burner for many years, until the past came rushing back in the wake of the Charlie Hebdo cartoon and killings. This time the issues were wider and had greater ramifications. Murder can never be condoned. But on the one side, here was the question of absolute right to freedom of expression and on the other, yet again, was the stereotyping of the community. For a moment, forget the reprehensible work of Charlie and the crushing of the sentiments of people, across faiths and continents, men and women who enjoy freedom with responsibility. And no, the argument of absolute freedom of expression does not hold with the French. Wasn't cartoonist Maurice Sinet forced to resign for suggesting that Sarkozy's son converted to Judaism for pecuniary benefits? Smirk, smirk, countrymen! We have had our instances of conversion and reconversion—*ghar wapsi* and all that—the only difference being here poor, unlettered people agreed to adopt a new religion for a ration or BPL card! And Holocaust, keeping in mind the sentiments of millions, is a no-no as far as satire goes.

At another level, look at the wider expanse of the work of French cartoonists: the Muslims in their depiction, all sport a beard, have fierce eyes and often run in anger with not much else than murder on their mind. They dress up like the Arabs. Impervious to reason and civilized communication, they brook no dialogue, and are not much removed from being barbaric. Arabs, as a race, have reason to take offense. Muslims who hail from say, the United Kingdom, India or Indonesia, as a community have reason to take umbrage. We don't dress up like the Arabs; we don't talk or eat like them; and Arabs don't eat, drink or dress up like us. And even within a country, Muslims are not necessarily alike. A Muslim from Delhi is likely to have more things in common with a local Hindu than a Muslim from, say, Kerala or Tamil Nadu.

This convenient stereotyping of a community creates false impressions, and conveys, at best, a lopsided picture of a faith followed by approximately every fourth human being on earth. Yet, rather than showing the followers of the faith in poor light, the propagators of this stereotype expose themselves as hypocrites, as men and women who choose not to see or show the complete picture.

For instance, they never talked of the prophet as the first feminist; the man who worked against female infanticide centuries before it became fashionable for the rest of the world; the man who gave women the right to education, property and the freedom to choose their marital partner, the man who acknowledged the helping hand his wife Khadija gave after he was visibly disturbed following the first revelation.

In his last sermon, the prophet emphasized the equality of mankind, telling the faithful, 'No Arab has superiority over non-Arab, nor a white man over black'. Even on the subject of satire, the Quran expressly prohibits it through Surah Al-Hujurat, Verse 11: 'Believers, let not some men among you ridicule others ... nor should some women laugh at others—it maybe that the latter are better than the former—do not defame or be sarcastic to each other, or call each other by (offensive) nicknames'.

For the misguided cartoonists and the proponents of total free speech, faith is only to be lampooned, not appreciated. And, if it is the faith of the economically poor and the marginalized, it is better. What Charlie and company stand for is not freedom of expression but sick conformism. 'If you are like us, you share our values, you are liberal and modern', is their message. It took more than a year and an editorial in French, loosely and inaccurately translated into English to prove that all arguments of freedom of expression, equality and liberty were just a facade, a cloak to hide their blemishes. The editorial, calling for total criticism of Muslims and non-tolerance of their ways of living, gave examples of several Muslims, pious and law abiding, who, by their insistence on publicly practising their religion—women with a hijab, men with a beard—sell only halal food items. The editorial said,

> You dare not tell the woman her veil bothers you, that it is a throwback to medieval times, an anachronism in a modern democratic state; you dare not tell the baker that in a secular republic he should not impose his religious beliefs on what food is sold in his shop and force his religious beliefs (literally) down your throat.

The remarks about Muslims in general, all Muslims, betrayed Charlie Hebdo's lack of powers of tolerance, the very values it wants the Muslim world to follow. That these remarks came even as refugees, largely Syrian Muslims, struggled to eke out a living in Europe made the word even more callous.

Charlie Hebdo respects it not but I exercise my right to differ, to criticize, to expose the shallowness of their argument. They need to get rid of their blinkers, their prejudice. There are many ways of living.

Unlike them, I do not follow a one-size-fits-all policy. That is why I get a sense of revulsion when I think of the Hindi author even 20 years later. He had a blinkered vision. He had his stereotypes. The French cartoonists have theirs. If anything, our author was better—he had no malice.

PART 3

The Idea of India

EVERYBODY AN IMMIGRANT

IN THE LAND OF THE BUDDHA, divinity resides in every nook and cranny. Someday, if you hit the national highway, every few kilometres you will find a little temple under a peepal tree (sacred fig). Far from the madding crowd, a Hindu priest would be chanting his verses. So many motorists would slow down, bow gently and move on. The same thing happens when they cross a bridge over the Ganga, Yamuna or Godavari. India, and Indians, cannot have enough of gods and goddess. The mundane makes space for the divine. The profane is just an aberration.

Another day, hit the same national highway, and every few kilometres you will find a green dome and a green door surrounded by white-washed walls. It will be either a masjid or a madrasa. Cometh the prayer hour, and almost out of nowhere, men start trickling in. Meanwhile, many motorists, usually Hindu, slow down their vehicle as they pass by the masjid. Again, almost naturally, they bow their head in reverence for a second and drive on. Divine transcends the barrier of religion in the land, about which Prophet Muhammad (PBUH) himself is reputed to have said, 'I can sense cool winds coming from Hindustan'. No surprise then, Sir Muhammed Iqbal called a popular deity of India, Shri Ram, as Imam-e-Hind. Unfortunately, vast multitudes of Muslims, who swear by '*Saare jahan se achcha Hindustan hamara*' penned by Iqbal, have forgotten that the same man called Ram as the leader of the country. And the Hindus? Well, they have forgotten Iqbal altogether. Many have even stopped singing '*Saare jahan se achcha*'.

Yet the spirit of India proves stronger than many of its citizens. Sectarianism, caste conflicts, class discrepancies may not be all that rare, but there are Indians, of every faith, every religion, who are surmounting the odds and holding on to the idea of India, a land made rich by Bhakti saints and sufis. The modern-day sufis need not necessarily come in a divine cloak, but dressed up like any other Indian. It seems, no travesties, no challenges, no odds, ever shake them from their Indian-ness. For proof, just look closely at the Hajis who go for pilgrimage through All India Haj Committee. Comprising men and women from almost all states of the country, for many of them, Haj is their first air journey. Some cannot even fill the immigration form. A few do not even know the verses they are supposed to recite during Hajj, leave alone knowing the Arabic language used in Saudi Arabia. Yet, they go for pilgrimage, driven by faith, united by the Tricolour. As many semi-literate men and women undertake the journey along with some 30 lakh people from across the world, there is a real danger of being lost. And in the absence of an ability to converse in Arabic or English, it could as well be curtains for many of them. Yet, they not only survive but also come back for Hajj later in life. All thanks to the Tricolour band they sport on their wrists. Wherever they might be lost during Hajj means only momentary problem. Soon, the Hajj officials and local volunteers recognize them by the Indian flag and take them to the Indian camp. No wonder, it is not uncommon to hear unlettered women going for Hajj, saying, 'In prayer I will do what the woman ahead of me does. And if there is commotion due to lakhs of people, I know, the volunteers will recognize me with the Tricolour wrist band'.

Their faith is never shaken. Nor has it even been misplaced.

At another extreme is Salim Shaikh, the bus driver who saved the lives of Amarnath pilgrims in 2017, or the horse riders who take the pilgrims to the shrine. Every year, the quest for the divine is assisted by local Muslims in Kashmir. And when the shadow of violence looms large over the strife-torn state, it is not unusual to find the Grand Mufti of the state visiting the base camp of Hindu pilgrims and assure them that their pilgrimage would go on. Just as it was when the Grand Mufti of Varanasi visited the Sankat Mochan temple immediately after serial bomb blasts struck the city in 2006. With each step he climbed of the temple, the forces of terrorism were defeated. Aptly, as he tried to take the final few steps, the chief *purohit* (priest) of the temple, came down to lend a helping hand. Any forces looking to fish in muddied waters of communalism had to look elsewhere.

Just as they had to in Uttarakhand where the Sikh community came forward to lend gurdwara premises for Friday namaz in the monsoon of 2016. The mosque was full of stagnant waters, it was impossible to hold a prayer for a large congregation. The local Sikh community, and its religious leaders, rose as one to offer their premises for Islamic prayers.

India reasserts itself over and over again. Much like life which defeats death every day to see a new sunshine, India too shall rise from the ashes of hate violence, bigotry and exclusion. After all, inclusive India has always won against the forces of exclusion. The Hunas attacked and went. As did the Mongols. And the British conquered, exploited India's wealth before being forced out by the power of non-violence. But for all those who wanted to build their nest in India, the land offered its branches, its leaves, its flowers. Didn't we embrace the Delhi Sultans and the Mughals the way we embraced the Aryans earlier? Everybody here is an immigrant; it all depends on how far back you go in time. Pray what do immigrants do best? Lend each other a helping hand. And never waver in their commitment to their land, their nation. Immigrants always have a longing to belong. It is then no surprise that Iqbal called India the best of lands in the world. It is no shocker that Aamir, an innocent boy who lost more than a decade under imprisonment, would like nothing more than equality for all prisoners, irrespective of their religion. Or the Malegaon medical practitioner continues to repose faith in the judiciary of the country following his acquittal after a little under a decade in jail. Nor does it surprise when a survivor of the grim Hashimpura massacre uses '*Chak De*! India' as his ring tone. The sound of India is difficult to ignore.

INNOCENT ACQUITTED, BUT HOW?

'We were framed. It took almost 12 years and finally Supreme Court acquitted us of all charges. I am thankful to Supreme Court for giving my freedom back', said

Nisar-ud-Din Ahmad on being released after spending 23 years in prison.

Nisar's faith in the Supreme Court of the land was touching. It was no shallow homily of a politician. Here was a man who had spent the best years of his life inside jail on false charges. Yet saluting the highest court of the land for giving his freedom back. As luck would have it, Nisar is not the only one to have spent considerable time in jail before being acquitted. Nor is he the only Muslim to be so framed. In fact, there are scores of them. This reality came to light when *First People's Tribunal on Innocent Acquitted* released its report towards the end of 2016. The jury was headed by retired Chief Justice of Delhi High Court A.P. Shah and included senior journalists Neena Vyas, Vinod Sharma, filmmaker Saeed Mirza, and academic activists Nandini Sundar and Abdul Shaban. Pulling no punches, the jury which spoke to a number of men who did jail-time before being declared innocent, spoke out loud and clear about possible discrimination against Muslims at the initial stage of arrest itself. Every bomb blast is followed by the arrest of Muslim youth, even if the blast takes place in a mosque, they argued.

The report observed,

It is routine for police and investigating agencies to round up and arrest Muslim youth in the aftermath of any bomb explosion or attack. The most striking example of this is the manner in which investigation into the Malegaon blast 2006 was carried out. Members of the Muslim community were rounded up, trumped as SIMI activists and shown as key suspects despite the fact that at least one of them was already in police custody at that time, and another key accused was hundreds of kilometres away leading the Shab-e-Baraat prayers in Yavatmal on that very day. The testimonies lend credence to the charge that the investigating agencies are prejudiced and that they manipulate and fabricate evidence to make unnecessary arrests, only for the reason that the accused belong to a minority community.

The jury also pointed out the need to give adequate compensation to those pronounced guilty for the loss of livelihood opportunity, education, etc. Quoting the Supreme Court, it said, 'It is the duty of the state to apply the healing balm.... Alongside compensation that the state must offer in recognition of its liability and victim's rights, those guilty of falsely framing innocents in terror cases must suffer penal consequences'. The jurors also recommended that the 'dignity of those acquitted must be restored'. Importantly, they sought punishment for those guilty of fabricating evidence and subverting the law. 'Those who had been wrongly convicted should be entitled to compensation from the state. Those who are responsible for subverting the rule of law—police, prosecutors etc.,—must be held accountable'.

Tragically, all the victims of delayed justice the jury spoke to talked of custodial torture, constant violence. So rampant was the torture of the accused that the jury observed,

> In every single testimony, we heard sordid tales of torture, narco-analysis, manipulated evidence. This is not a case of 'some bad officers' but points to a widespread institutional crisis, where violence against suspects has become entrenched, where false arrests are condoned, where investigators guilty of framing innocents are not punished—but rather decorated and feted. One of the key

features of all testimonies was the systematic torture that the suspects were subjected to by the agencies. Torture is endemic to India's policing culture. In terror investigations, however, it seems to be the very cornerstone. Part of the reason may be the admissibility of confessions as evidence under TADA and POTA previously, and currently under MCOCA.

The jury emphasized that the dignity of those acquitted must be restored. Thus,

> It is imperative that the harms inflicted on them must be redressed within the framework of rights rather than charity. Those who had been wrongly convicted should be entitled to compensation from the state. The Government of India should grant compensation to the exonerees for the loss and harm caused to them and for violating their right to life and liberty and the torture under Article 21 of the Constitution of India. The amount should be calculated on case-to-case basis, weighing in both pecuniary and non-pecuniary factors such as the length of incarceration, loss of income and opportunities of education, possibilities of livelihood, skills, etc. Also, the amount spent on legal fees besides intangibles like the loss of family life, stigmatization and psychological and emotional harm caused to accused and his family. The said amount may be recovered from the officers responsible for the wrongful arrests and prosecution. (*First People's Tribunal on Innocent Acquitted*)

Yet many of those released after spending years in prison, retained their faith in our judicial system, the same system that, at times, took years to deliver justice. Whether Nisar or Mohammed Aamir or Salman Farsi, all the men released after detention thanked the courts. Their tales of horror notwithstanding. For instance, Nisar, along with his brother Zaheer, was arrested in 1994 in the Bombay Railway Blast case, coinciding with the anniversary of Babri Masjid's demolition. While Zaheer was released in 2008, Nisar was acquitted only in 2016, 23 years after being in jail. Both Nisar and Zaheer were convicted for the railway blast cases in 1996. The charges against them were under various sections of TADA, IPC, Explosive Substances Act, Arms Act and Railways Act for planting bombs in five trains.

> [Nisar's] case presents us with all that is wrong with the criminal justice system when it comes to dealing with terror cases. Arrested by Hyderabad police in January 1994 for carrying out multiple train bombings that had taken place across the country in December 1993, Nisar was kept in illegal detention for over a month. The only evidence police produced was the alleged confession— the provisions of Terrorist and Disruptive Activities Act (TADA) were later invoked to make these admissible. But the confessions themselves told an interesting tale.
>
> While arresting Nisar, the Hyderabad police had made out a confessional cum recovery memo. However, since the so-called confession was made before an inspector rank officer, it was not admissible as evidence even under TADA. Nisar's confessional statement was thereafter recorded before a senior police officer as required by Section 15 of TADA. Strikingly, the confession as recorded under Section 15 of TADA, and the inadmissible 'confession' were identical, word for word, comma for comma, full stop for full stop. By a strange chance, Nisar found both the documents in his charge sheet—someone had mistakenly annexed the confessional–recovery memo in his copy. If this wasn't enough, in May 1996, the designated TADA court in Hyderabad ordered discharge of the accused under the provisions of TADA, directed the trial to be conducted under ordinary IPC sections. The state

government of Andhra Pradesh appealed against the local court's rejection of TADA charges in the Supreme Court but received no reprieve. In fact, the Supreme Court was of the opinion that the exercise of power under Section 20A(2) of TADA Act by the then Commissioner of Police was in a very casual manner and even issued notice to the concerned Commissioner to show cause why adverse remarks against him be not made in the judgement. The state of Andhra Pradesh therefore withdrew their appeal in 2001.

But by now, Nisar and other accused, including his brother Zaheer, were undergoing trial in the TADA court of Ajmer, where again the confessional statement was the principal piece of evidence against him. Nisar produced certified copies of the confessional statement to demonstrate its likeness to the custodial confession as well as proof that the state of Andhra Pradesh had withdrawn their appeal against the TADA court's order to show how confession recorded under TADA should not be used as evidence against him. Yet, disregarding all this, the designated TADA court in Ajmer sentenced him to life imprisonment.

The Supreme Court in 2016—by which time Nisar had already spent 23 years in jail—observed that the document on the basis of which Nisar was convicted should not have been admissible as evidence.

But the question that Nisar, his brother and co-accused Zaheer ask is what of the 20 years lost in between, when the document was first rendered inadmissible by the Hyderabad TADA court and the SC's recognition of that inadmissibility.

In fact, when Nisar was released after long incarceration, he could not come to terms with his newfound freedom. As a report in *The Indian Express* quoted him, 'I felt a terrible heaviness in my legs. I froze. For a moment, I had forgotten I was free'. Incidentally, Nisar, along with three others, was booked for five blasts on board trains on the first anniversary of Babri Masjid demolition. By the time he was released, he had 'clocked 8,150 days of the prime of life inside the jail'.

Nisar was a second year student of Pharmacy when he was picked up by police on 15 January 1994 near his home in Gulbarga, Karnataka. He was on his way to college where a police vehicle was waiting for him. Shoved inside the vehicle, he was taken to Hyderabad. But, according to records, he was produced before a court only on 24 February 1994, nearly a month and a half after his initial arrest. That's when his family got to know about his whereabouts. That started a long journey towards justice, a journey that reached fruition in May 2016. Finally, India's judiciary upheld the traditions of justice. And Nisar was acquitted of all charges. His faith in the system redeemed.

ONCE FRAMED FOR TERRORISM, NOW A SYMBOL OF NATIONALISM

Late Justice Anand Narain Mulla of the Allahabad High Court famously observed, 'There is not a single lawless group in the whole of the country whose record of crime comes anywhere near the record of that single organised unit which is known as the Indian Police Force'. The quote of Justice Mulla would have rung in the ears of Mohammad Aamir Khan for 14 long years as he was accused of crimes he never committed. Kidnapped by the police, he was tortured, stripped, humiliated, made to sign blank sheets of paper, admitting to crimes he had not even heard of. His nails were pulled out; he was given the roller treatment. At times given water with detergent to drink, at others, water was flushed into his nostrils with a pipe at great pressure.

As Khan recalls in his book *Framed As A Terrorist* (2016) that he has co-authored with Nandita Haksar,

I went for namaz and then started walking towards Bahadurgarh Road in Sadar Bazar.... Suddenly I was pushed violently from the back and fell. Some people came out of the Gypsy and pulled me into the car. I was pushed down onto the floor of the car. My hands were quickly tied and I was blindfolded. Although I was very scared, I managed to ask why they were kidnapping me. I thought they were criminals.... After about half an hour, the vehicle stopped and I was taken down. After that I could feel I had been brought into a room. Here they removed my blindfold and untied my hands. I saw ten to twelve men standing facing me. They looked strong and muscular and dehumanized. No one said anything, except one who ordered me to take off my clothes. I was so embarrassed. They had no shame. They made me take off all my clothes and when they saw I had no underwear, one man remarked: '*Saale yeh underwear bhi nahi pahente*'. I assume by 'they' he was referring to Muslims. Then all of them started hitting me. I was slapped, kicked, elbowed, boxed and my hair pulled so hard that I thought my neck would break. All the while they abused me verbally. I had never heard such dirty and violent language. The abusive language was full of anti-Muslim innuendos.

That was in 1998 when Khan was picked up and framed in 18 bomb blast cases. It took him 14 years to prove his innocence. Now he is a free man. When he finally came out of jail, he stepped out into a drastically changed world—his father was dead and his mother paralyzed. He had no job and no security.

Yet, all this failed to shake Khan's faith in the nation. Rather than being embittered with the nerve-wrecking experience or holding the state responsible for the torture, he retains his faith in pluralist democracy. For somebody who has gone through a lot, Khan is a remarkably level-headed man. He retains no grudge towards those who put him in jail; rather, in jail, he discovered the real meaning of shared living. In Old Delhi where he used to live before he was put in jail, his social circle was all about Muslims in the neighbourhood. The Muslims had their ghettoes, the Hindus theirs. And Khan did not mingle much with those from other ghettoes. Yet today Khan recalls with a touch of emotion some of the prisoners in Tihar Jail who kept alive his faith in humanity. Some were Hindus, others Christians, Sikhs and Muslims. The way they helped each other and respected each other's customs and traditions kept Khan away from hatred.

In his book, Khan talks of a prisoner called Devinder, who used to give him dates and milk during Ramadan, and Deenu, who used to fast with Muslims in Ramadan.

In my long jail journey I had various bitter-sweet experiences. On the basis of such experiences I can say that in our country even today there is no dearth of humanists, secularists and positive thinkers. You might have noticed that outside the jail communal riots take place but inside the jail there are no riots based on faith. Inside not everybody is a sinner, there are good people, innocent people too. Based on mutual love and respect, prisoners often fast together. This Ganga-Jamuni culture is alive in many a sad soul. It is true that if I have understood humanity well then I have learnt it in jail.

Khan has penned similar things in the book,

> In the barracks, the prisoners showed great respect for each other's religions. During the first days in jail when I was in the Mundakhana, I came in touch with Hindus, Sikhs and Christians. In the first days in jail there were three prisoners with whom I shared food and had discussions. One was James, who was an accused in a dacoity case in south Delhi; Surendra who was from Agra, I don't remember in what case, but I remember that he could speak Japanese. Surendra was about nineteen years old and even the jail officers talked to him.... And then there was Manoj who helped the *nambardars*. Later I found James and Manoj had been told to keep an eye on me.... Surendra and Manoj was the first Hindus of my age group I got to know closely; while living in Sadar Bazar I had never had any occasion to make Hindu friends of my age.... Then there was a Muslim prisoner called Aarif. We, Muslim under trial prisoners, offered namaz together in one corner which we had reserved for ourselves. I noticed that whenever it was namaz time the Hindu prisoners would lower their voices and switch off the television. The Muslim and Christian prisoners would remain silent if the Hindus were praying or when the Sikhs did their ardas early in the morning.

Yet the officials continued to be blatantly communal in their approach. Khan faced many anti-Muslim remarks, both during interrogation and otherwise. And namaz in congregation was disallowed too.

> We were not allowed namaz by jamaat (congregation) inside Tihar jail. We were just told that it is due to security reasons. What was the fear particularly when Satsang/Vipasna/Yoga were allowed in congregations, which I consider a good thing. But they did not allow even Friday prayers though the Constitution gives equal rights to all.

That was a little dampener. Otherwise, Khan retained his faith in multihued, multilayered society. Following his acquittal and release from jail, although the state failed to step in, Khan was helped in rehabilitation by non-governmental organizations such as Anhad and civil rights activists.

> I am grateful to civil society and media for helping me live, stand on my feet. They fulfilled what was to a large extent, the State's responsibility. The recent order of the National Human Rights Commission gives me courage. When I met the President with Mr Prakash Karat, then also I said that we are Indian citizens and you are our guardian. We want to forget out past and begin life afresh. We need your help in this. I would like to add that for those who are acquitted by the courts after long imprisonment there should be a system in place so that they fulfil their responsibilities towards their family and the nation. The acquitted too are Indian citizens and they too have the right to life.

Indeed, Khan's persistence paid off when the National Human Rights Commission instructed Delhi Police to award him a compensation of ₹5 lakh. When Khan was finally given the compensation in April 2018, he said, 'Rupees five lakh can't buy my 14 years back, but it can help me provide a better education to my daughter who is just four-year-old', said Khan, adding, 'I am thankful to the judicial system, the NHRC and the Delhi Police for the compensation that I have received, but I demand a rehabilitation policy for people like me. Society should change its perception and treat us like any other normal person. Like me, there are many people who want to live a simple and respectful life'.

If on the one side, his story shows how the police, the doctors, the magistrates and the civil society are responsible for the systematic subversion of the criminal judicial process, on the other it tells us that at the ground level, the common Indian refuses to be communalized. Khan bears no grudge towards the media which labelled him a 'terrorist' without bothering to find out the truth, or towards the system which granted bail to alleged perpetrators of the Hashimpura massacre where 42 Muslims died but denied him bail for 14 years in fabricated case with two casualties.

One silver line that emerges from Khan's harrowing experience is his continued faith in the pluralist fabric of the country. His wedding card with one Mr Chawla's name as the guardian is a testimony to that. Today, Khan is part of a National Human Rights Commission project on jail reforms and prison rights and visits universities addressing students who show solidarity with him. 'Young people cry on hearing my story. They show solidarity. That is why I respect our secular democracy. For Indian Muslims, India is their country by choice—I am grateful to my ancestors for making that choice', he said in a media interaction. And therein lies hope for continued shared living.

A HUMANIST DESPITE BEING CALLED A TERRORIST

It is purely by chance that I came across a little booklet in Urdu that talked of the plight of the nine accused of Malegaon blasts. Printed on recycled paper, I picked it up at Barabanki in Uttar Pradesh during monsoon time in 2015. With the printing quality leaving a lot to be desired, I could not finish the book authored by one Fasihur Rehman. That there were copies in Hindi too did not help. But it did set me thinking about the innocent men who were jailed for a crime they did not commit. Finally, with a degree of luck and patience, I managed to get across to Dr Salman Farsi, a Unani doctor, accused of abetting in the crime and conspiracy of Malegaon serial blasts. The blasts that occurred soon after the Friday prayers near the Hamidiya Masjid on 8 September 2006, killed more than 30 and left more than 125 injured. The Anti-Terrorism Squad (ATS) arrested nine Muslim men, among them being Dr Farsi. After being picked up on 5 November 2006, he was to spend the next five years in Maharashtra jails before being granted bail in 2011. And then had to wait for another five years before being absolved.

In April 2016, a sessions court discharged Dr Farsi and all other accused Muslim men of all terror charges in the case. Sessions Judge V.V. Patil declared that the eight men be 'set at liberty'—the ninth accused, Shabbir Ahmed, had passed away. Criticizing the ATS for the arrests, Patil said,

> In my view, the basic foundation or the objective shown by ATS behind the blast is not acceptable to a man of ordinary prudence. I say so because there was 'Ganesh immersion' just prior to September 8, 2006.... Had accused no. 1 to 9 any objective that there should be riots at Malegaon, then they ought to have planted bombs at the time of Ganesh immersion which would have caused death of most Hindu people. It seems to me highly impossible that accused no. 1 to 9 who are from Muslim community would have decided to kill their own people to create disharmony between the two communities, that too on a holy day, i.e., Shab-e Barat. (Sessions Judge V.V. Patil's judgement, April 2016)

The order was greeted with relief and joy by the accused. Dr Farsi although remains a deeply hurt man on the one side and a true humanist on the other. One moment he is angry with ATS, next moment he is ready to sacrifice his New Year Eve to look after the ailing. You mention the ATS and Dr Farsi, who now works as an emergency medical officer for the Bharat Vikas Group in Nampur, 30 kilometres from Malegaon, gets all agitated. 'It is an anti-national body. They target one section of Indian citizens based on their faith. If they are against a section of Indians, they have to be called anti-national'.

He believes that the body deliberately launched a witch-hunt against the Muslims after the blasts though, as the subsequent judicial order also proved, it was against all logic and common sense. The ATS, believes Dr Farsi, is both communal and casteist. 'They picked up people on the basis of religion. Then they tried to play the caste card, passing snide remarks about Ansaris because they are weavers. It was humiliating'. Dr Farsi, like others, was subjected to third degree treatment. Five years after he was granted bail, he is still to forget the treatment and it pains him to go back in time. 'All I would say is there was torture. We were subjected to great torture, great brutality. I would not like to go into the details as the thought even today brings back the pain of those days. The ATS people are truly anti-national'.

Yet the same doctor retains a ray of hope for the nation, a little glimmer for the larger society. 'What I and other accused experienced at the hands of ATS was different from what I experienced in jail. Inside the jail, the things were very different. The fellow prisoners all thought that we were innocent and framed in wrong cases. There was never a communal slang'.

Dr Farsi is a hafiz, one who has memorized the Quran. He has been an imam as well. Inside the jail, he used to lead the Friday prayers and also the special prayers on Eid.

'Prisoners who were Muslims, used to participate. Those from other faiths used to gather to listen to my *khutba*'. Incidentally, *khutba* is a brief sermon given before the Friday prayers. 'At the time of namaz, all used to gather. Maharashtra jails have international prisoners too. They would come over as well to listen to me when I would read from the Quran. Many accepted Islam as their way of life on my hand'.

The curiosity to know about other faiths extended beyond the prisoners to the jail staff too. 'At times inspectors and constables used to listen to my recitation of the Quran. Nobody passed snide remarks. Everybody listened respectfully'.

In the jail, there was no communal feeling. 'People used to share sweets on each other's festivals. And they did not doubt my integrity. They genuinely believed I and other accused in the Malegaon serial blast cases were innocent'.

This—as he does not tire of reiterating—was in stark contrast to the communal and casteist filth that was thrown at him by the ATS. Little wonder, he considers the body responsible for freeing Brahmin terrorists while arresting innocent Muslim men. Since he had to attend to a patient in an emergency, he asked for a little break in conversation by saying

People were arrested in Malegaon blasts case through anti-national elements with anti-national mindset. Now such elements have entered the NIA—National Investigation Agency—which has led to the support for the likes of Sadhvi Pragya and others. My point is proved by former public prosecutor Rohini Salian who has said that she was asked to go soft on the Hindu accused by an NIA officer. The Government needs to step in and take action. (Author's interview with Dr Salman Farsi)

Back after administering first aid to the patient, he reveals that although he retains his faith in the shared value system of the society, life, consequent to the bail has not been easy. His attempts to resume his medical practice in Malegaon did not bear fruit—he had been arrested in 2006 from his clinic in Govandi, Mumbai, and often the thoughts would cloud his mind. He grazed sheep and goats for a year too. 'I am a hafiz. So I joined a masjid as an imam. But the income would be too little. So I started herding sheep and goats from morning to evening'. Incidentally, he claims to be a qualified goat milk therapist. All along, there has been precious little support from the government or the civil rights groups for rehabilitation. 'No organization has come forward to support me or other accused who have now been discharged. I am happy with my job as it gives me a chance to work for humanity. But for six days a week I am away from my family'.

His story needs to be told, and read, hopefully in a better way than managed by Fasihur Rehman.

HASHIMPURA: *CHAK DE!* INDIA

A group of Uttar Pradesh's armed reserve police force selected forty two youngsters, in full public view, from among a crowd of more than 500 people, loaded them into an official police truck, took them near the water canal, killed them one by one, threw them into the water, hopped on to the truck, reached their camp and went to sleep. Twenty-eight years later, the court acquitted them. Yes, it all happened, but the investigators did not have enough meat in their material to make the killers sleep in jails.

These are Vibhuti Narain Rai's (2016) words about the brutal Hashimpura massacre, one that was probably part of a conspiracy to instil a sense of fear among the Muslims. After all, as often observed, communal riots in India are often between the Muslims and police and not versus the Hindus. Hashimpura, along with Maliana, was to Congress rule what Gujarat 2002 was to the BJP government in the state.

Rai knows what he is talking about; he was posted as a senior superintendent of police and inspector general of police in many communally sensitive areas of Uttar Pradesh, including Ghaziabad district, where the Hashimpura massacre took place. It was the bloodiest instance of custodial killings in independent India. As Rai says in his book *Hashimpura: 22 May* (2016), 'Hashimpura remains a disgraceful instance of the merciless and barbaric use of brute state force and a spineless, politically expedient government lying prostrate before its own men—the killers'. On the fateful day, young Muslim men were packed in a truck, URU 1493, driven to a canal and shot dead one by one by 19 Provincial Armed Constabulary (PAC) men.

The acquittal did not surprise anybody who had watched the proceedings unfold. For instance, well-known news photographer, Praveen Jain, who had taken pictures of the most barbaric actions of the PAC men, was never called to give his account until he himself stepped forward. This despite the fact that his photographs were submitted in the court with the charge sheet and his name was included as one of the witnesses. Surprisingly, no one on behalf of the prosecution or the victims' advocates contacted him for evidence. When he came to know that the case was going on in Delhi's Tis Hazari court, he himself approached the prosecution advocate and offered to tender his evidence. This shows how the case was handled on behalf of the prosecution/victims. His statement in the court proved to be formidable evidence to enable the judge to come to the conclusion, 'It is painful to observe that several innocent persons have been traumatized and their lives have been taken by the State agency....'

Not much changed between 1987 and 2015 when the judgement was finally delivered, except that Platoon Commander Surendra Pal Singh, said to be the man behind the carnage, died. As did two others. The remaining 16 men were all acquitted. However,

> The relation between the India state and the minorities is almost the same now as it was then in 1987 or even earlier, in the 1950s and the 1960s. The same absence of trust, the same hatred, the same prejudices, the same notions, and the same the requirement and attempt to prove their 'Indian-ness'. Nothing has changed. It is as if the more things change, the more they remain the same. Or perhaps, worsen. (Rai 2016)

Most men picked up by the PAC killers in uniform were shot dead. Just a few of them survived. Just about. In a way, their case was worse. They survived the bullets of PAC personnel but their hopes of justice were defeated with the acquittal of the accused after proceedings had dragged on for 28 years.

Among them, surprisingly, was Zulfiqar Nisar, a man who had as little reason to cheer India as any. Or so one thought. Yet when Rai called up Zulfiqar who now sports a beard and wears a traditional skullcap associated with devout Muslims, '*Chak De*! India' was indeed his ringtone—the PAC personnel's gory crime failing to shake his love for the country. Zulfiqar was no ordinary man. He was a rare survivor (and witness) of the Hashimpura massacre, a man slaughter that earned the PAC such disrepute that post 22 May 1987, whenever the PAC was deputed to a town that had just witnessed a communal flare-up, the minorities braced for the worst, the wounds of 1987 fresh in everybody's minds. Zulfiqar, along with the likes of Babuuddin and Qamaruddin was a witness to the gory killings of able-bodied, innocent young men who, hours before being shot dead and thrown into the canal in Ghaziabad by the PAC men, had been rounded up in their village by the outfit. The old men and children were segregated in one section, robust young men in the other. The old men were let off with a warning and a volley of expletives; the younger men were not so lucky.

Zulfiqar's story says something not just about his love for the nation but is actually a comment on our society as well. Sample these words of Zulfiqar:

> It was around 6.00 in the evening on May 22, 1987, when I went to the terrace of our house to offer namaz, when some policemen came in. They brought me, my father and my two uncles outside our lane on the road where some 400 to 500 people were squatting. We were made to sit with them.... The PAC men divided the people into two groups. On the one hand were youngsters and on the other were old men and children. They left out the old people and kids, and whisked away many others, including my father and two uncles, in PAC trucks. The remaining forty-five physically strong people, including me, were ordered to board the last waiting truck.... The PAC men surrounded us in the truck in such a way that our view of the outside was blocked. After about an hour and a half, the truck turned towards a road running parallel to Ganga Canal in Muradnagar and came to a halt after about a one and half kilometres. (Rai 2016)

It is there that the young men were asked to alight. First Yasin. Zulfiqar saw him fall and then two people lifted Yasin by his hands and legs, and flung him into the canal. Other occupants would meet the same fate. And Zulfiqar too. Well, almost.

> A bullet ripped through him, near his chest and ejected from the back. He fell and, realizing that the only way to survive would be to pretend that he was dead, he remained still on the ground. Zulfiqar was picked up and flung into the canal. As fate would have it, he did not land in the middle of the canal, where the water current was strong, but near the thick bushy growth where the flow was slow. He floated for some time and then clung to the thick bushes. (Rai 2016)

A little later, after the PAC men had driven away, he felt somebody touching him. 'He stiffened, terrified. The man touching him was his neighbour Arif who, too, had miraculously escaped death'. Shortly, Arif and he found Qamaruddin in worse state. Soon, Arif disappeared, never to be seen again. Of course, fellow survivor Qamaruddin prevailed upon Zulfiqar to leave him in the dead of night and escape to save his life. It is the heroic stuff seen in movies, but here Qamaruddin and Zulfiqar lived through this in real life. It makes for a nerve-jangling experience how a man in acute distress attempts to help another similarly placed, and how a man staring at death in the face wants to save his compatriot's life. Zulfiqar who somehow escaped with his life was turned down by senior Congress leader Mohsina Kidwai, MP, Meerut when he first sought help. Instead, he got a helping hand from Syed Shahabuddin, then very much the voice of the active Muslim Indian or Indian Muslim, as he used to debate then.

Yet when the case reached its conclusion in 2015, there was shock in store for Zulfiqar and all others involved with the proceedings, including Rai. In Rai's words,

> It was 21 March 2015. My mind was too tense to let me fall asleep. Twenty-eight years after the massacre the verdict on Hashimpura was finally expected. I was some 800 kilometres away from the Tis Hazari court in my village Jokehara, in the Azamgarh district, but my heart and mind were in the court.... I called up Zulfiqar Nasir who assured me that he would inform me the minute the judgement was out. At around 3.00 p.m. Zulfiqar gave me the shocking news—all the accused were acquitted. I was left speechless. What a tragic end to our gruelling efforts spread over twenty-eight years! (Rai 2016)

The judgement was merely disappointing, not shocking. The CID, which was given the task of investigating the Link Road and Muradnagar massacres by the Chief Minister, Veer Bahadur Singh, was engaged in a virtual mission to save the culprits. The CID succeeded in its politics of obfuscation and deflection. Indeed, additional sessions judge, Sanjay Jindal, put it aptly,

> The defects in the investigations are of such a nature which go to the very root of the prosecution case and if ignored the same can cause a serious prejudice to the accused persons, and such ignorance may result in the miscarriage of justice.... It is very painful to observe that several innocent persons have been traumatized, and their lives have been taken by the State agency, but the investigating agency as well as the prosecution have failed to bring on record the reliable material to establish the identity of culprits. (Rai 2016)

Hashimpura and Maliana shall remain more than unfortunate footnotes in secular India's annals. An officer such as V.N. Rai, recipient of the President's Police Medal for Distinguished Services, through a book such as *Hashimpura:22 May* ensures that the faith of the minorities in the state is merely shaken, not crushed. Amid all the gloom, there is hope though. Remember Zulfiqar's ringtone? *Chak De*! India. Indeed. Meanwhile, he still waits for justice.

SIR MOHAMMED IQBAL

Day in and day out, I came second in a literary soiree with my *shareek-e-hayat* (life partner). It seemed destined to last a lifetime. Then one day, just that one day, I pulled off a Zimbabwe on her Australia. As she sat all by herself at home, her eyes were moist. She apparently had one battle too many in her office and seemed ready to throw in the towel after all her work had failed to get the desired recognition. I urged her not to give up the fight. Fight one more round. In vain. Then in a moment of divine intervention, I quoted Allama Mohammad Iqbal, '*Khudi ko kar buland itna ke har taqdeer se pehle Khuda bande se khud pooche bata teri raza kya hai?*' (Develop the self so that before every decree God will ascertain from you: What is your wish?).

Her sorrow disappeared in a minute. Iqbal, more than 60 years after his death, had helped me cheer up my spouse. I could finally quote a couplet she could not better!

On another occasion, Iqbal came to my rescue. Back in June 2001, some right-wing fringe elements stood exultant at a central Delhi theatre after watching the first day first show of Anil Sharma's *Gadar*—as jingoistic a film as Hindi cinema has ever dished out. Cries of '*Jai mata di*' rent the air after the screening. The security personnel's pleas to maintain decorum were ignored and one of the men blurted out, '*Jai mata di*', adding, '*Ajee saare jahan se achcha Hindustan hamara ... maaro ... Pakistaniyon ko*' (O, India is better than any country in the world ... Let's hit them ... These Pakistanis).

Stunned, I mustered up all my courage and shouted back, 'Do you know who has written "*Saare jahan se achcha*"?' There was stunned silence. 'It was Mohammad Iqbal', I said in a tone considerably mellower. The crowd dispersed with some mumbling, '*Jo bhi ho, "Saare jahan se achcha Hindustan hamara" likha to ek Hindustani ne hi hai*' (Whatever, "Saare Jahan Se Achcha Hindustan Hamara" was written by an Indian). A little under a hundred years after the composition of 1904, Iqbal had yet again helped calm frayed nerves.

On such experiences is built my treasure of Iqbal moments. The trove just got richer when I got a copy of the absolutely fascinating biography *Iqbal: The Life of a Poet, Philosopher and Politician* by Zafar Anjum (2014). It was time to read anew about the man to whom we as a nation have done little justice. '*Saare jahan se achcha*' has all but been forgotten by a generation that settles scores on patriotism by screaming '*Bolo! Bharat Mata ki jai*'. The ode to the nation and its eternal beauty is a silent loser in this display of lungpower. It takes but the son of Akhlaq, the man who was murdered in Dadri, to bring alive feelings of patriotism by singing '*Saare jahan se achcha*' on television. That he happened to be working with Indian Air Force only added to the poignant moment.

A little departure from the past is understandable, probably inevitable. After all, we are living in an age when Urdu has come to symbolize a religion, a community, a culture. Predictably, '*Saare jahan se achcha*' is not on every school-goer's lips today. Also, in a cruel twist of fate, Iqbal was made the national poet of Pakistan while we Indians got busy singing hosannas to Rabindranath Tagore, and today Iqbal stands banished from public consciousness. For some, he belongs to Pakistan, as our neighbours consider him the spiritual father of their nation. Interestingly, Iqbal had passed away almost a decade before Pakistan came into being. For others, his best work came in Persian, a language no longer heard that often in the subcontinent. Never mind that he did not ever go to Iran yet got maximum following in that country. In fact, he started penning Persian ghazals following a chance meeting in England where a discussion prompted him to pen ghazals in the language to find more takers beyond the subcontinent. Then there are those who lay stock by his poetry that not only draws its inspiration from the glorious Quran but also gives an explanation for many of the verses. His 'Shikwa' and 'Jawab-e-Shikwa' have become cornerstones of discussion on the world of believers; when the former was considered too arrogant in tone, he penned the latter.

In Pakistan, for long years, Dr Israr Ahmed, founder of Tanzeem, and a noted tele-preacher quoted Iqbal in his talks. He, in fact, based his definition of materialism as a grave sin of modern times largely on Iqbal's concept. Iqbal, it may be recalled, considered the West too devoted to material pursuits, too keen to fulfil body requirements, to care for the heart. Iqbal's idea of *khudi*, or self, inspired millions. Akin to German philosopher Nietzsche, he rejected the idea of weakness and urged man to overcome all odds with his willpower. For him, it was a mantra of action for any individual or nation to succeed. He believed in constant struggle.

Yet, in many ways, Iqbal has become a prisoner of interpretation. A man who composed a long poem 'Aftaab' (The Sun), which is a translation of the Gayatri Mantra, is today seen only with a certain slant. Forgotten too is his 'Naya Shivala' (The New Temple) where, as Anjum says, Iqbal asks 'the Muslim nation to unite with Indian Hindus. It is in this poem that he says, "*Khak-e-watan ka mujh ko har zarra devta hai*" (Each dust particle of my motherland is God to me)'. Indeed, Iqbal was a genius without a parallel, a diehard nationalist who, over time, transformed into an internationalist, a man once won over by the West who went on to be at the head of Eastern revivalism. Yet for a young man or woman growing up in this millennium, Iqbal remains a mystery with most having nothing more than a passing acquaintance with his works. For entirely non-literary reasons, he has been denied a place in the pantheon of modern Indian giants. A generation that considers '*Bharat Mata ki jai*' as the only slogan apt for expression of nationalism is being tacitly groomed to forget Iqbal. Not many schools begin their morning assembly with '*Saare jahan se achcha*' anymore; it is such a stark contrast to what happened when Iqbal returned from Europe in July 1908. Having landed in Bombay, he took a train to Delhi. Along the way, at various stations, students greeted him by singing '*Saare jahan se achcha*'. Interestingly, around the same time, he recited his famous 'Shikwa' to the public for the first time. Talking of the condition of Muslims across the world, he complained to Allah (quoted from Zafar 2014),

We who removed from this world's book the leaves
which were with falsehood stained,

We who from a tyrant's ignorance, the imprisoned
human race unchained,
We who with myriad *sajdas* filled Your Holy Kaaba's
hallowed shrine
Whose bosoms reverently held Your great and glorious
Book Divine—
If our meed still the obloquy that we have shirked the
faithful's part,
How then cans't You make claim to the kindly faith-
compelling heart?

Yet his words angered the clerics who questioned his lament to God! Of course, they were all silenced a few years later with 'Jawab-e-Shikwa'.

Yes, Iqbal was a product of many cultures, a man who refused to fall into stereotypes. Europe infused Iqbal's life with a singular mission—to revive the dynamism of Islam to save humanity from the ills of materialism. A transformed Iqbal stopped considering himself a poet; to his mind, he became a messenger who used poetry to awaken humanity, especially Muslims, to its ills, as Anjum says.

On his philosophy, his internationalism, his relation-ship with God, passionate debates take place across the world. What is often forgotten is his address on New Year's day in 1938 on All India Radio, Lahore.

Only one unity is dependable, and that unity is the broth-erhood of man, which is above race, nationality, colour, or language.... So long as men do not demonstrate by their actions that they believe that the whole world is the family of God ... the beautiful ideals of liberty, equality, and fraternity will never materialise.

History and its endless debates. Many summers ago when I was a student of history, our teachers used to encourage us to read Romila Thapar. Her books *A History of India* and *Asoka and the Decline of the Mauryas* were insightful as well as light on the mind, carrying not a trace of academic jargon which makes much of our history writings unreadable. Of course, we read with interest D.N. Jha too, in particular, his take on the issue of cows in the Vedic Age. Only some of us who looked for quick fix solutions went anywhere near L. Mukherjee's *Ancient India*. Later, it turned out that Mukherjee was the author almost all civil services aspirants read for their instant dose of ancient Indian history. To each his own.

I loved my Romila Thapar books. Putting bookmarks, underlining passages, making asterisk mark in the contents section, I did it all. The other day, I revisited the book. Its pages unavoidably yellow, it still does not quite smell of old books simply because it is never too far from the sight or hands. This time, I felt the need to re-read her after reading Vamsee Juluri's latest, *Rearming Hinduism* (2014).

With a book that demands, and deserves, attention and encourages debate, Juluri seeks to demolish the theory that Hindus, like the Muslims and Christians later under different guises, invaded India. Scoffing at Wendy Doniger's story of how 50 million years ago a piece of land broke off from Africa and voyaged across primal oceans to smash violently into what is now Asia, and became India, Juluri argues with a lot of passion why the Aryan invasion theory does not hold. Questioning the historians who hold that Hinduism came to India with the Vedic civilization, he writes, 'The arguments today about Hinduism's origins largely revolve around geography. The dominant, academically sanctioned history maintains that Hinduism began with the composition of the Vedas by a gang of violent horsemen who swept down from Central Asia into the Punjab'. He then goes on to favour the view of the other school which believes that Hinduism was already in place in the subcontinent by the time of the Indus Valley Civilization. Juluri argues that the Aryan invasion story is part of a Eurocentric view of history wherein European historians believed that Hindus were 'once of their own kind, now grown dark and dull in the sun'. He then questions the 'Hindus as conquerors' theory, arguing that the myth of the Vedic violence was just that.

Considering Juluri treads too close to the view held by right wingers, I decided to go back to Thapar's work for a more rounded perspective. And this is what she writes in *A History of India* (1990): 'By 1700 BC, the Harappa culture had declined and the migration of the Indo-Aryans from Iran in about 1500 BC introduced new features into the cultural background of northwestern India'. Without using words such as 'attack' or 'invasion', she hints at the foreign origin of the Aryans. Initially, she focuses on the similarities in the Indo-European languages, pointing out the surprise of some Europeans on finding out that Sanskrit was related in structure and possibly in sound to Greek and Latin. Later, she writes, 'The Aryans came as semi-nomadic pastoralists living chiefly on the produce of cattle, and for some time cattle-rearing remained their main occupation'. She also points out that the Aryans regarded the elephant with curiosity, calling it a beast with a hand—the elephant was not known to people in Central Asia then but was very much a part of our geography. Mukherjee, on the other hand, simply calls the coming of the Aryans as 'the Indo-Aryan conquest of Northern India', implying that the Aryans originated elsewhere. 'After crossing the mountain passes, the Aryans first settled in the valley of the Kabul river and the Punjab', Mukherjee writes of the initial Aryan settlements.

On similar lines to Thapar's Sanskrit syntax ran Max Mueller's view that the ancestors of the Indians, Greeks, Persians, Romans and Germans must have lived together at some stage. This was revealed by a study of the languages of these peoples. For instance, roots words such as *pitri* and *matri* in Sanskrit for father and mother respectively were the same as *pidar* and *madar* in Persian, *father* and *mother* in English and *patar* and *matar* in Latin.

Mueller mainly held that the main stream of the Aryans flowed towards the North West. Accordingly, it is believed that 'the original home of the Aryans must have been nearest to the lands occupied by the Indians and the Iranians, and that probably was Central Asia'. Much later, Bal Gangadhar Tilak held the opinion that the original home of the Aryans was the Arctic region, a view he expressed in the book *The Arctic Home of Aryans*. He argued that the Vedas referred to days and nights lasting up to six months, a reality of the Arctic region. Interestingly, Hindu reformer Dayanand Saraswati was of the belief that the original home of the Aryans was Tibet, a view he expounded in *Satyarth Prakash*.

But then there are others who propound the theory that the Aryans' original home was India and they must have migrated from here, a club whose membership now Juluri can claim. They argue that the Vedas were composed in India and the social structure of the civilization can be traced to Vedic institutions. As Juluri goes about delineating his theory, he also opens a little window to Hindu nationalism, as distinct from Hindutva. Writes Juluri (2014),

> Liberal Hindus, normal Hindus, when they are not being angry about being talked at and talked down to by self-proclaimed liberal secularists, would probably be the first to agree that the invasion of India by Turks and Mongols centuries ago does not justify hatred towards Muslims today. If that was the point that had to be made, the alternative historians and secularists could have made it easily, elegantly, and effectively. But they didn't. They presume that whatever Hindus are trying to discover about their own history after centuries of distortion and confusion, is part of a Hindu nationalist conspiracy. Rather than simply agree with reality and say, yes, Islam came to India from elsewhere, but it is Indian now and let's respect that instead of dreaming about expelling Muslims to Pakistan. That is all that really needed to be done about Hindu nationalism. It was as argument in the present, about the future.

As for the past, Juluri is angry. And clearly on a different page.

> We, Hindu, a billion of us, nearly one-fifth of humanity today, are supposedly the children of a group of violent horsemen from Europe and Central Asia who invaded India. Our Hinduism, one of the oldest unbroken ever-adapting spiritual and cultural traditions of celebrating non-violence, animal life, and religious diversity and pluralism in the world, is supposedly rooted in a set of holy texts that describe killings and mutilating.

He reserves his ire for Doniger, 'The Hindus-as-conquerors trope does not end with comparisons to genocide. For good measure, Doniger also informs us that the Vedic "cowboys" denigrated the natives of India as "barbarians" not unlike the American cowboys who denigrated the native people of North America'.

It was a view vehemently contested by those who reason that the Aryans came from Central Asia. They point out that the early Aryans were familiar with oak, pine and birch trees which did not grow in the plains of India. And they were not acquainted with the elephant, lion and tiger.

So, thanks to Juluri and all the predecessors, the debate rages on. As for me, I stay in Thapar's quarter. If the Aryans came from Central Asia and composed the Vedic hymns, the Muslims came via Kerala and Sindh, and the Christians via Bengal, then who is an immigrant? All are immigrants. All that matters is how far back do you go in time. And whose home is it? Well, everybody who regards it a home.

REALITY OF CONVERSIONS

India woke up to the reality of conversion in the summer of 2016. For long considered a phenomenon more likely to be found in the hinterland, the conversion of some 100-odd Dalits from Bhagana village near Hisar, Haryana, surprised many. The families embraced Islam in New Delhi and offered prayers at Jantar Mantar, a few metres removed from Parliament House, reviving the age-old debate on conversion.

The Dalits did not convert as much out of regard for the egalitarian principles of Islam as an attempt to avoid exploitation in the Hindu caste hierarchy. Interestingly, some local dailies splashed a photograph of the new converts standing shoulder to shoulder to offer prayers. It was a symbolic representation of their fight for equality.

The newly converted Dalits claimed that the local Jats, the dominant caste in the village, staked claim to a playground that the Dalit families used. As the Dalits did not cede the ground, unlike what would have happened a few decades ago, it was followed by their women's harassment and molestation, much like what has been projected by many Hindi films in the days of black-and-white cinema. The village's khap panchayat supported the Jats and announced a socio-economic boycott of the Dalit community. After some girls were assaulted in the village, the Dalit families moved to the Capital and changed their faith. The conversion was a weapon of protest, not so much as a tool for social equality. Importantly, they needed to leave the village to even change their faith publicly.

Interestingly, similar sentiments were echoed by Chandra Bhan Prasad, noted Dalit voice and author of *Dalit Phobia: Why Do They Hate Us?* (2006), who said, 'Dalits haven't embraced Islam in search of an alternate system of faith, but more as a social rebellion'.

Yet, in a land where terms such as Dalit Christian and Dalit Sikh, anomalies by themselves, are used without a sense of irony, won't the conversion just add a new term, Dalit Muslims? As for those Dalits who did not convert, they stay on as 'Hindu Dalits' and remain part of the hierarchical structure of Hinduism. While they suffer exclusion in the age-old caste order, they remain handy vote banks in the growing politics of Hindutva. For long periods they suffer in silence, but are offered an opportunity to cash in on their caste status at the time of elections—panchayat, Vidhan Sabha or Lok Sabha. But it is a long haul, requiring abundant patience and grit, something not everybody is endowed with. For them, conversion is a more viable option.

Does conversion then necessarily guarantee a life of equality? Far from it. In our country, a person can leave his religion, adopt another faith, but his caste follows him. Caste is a reality which transcends the seemingly egalitarian tenets of Islam, Christianity and Sikhism too. Writing about Islam, illustrious sociologist M.N. Srinivas (1980) had observed in his much acclaimed book, *India: Social Structure*,

> Islam proclaims the idea of equality of all those who profess the faith, but in India it has been characterized by caste. Muslim caste differs in some respects from the Hindu caste system; there are no ethico-religious ideas justifying the hierarchy or regulating the inter-caste relations through ideas of purity and pollution; there are no *varna* categories. What we have is a hierarchy formed by several *jatis*.... Muslims who have a tradition of foreign ancestry are called Shurafa or Ashraf and are considered to be the highest. After them come converts from high-caste Hindus, such as Rajputs. Next come occupational castes such as the weaver (Julaha), barber (Nai) and oilman (Teli). Last come the sweepers.

Under the circumstances, what exactly do newcomers to another faith, Islam as in this case, stand to gain? Not much. The chances of any detailed study of the new faith leading to a change of heart are negligible. And the gains, if any, are likely to be not much more than brownie points in local social equations with the dominant caste. It all stems from tension between different castes within the fold of Hinduism rather than a ready and willing espousal of a non-casteist, non-hierarchical faith such as Islam or

Christianity. So long as Dalits don't defy the twin principles of caste—occupation and blood purity—mere change of faith does not free them from the caste order.

In recent times, as indeed in the Hisar incident, the marginalized caste's attempt to overcome oppression has taken the form of religious conversion. The act of religious conversion needs to be unpacked not entirely in terms of what is on offer from the other system of religion. There is also an aspect of reconfiguring self-identity for greater self-assertion. Recourse to a different religion cannot be and should not be interpreted as a mere acceptance of a different belief system. Rather, it's also to be seen as a community's struggle to overcome its backwardness through the social capital and political network, notional or substantial, from an outside system for a possible relief from local injustices.

Historically, there have been occasions when the downtrodden groups have managed to come up in hierarchy. For instance, Raj Gonds of Central India claimed for themselves Kshatriya status. Then there have been instances of spatial movement through which the oppressed leave their home and hearth for another place where they start their life under the cover of anonymity. The phenomenon is more specifically seen in instances of mass urbanization. Historically, caste frames have always been quite porous allowing exit routes to members to opt out of the situation. Caste-based communities have escaped the stigma of caste and its attendant oppression through instant anonymization by moving away from their places, migrating to cities. Alternatively, the oppressed communities remain at their place and struggle against the regime of caste-based injustice. This is exactly what has happened in Hisar.

The phenomenon of caste here needs to be looked at in a more grounded sense. The Dalit community in the village was seemingly entangled in the hierarchical inter-group relations and in a struggle to survive on the margins of village economy and society. It's a sad story of being a Dalit in a village where the general story of dominant caste's oppression is repeated. A socially backward caste being subjected to worst oppression without respite from law, state or any other controlling mechanisms in society.

Most of the time in our country, conversions follow caste oppression where the state prefers to turn a Nelson's eye to the goings-on. A wilful non-enforcement of law against its gross violations should not be read in terms of the prevalence of an archaic custom. Rather, caste injustices are part of gross legal violations in modern times. For a variety of reasons, the existing state hasn't been able to attend to them.

However, neither does the marginalized caste exist in a permanent social trap nor is its recourse to a different religion likely to lead to an enduring resolution of the issues threatening collective existence. The conversion is merely an attempt at inching away from oppression at the local level. Caste-communities have adopted religious conversion as self-help mechanism to seek social equality as if the state was absent, as if the agencies that are supposed to be overseeing the provisions of development provisions in the medium of social justice are powerless to do so. Much of religious conversion is about the faith reorienting itself. In social terms, it's also about a leap of faith in the real world. Expecting a religious system to provide social equality is vain hope. Not expecting the same from the modern secular system is a sign of community's alienation and a measure of its distance from development and law and order.

The recourse to Islam with its concepts of egalitarianism brings about some reconfiguration of self-image, as well as mobilization of public opinion against local violations. What it does help perpetuate is the unity between the minorities and those at the lower end of Hindu caste hierarchy. As shown by the religion- and caste-driven politics of Bihar and Uttar Pradesh, Muslims and Dalits or Muslims and Yadavs make for fine electoral arithmetic.

UNIFORM CIVIL CODE

For years, the Hindutva brigade has gone to town with claims of minority appeasement—the term minority being just a euphemism for Muslims. For years, there have been unsubstantiated claims of Muslims indulging in polygamy, of Muslim women being denied their share in inheritance, of the community refusing to join the mainstream. If sadhus and sadhvis with anything but faith on their mind urged the Muslim community to give up its claims to the Babri Masjid site, a leader such as L.K. Advani who failed to honour his word when it came to Babri Masjid's protection wants to be taken seriously, when he assures that a uniform civil code does not mean Hindu law being imposed on all Indians. Indeed, for years, our media has faithfully reproduced allegations of Muslims being an impediment towards uniform civil code. And political parties such as the BJP have had it as part of the manifesto— more recently, the Union Law minister D.V. Sadananda Gowda termed the implementation of Uniform Civil Code as 'duty of the state', adding that the issue is under examination. His colleague in the party, Vinay Katiyar, added for good measure, 'A uniform civil code is required for strengthening the Indian republic. Consensus on the population policy is not possible due to lack of a uniform civil code resulting in imbalance in population'.

Indeed, in the common man's eye, Article 370 and Uniform Civil Code are two great obstacles in the path of national integration. In some cases, even secular forces have joined the chorus. Some distinguished judges have not kept away either. Yet the reality is far removed from the rhetoric. The help though comes from unexpected quarters. Professor Tahir Mahmood is a legal eagle like few others in the country. His tenure as the Chairman of the NCM was notable for its proactive approach and steadfast effort to get the NCM more punitive powers. His book on uniform civil code was not often quoted beyond legal circles when it first hit the stands, partly because it did not have the distribution network of a major publisher to thrust it to public eye. But really should Mahmood's *Uniform Civil Code: Fictions and Facts* (1995) were to be widely read, it would help clear a lot of misconceptions, many of them passed on from one generation to another. A careful scrutiny of the legal instances he quotes and the various Acts and judgements he writes about bring one to a simple conclusion: We are living in a country guilty of majority appeasement. Among the minorities, the worst sufferers are Muslims, not the Parsis, numerically the weakest of the lot.

Mahmood (1995) in the chapter 'Reflections on Jorden Diengdeh Case' writes,

> The Parsi marriage law till this date contains provisions
> for special Parsi matrimonial courts—Parsi Marriage and
> Divorce Act, Sections 18–29; and the Parsi succession law

is still close to the Islamic law in providing for daughters half of the sons' shares in their father's property—Indian Succession Act, Section 51. The amendments of 1988–89, notably have introduced no change in these special features of the Parsi personal law. Social reformers, however, have never frowned on these provisions of the Parsi personal law which continued in force even after the two heavy doses of reform administered during 1988–1991.

The Christians, on the other hand, are not governed by a uniform law. 'Having a dominant majority in Mizoram, Nagaland and Meghalaya, a sizeable percentage of population in Goa, Kerala and Manipur ... the community has various kinds of religious laws and customs in force along with the central and regional statutory laws'. Yet no voice that local Christian customs are an impediments towards uniform civil code.

Furthermore, he is ready to shock all those seeking a uniform civil code as the way forward for a nation to treat all citizens as equals.

Had a Hindu Code Bill not been pending for enactment in the central legislature at the time of the advent of Independence, there would have been no provision relating to a uniform civil code in the Constitution of the Republic. The idea of a uniform civil code had its origins not in the support for, but in the opposition, to the Hindu Code Bill. To say so I have the authority of none else but Dr. B.R. Ambedkar—some of whose words spoken in the Constituent Assembly in favour of the uniform civil code proposal are often fondly quoted—who had once emphatically said on the floor also that opponents of the Hindu Code Bill were demanding a provision for uniform civil code not on principle but by way of a stalling tactic. It was demanded by the critics of the Bill that it be withheld till it was modified so as to be made applicable to all Indians.

Dr. Ambedkar, a staunch supporter of the Hindu Code Bill did not agree. The opponents of the Bill also did not budge. Eventually, while the Hindu Code Bill could not be passed until finalization of the draft of the Constitution, to meet the obstinacy of its opponents a directive principle on the advisability of 'uniform civil code for the citizens' found a place in the Constitution. (Mahmood 1995)

Then comes a clincher, something which reeks of discrimination, even if unintended. Here Mahmood repeats what he had written in *Radiance Viewsweekly* in January 1986,

There are historical reasons why the Muslims had failed, despite their best efforts in the Constituent Assembly, to secure inclusion of any specific provisions in the Constitution in respect of their personal law. For the Sikhs, the kirpan was as sacred as the cow for the Hindus. Both the communities could easily get their sacred things fully protected under the Constitution. For the Muslims their personal law was as much sacred: yet, they were denied its statutory protection.

Incidentally, for all the political talk of the need to take steps towards Uniform Civil Code and open declaration in party manifestoes, the Centre and state governments have taken steps to the contrary. Personal laws, including their family-law contents, have been placed in List III or the Concurrent List of the Constitution. In *From the Heart*, a compilation of his speeches, Mahmood argues,

Regional diversity in family has thus been legally sanctified, and the scope for countrywide uniformity—as enshrined in the judicially unenforceable Article 44—is restricted and curtailed by the Constitution itself. Accordingly, Parliament and State legislatures both can make laws, and have made mutually contradictory laws.

The Hindu Succession Act 1956 enacted by Parliament, has been, for example, drastically amended by the State Legislature in Kerala through the Hindu Joint Family Abolition Act, 1975. Parliamentary legislation on family law matters is, moreover, often supplemented with additional provisions by the State Legislatures—e.g., State amendments of the Hindu Marriage Act 1955 in Uttar Pradesh and Tamil Nadu. (Mahmood 1998)

Then there are instances of states having their own set of laws. If Jammu and Kashmir has its own family laws, both statutory and non-statutory, Pondicherry, which became part of India in 1954, gave the local residents a choice of continuing to be governed by the old French Civil Code or their own religion-specific laws. Those who opted for the former are known as Renoncants and are not governed by the general Hindu, Muslim or Christian laws. In Nagaland, the Naga Customary law and procedure and the religious practices of the Nagas were specifically protected by a special provision incorporated in the Constitution in 1962 through the 13th Amendment. Similar rule was applied to Mizo customs and social practices.

The biggest contradiction came with the Hindu Code Bill which was inherited by the Republic from pre-Independence days.

Parliament retained it and eventually enacted it in fragments. In 1954, the old Special Marriage Act of 1872 was replaced by fresh legislation, incorporating a new secular law of marriage and divorce. The State, however, failed to compulsorily apply it to any group of people including the predominant Hindu community. Within one year, Parliament enacted a separate Hindu Marriage Act 1955. The new Special Marriage Act enacted earlier had to be relegated to the status of an optional law which any

Indian could adopt or reject at one's sweet will. Since then, a number of steps have been taken to establish by legislation a separate Hindu personal law, often by curtailing the scope of the secular family laws enacted in pre-Independence India. (Mahmood 1998)

With the Hindu personal law often prevailing over the secular family laws, Muslim personal law not even being codified, so who is a beneficiary of appeasement?

AGE-OLD GLUE: COMMONALITIES IN FAITH

In a travesty of our times, while we treat a slogan as a benchmark of nationalism, that modern concept of people occupying a contiguous piece of land with similar race, language and culture considering themselves a united community and putting the nation ahead of the rest, we have forgotten the age-old glue we have been blessed with. In a country where people practising different faiths have often been at each other's throat, there has been little effort to understand different religions. Had we done so, we may not have needed a catchy slogan or two to unite the masses. While some pacifists have tried to find the clichéd commonalities in different religions, only a handful of hardy souls have attempted to study religion beyond their own, that is, the religion they are born in.

It is particularly galling when one considers that almost all of us believe that Unto Him shall we all return; he who has taken a breath shall taste death too. Why then does man build boundaries? Why then does man even try to find different ways of reaching the Almighty? He is One. The most beautiful of names belong to Him. Doesn't the Rig Veda tell us all He is in the East; He is in the West?

Does not the glorious Quran tell humanity, 'To Allah belongs the East and the West. To whichever direction you turn, you face the countenance of Allah. For Allah is All Embracing and All Knowing'?

A thousand years ago, we had Al-Beruni who studied Vedanta like none else. Then we had a flowering of inter-religion dialogue during the Mughals with not just Dara Shukoh but even Abdur Rehman Chishti as also Mazhar Jan-e-Janaan, a Naqshbandi sufi who attempted to bring Indian Muslims and Hindus closer ideologically, they all spent time not only studying various *granths* (scriptures) of Hinduism but also in essence told us about the one-ness of humanity. Never for a minute did they doubt that Prophet Mohammed (PBUH) was the last prophet, but they were prepared to look for an Indian prophet consid-ering that Quran says that a messenger had been sent to every community, and no community was ever destroyed without a guide being sent to it, to show the right way. Then there was the peerless Sarmad, fearless and frank and extremely popular. In fact, Sarmad's popularity irked the Mughal emperor Aurangzeb so much that he believed Sarmad's views were gathering public opinion in favour of his brother, the formidable Dara, who was also his political foe.

But these have been rare voices. One is yet to find a contemporary Hindu scholar who has attempted to study Islam. Likewise, there is scarcely an Islamic scholar who can be dubbed as an authority on Upanishads or the Bhagavad Gita. Little wonder, career bureaucrat, now Chairman, South India Education Trust, Moosa Raza, when he decided to pen *In Search of Oneness: The Bhagavad Gita and the Quran through Sufi Eyes* (2012), his first lament was the absence of scholars studying religions beyond their own. As he says in the introduction,

> It is very unfortunate that though the Hindus and the Muslims in India have been living together for more than a thousand years, knowledge about each other's religious books is often absent and, if present, it is generally superficial. After Al-Beruni's book on India, the *Kitab-al-Hind*, and the fourteen chapters he devoted to the Indian religions, hardly any Muslim writer has studied Sanskrit and read the Hindu texts in the original. Similarly, I am yet to come across a Hindu writer who is capable of writing authoritatively on Islam and the Islamic texts—the Quran and the Hadith in particular. European scholars have devoted considerable attention to Islam and its religious texts as well as to Hinduism and its texts. They have produced well-researched and erudite works for at least over a hundred years.

Not so Indians. More is the pity. People have fought political battles in medieval times, arrayed on political lines in modern times, but not many have bothered to find out what makes a man, irrespective of his religious denomination, tick.

Raza's is not a scholarly work by any stretch, but it is a work that provokes you to study, to explore, to find out. All along, he uses the tools of a scientist to find an answer to a question of belief. At one place, he happily tells us that the Quran says, '*Inna khalqnaakum min nafsun wahida*' (verily we have created you from a single soul). He goes on to tell that the Quran says that mankind is but a single community, *ummatan wahida*. Isn't it very similar to *Vasudhaiva Kutumbakam*? Then Raza expounds the virtues of the Gita. Quoting the Gita, he says, '*Sarvabhutasthitam*' (abiding in all beings). Then he draws a parallel with the Sufi who sees God in every atom, every speck and every drop of water. Of course, he finds an easy echo in the words of Sankara, who moaned, 'O Lord! Pardon my three sins. I have in contemplation clothed in form Thee who are formless. I have in praise described Thee who are ineffable. And in visiting temples ignored Thy omnipresence'.

Raza's search for Oneness deserves moments of quiet contemplation. Some, like Panditji, whom he quotes, might find that within. Others might yearn to find it all around. But, today, if friends in groups endeavour to read texts of different religions, they will come back with gems very similar. For instance, as Raza (2012) informs us,

> The Bhagavad Gita, one of the significant religious texts of the Indian subcontinent, has been read, paraphrased, expounded on and translated many times by Islamic scholars, beginning with Al Beruni whose paraphrases of the Gita sound almost like a commentary on the Quran, to Abdur Rahman Chishti's commentary on the Gita. Chishti claims the text to be Krishna explaining to Arjuna, by analogy, the secrets of *tawhid*—the oneness of God. 'To God belongs the East and the West. To whichever direction you turn, you face the countenance of God. For God is All-Embracing and All-Knowing', says the Quran. 'Call "Allah" or call "ar-Rahman", whatever name you call, to Him belong the most beautiful names'. Much earlier, the Rig Veda had said, '*ekam sat, vipra bahuda vadanti*'— truth is one and the wise call it by many names.

Many may draw solace from His word itself. After all, Raza is talking of God. Does not Surah Ikhlas tell us, 'Allah, the One and Only! The Eternal, the Absolute. He begeteth not nor is He begotten. And there is none like unto Him'? Or what the Bhagavad Gita says about Ishwar, 'The

Unmanifested, the Imperishable'. On such commonalities, one finds a bridge to happy coexistence. Recalling a verse Muslims say when they hear of somebody passing away, '*Inna Iillahi wa inna ilaihi rajioon*', there is a parallel in Hinduism. Taking help from Al-Beruni quoting Vasudeva's peroration at the very beginning of the Bhagavad Gita, he writes, 'Both life and death are not your concern. They are in the hands of God, from whom all things come and to whom they return'. Yes, unto Him shall we all return.

From Him to Him. It is all in the path of the journey that the differences lie. It is the differences that need to be better understood and appreciated than swept under the carpet. Just the way the Jamaat-e-Islami Hind volunteers did the other day at the height of summer in May 2016. Raising awareness about the dire need to save every drop of water in the wake of drought in Maharashtra and Karnataka, the volunteers distributed pamphlets quoting from religion. A pamphlet reproduced Prophet Mohammed's (PBUH) saying, 'Do not waste water even if you are at a running stream', another quoted from the Atharvaveda to tell us that there is only one God, whatever one might conceive Him to be. 'Verily He is one—single, indivisible, supreme reality'. Jamaat quoting the Vedas? Indeed. Yes, unto Him shall we all return. And on that day, nobody shall intercede with the Imperishable, the Unmanifested on behalf of another.

INDIA FOR INDIANS

A shade softly, a little bit nervously, but India is surely speaking up for the soul of the nation. The shared past is being talked anew. And people, often guilty of silence, are finding their voice boxes. Going away is the indifference one noticed when seasoned author Nayantara Sahgal pointed out that the soul of India was in danger in front of onslaught by Hindutva forces. It was the summer of 2015 when Sahgal first made herself heard on the challenges facing the nation.

It was a voice not many paid heed to then. Some read in it, in a rather sexist manner, the moaning of an old woman. Others found her just as a shadow speaker for the Congress. So much so, a little under three years later, on the 25th anniversary of the Babri Masjid demolition, Sahgal (2017) had to remind us,

> India is a bruised, battered and bleeding democracy. In the past three years, the country's multi-cultural inheritance has been torn to shreds. Indians have been partitioned into Hindus and Others, and Hinduism has been replaced by a martial creed called Hindutva, invented by Savarkar and now put into practice by the RSS, whose government is waging war on Indians outside the Hindu fold and on those within it who oppose its ideology.... An ideology that had been rejected by Indians since its inception in the 1920s—when Indians chose to follow Mahatma Gandhi instead in the epic non-violent fight for freedom from British rule, and afterwards to stay staunchly secular—now governs us. We are told this is a new India and so it is.

> It is now a country in which being different—in belief or lifestyle—is punishable, and one in which Muslim means enemy. The word is out that Muslim numbers must be reduced and the ominous impact of this statement is visible on the streets. We have seen defenceless Indians of the Muslim faith beaten and lynched in public view. But blood sport is not confined to Muslims. Well-known Hindu writers have been killed by gun-toting vigilantes and their murderers have been left free to kill again.

By December 2017 though, she had plenty of support. Sahgal's was no longer the voice of a lonely, helpless Indian, seeing the ship sinking. Soon, it became a chorus, as more and more Indians, cutting across religion, caste and region, spoke up against constant smothering of the minorities and a relentless bid to replace the expression 'unity in diversity' by 'uniformity of belief'.

The tide began to turn with a seemingly innocent message by documentary filmmaker Saba Dewan who, in the wake of Junaid Khan's brutal murder—he was killed on a train on his way home after Eid shopping—declared online, 'Not In My Name'. She asked on Facebook,

> Shouldn't there be protests against the lynchings especially after the murder yesterday in Delhi NCR by a mob of a 16-year-old Muslim boy? If not now then when? Why wait for political formations to organize a demonstration? Why can't all of us as citizens repulsed by the violence get together in protest at the earliest next week at Jantar Mantar under the banner—Not in my Name.

And thousands of people nodded in affirmation.

The message soon went viral. And a protest was planned at Jantar Mantar in New Delhi where a cross-section of people gave the rallying cry, 'Not in my name'. It was for the first time that common Indians, largely Hindus, but including Muslims, Christians, Buddhists, Sikhs, Jains and Dalits dissociated themselves from the constant attacks on members of Muslim and Dalit communities in the name of preserving the sanctity of Hinduism. Not in my name was an apt expression, as most Indians did not subscribe to the hate all–love none ideology. So powerful was the response to the call that 17 cities across India decided to hold simultaneous protests. Ranging from Thiruvananthapuram and Kochi to Patna and Chandigarh, common Indians stood shoulder to shoulder to negate the aggressive, even violent expression of Hindutva.

The #NotInMyName protests caught international attention in June–July 2017. They were a rage, but the breeze of protest continued to blow, gently, quietly, and persistently. Soon army veterans and later civil servants found their voice. Social activists, authors, retired army men and civil servants all took it upon themselves to speak up for the idea of India, a nation built on pluralist ethos and a shared past. As instances of lynching and public flogging of the Muslims and Dalits continued with barely a gap, the who's who of India decided enough is enough. In July 2017, a group of 114 veterans of the Indian armed forces wrote an open letter to the Prime Minister besides various chief ministers and governors. They expressed their distress at the killing of the innocent which went 'against the secular and democratic values enshrined in the Constitution'. Stating at the beginning that they were writing as Indians without any political allegiance, they wrote,

> We are a group of veterans of the Indian Armed Forces who have spent our careers working for the security of our country. Collectively, our group holds no affiliation with any single political party, our only common commitment being to the constitution of India. It saddens us to write this letter, but current events in India have compelled us to register our dismay at the divisiveness that is gripping our country. We stand with the 'Not in My Name' campaign that mobilised thousands of citizens across the country to protest against the current climate of fear, intimidation, hate and suspicion.

The armed forces stand for 'unity in diversity'. Differences in religion, language, caste, culture or any other marker of belonging have not mattered to the cohesion of the armed forces, and servicemen of different backgrounds have fought shoulder to shoulder in the defence of our nation, as they continue to do today. Throughout our service, a sense of openness, justice and fair play guided our actions. We are one family. Our heritage is like the multi-coloured quilt that is India, and we cherish this vibrant diversity.

However, what is happening in our country today strikes at all that the armed forces, and indeed our constitution, stand for. We are witness to unprecedented attacks on society at large by the relentless vigilantism of self-appointed protectors of Hinduism. We condemn the targeting of Muslims and Dalits. We condemn the clampdowns on free speech by attacks on media outlets, civil society groups, universities, journalists and scholars, through a campaign of branding them anti-national and unleashing violence against them while the state looks away.

We can no longer look away. We would be doing a disservice to our country if we do not stand up and speak for the liberal and secular values that our constitution espouses. Our diversity is our greatest strength. Dissent is not treason; in fact, it is the essence of democracy.

We urge the powers that be at the Centre and in the states to take note of our concerns and urgently act to uphold our constitution, both in letter and in spirit. (*The Indian Express*, 31 July 2017)

The letter was signed, among others, by Lt Col E.N. Ambre, Brig. V.K.S. Antony, Maj. M.K. Apte, Col C.T. Arasu, Lt Col Israr Asghar, Cdr C.R. Babu, Lt Gen. C.A. Barretto, Brig. Noel Barretto, Col T.S. Bedi, Lt Col Muzaffar Hasan, Maj. Gen. M.P.S. Kandal, Col M.S. Kapoor, Maj. Gen. T.K. Kaul,

Brig. Baqir Shameem, Lt Gen. Y.N. Sharma, Lt Col J.K. Thomas and Maj. Gen. S.G. Vombatkere.

Six months later, our army men got support from civil servants. In January 2018, they too drew attention to the danger to life and property of an average Indian. It was no longer suicidal to speak on behalf of Muslims, Christians and Dalits. India was recovering its spirit. The letter, signed by 67 civil servants, highlighted continued incidents of violence. They wrote,

> We, retired civil servants belonging to different services and batches, wish to register our deep concern at the continuing incidents of mindless violence in the country, especially those targeting the minorities, and the lackadaisical response of the law enforcement machinery to these attacks.

> The killing of Mohammed Afrazul, a migrant worker from West Bengal in Rajsamund, Rajasthan, on the 25th anniversary of the demolition of the Babri Masjid has deeply shaken each of us. The recording of the brutal act on video and the circulation of the justification for the killing over the Internet cuts at the roots of an inclusive and pluralistic society drawing its inspiration from the teachings of Buddha, Mahavira, Ashoka, Akbar, the Sikh gurus, Hindu sages and Gandhi. The violent incidents in Udaipur in support of the alleged killer are a pointer to how deep the sectarian poison has spread among the population of this country.

> In the last nine months, we have seen the death of Pehlu Khan on 3rd April (2017) after he was attacked by a crowd of (the) so-called *gau rakshaks* near Behror, Alwar, on 1st April. The killers named by him have not been arrested so far. However, seven others have been arrested and subsequently let off on bail.

The second killing on 16th of June of Zafar Khan was in the name of Swachh Bharat Abhiyan. The Municipal Chairman and other Safai Karmacharis in Pratapgarh reportedly beat him to death while he was opposing the naming and shaming process for making Pratapgarh open defecation-free. There is no arrest so far with the police claiming that Zafar Khan died of a heart attack.

The third killing in June 2017, was that of 16-year-old Junaid Khan on a train returning after Eid shopping in Delhi following a dispute over seats on the train when following abuses and insults he was stabbed and thrown out of the train at Asoti station, where he bled to death.

Following an outcry against this incident both within and outside India, the Prime Minister made a statement that 'killing people in the name of "Gau bhakti" is unacceptable'. He repeated this a day before the Parliamentary session started on 15th of July, 2017, at an all India meeting of the BJP, where he placed the onus on taking stringent action in these cases on the State governments. However, the killings continue without any check.

The fourth killing happened on 27th August, 2017, when Anwar Hussain and Hafizul Sheikh, both 19 years of age, who were transporting cattle purchased from Dhupguri in West Bengal to Tufangunj in Cooch Behar. As they got lost on the way, a mob accosted them in the early hours and when they could not pay the 50,000 rupees demanded of them, beat them both to death. Though three persons were arrested for the lynching, efforts to identify others in the mob have not produced any result so far.

The fifth killing happened on 10th of November, 2017, when Umair Khan and his friends transporting cows were fired on by so called *gau rakshaks* in Govindgarh Tehsil in Alwar district. Umair Khan was killed and his body was carried to the railway track in an attempt to destroy all evidence. Of the seven killers only two were arrested.

However, two of the victims, Tahir and Jawed, were placed behind bars.

We are deeply concerned to see the acceleration of a process of ghettoisation through organised resistance to sale of properties to Muslims, or refusal by owners to have them as tenants. A recent case reported in the media relates to prevention of a Muslim buyer to take possession of a house in the Maliwara locality of Meerut that he had paid for. The daily indignities that the Muslims face in this and many other ways is bound to lead to an atmosphere of resentment in that religious community that will further vitiate an already poisoned environment. The love-jihad campaigns of right-wing Hindu groups are again symptomatic of the efforts by extremist elements of the majority religion to interfere in the basic constitutional rights of citizens to enter into marriage with a partner of their choice.

In the past few weeks in December (2017), we are witness to increasing targeting of Christians around the observation of Christmas. On 15th of December, police detained groups singing carols in Satna. When a group of priests went to make enquiries, they were also reportedly detained by the police. In Uttar Pradesh, the Hindu Jagran Manch warned Christian schools in Aligarh against observing Christmas. In Rajasthan, members of the Vishwa Hindu Parishad allegedly stormed a Christmas function on the grounds that this was an attempt at forced conversion.

We seek now and without delay a clear response from the Hon'ble Prime Minister and his government on these issues, along with immediate and firm action against the perpetrators of such hate crimes against minorities in this country by the respective law enforcement authorities. (*The Wire*, 28 January 2018)

The letter was signed by Bhaskar Ghose, former Secretary, Ministry of Information and Broadcasting; K.P. Fabian, former Ambassador to Italy; Javid Chaudhuri, former Secretary, Ministry of Health and Family Welfare; Surjit K. Das, former Chief Secretary, Government of Uttarakhand; Harsh Mander, Government of Madhya Pradesh, etc.

The two letters reminded one of the early days of the Congress in the late 19th century when the party still believed in the good intentions of the British. Then the Congress adopted the route of prayer, petition and protest to highlight the injustices towards fellow Indians. They believed that if the reality was brought before the British rulers, they would take corrective measures. The party was soon to be dispossessed of those notions, and, by 1905, extremist leaders such as Bal Gangadhar Tilkar, Bipil Chandra Pal, and later Lala Lajpat Rai, C.R. Das and others started moving towards *swaraj* (self-rule).

Today, the challenge is of a different nature. The protest is against the silence, amounting to collusion, of the elected government against attacks on the life and limbs of fellow Indians. The open letters demonstrate that the fight for the soul of India has started, an India where everybody has freedom to practice, propagate any religion or no religion, an India where everybody has the right to choose a vocation and to be treated equally before the law. The top-downwards approach may take time in reaching the masses, but it does tell us that the nation is no longer in slumber in front of an attack on its foundations.

All this is in stark, and heart-warming, contrast to what happened in 2016 when Sahgal returned her Sahitya Akademi Award, she had got for her work *Rich Like Us*, in protest against the killing of Kalburgi, Akhlaq and others, then only the authors spoke up, notably, Uday Prakash,

Rahman Abbas and Chaman Lal. But rest of the society was only too happy to read political motives behind the awards being returned by authors. Not many questioned the studied silence of the Prime Minister. So much so, it seemed it was easier to be the Prime Minister of India and keep quiet when the nation was crying for a word from him than to be an author and speak your heart out.

The winds of change may not yet be developing into a storm, but the gentle breeze promises lasting relief. Indians are beginning to speak for fellow Indians, irrespective of their religion, gender, caste, just as our Constitution visualized. Critically, Indians are speaking up for India, a nation whose soul has been under attack, a nation that could do with the balm of pluralism.

REFERENCES

Ambedkar, B.R. 1975. *Pakistan or the Partition of India*. New York: AMS Press.

Ananthamurthy, U.R. 2016. *Hindutva or Hind Swaraj*. Noida: HarperCollins.

Anjum, Z. 2014. *Iqbal: The Life of a Poet, Philosopher and Politician*. New Delhi: Random House India.

Azad, M.A.K. 1910. 'Sarmad Shaheed'. An essay in *Burhan*, Urdu fortnightly.

Baker, D., 2011. *The Convert: A Tale of Exile and Extremism*. Minneapolis: Graywolf Press.

Banerji-Dube, Ishita. 2014. *A History of Modern India*. New York: Cambridge University Press.

Basu, T., Datta, P., Sarkar, S. Sarkar, T., and Sen, S. 1993. *Khaki Shorts Saffron Flags*. New Delhi: Orient Longman.

Casolari, M. 2002. 'Role of Benares in Constructing Political Hindu Identity'. *Economic and Political Weekly*, 1413–20.

Chandra, B. 2016. *Communalism: A Primer*. New Delhi: National Book Trust.

Chandra, B., Mujherjee, A., Mukherjee, M., Mahajan S., and Panikkar, K.N. 1988. *India's Struggle for Independence*. New Delhi: Penguin Books India.

Chattopadhyay, B.C. 1882. *Anandmath*. Oxford: Oxford University Press.

Chaudhary, S. 1998. *Sufism Is Not Islam: A Comparative Study*. New Delhi: Daya Books.

Chopra, P.N. 2015. *The Collective Works of Sardar Vallabhbhai Patel*, 15 volume series. New Delhi: Konark Publishers.

Choudhary, Z. 2015. *Kashmir Conflict and Muslims of Jammu*. Jammu and Kashmir: Gulshan Books.

Dalrymple, W., and Sharma, Y. 2012. *Princes and Painters in Mughal India*. New Haven: Yale University Press.

Dalvi, M. 2012. *Taking Issue and Allah's Answer*. Translated by Muhammad Iqbal. New Delhi: Penguin Books India.

Engineer, A.A. 1991. *Sufism: Inter-religious Understanding*. New Delhi: HOPE India.

Fatah, T. 2011. *The Tragic Illusion of an Islamic State*. Pakistan: Vanguard Books.

Gandhi, G. 2010. *Dara Shukoh: A Play by Gopal Gandhi*. New Delhi: Transquebar Press.

Gandhi, N.M. 2013. *Alternative Realities: Love in the Lives of Muslim Women*. New Delhi: Tranquebar Press.

Gandhi, R. 2013. *Punjab: A History from Aurangzeb to Mountbatten*. New Delhi: Aleph Book Company.

Gayer, L., and Jaffrelot, C. eds. 2012. *Muslims in Indian Cities: Trajectories of Marginalisation*. London: Columbia University Press.

Golwalkar, M.S. 1966. *Bunch of Thoughts*. Bangalore: Vikram Prakashan.

———. 2006. *We or Our Nationhood Defined* (including a critique by Shamsul Islam). New Delhi: Pharos Media & Publishing.

Habib, S.I. 2013. *Jihad or Ijtihad: Religious Orthodoxy and Modern Science in Contemporary Islam*. Noida: HarperCollins.

Habibullah, W. 2015. 'Foreword'. In *Kashmir Conflict and Muslims of Jammu* by Z. Choudhary. Jammu and Kashmir: Gulshan Books.

Hiro, D. 2006. *Babur Nama: Journal of Emperor Babur*. New Delhi: Penguin Books India.

Islam, S. 2015. *Muslims Against Partition: Revisiting the Legacy of Allah Bakhsh and Other Patriotic Muslims*. New Delhi: Pharos Media & Publishing.

Jain, G. 1994. *The Hindu Phenomenon*. New Delhi: UBS Publishers.

Jeffrey, R., and Sen, R., eds. 2014. *Being Muslim in South Asia: Diversity and Daily Life*. New Delhi: Oxford University Press.

Jha, D.N. 2009. *The Myth of the Holy Cow*. New Delhi: Navayana Publishing.

Juluri, V. 2014. *Rearming Hinduism*. Chennai: Westland Books.

Jung, A. 1993. *Night of the New Moon: Encounters with Muslim Women in India*. New Delhi: Penguin Books India.

Kelkar, B.K. 2017. *Pandit Deendayal Upadhyayay: Ideology and Perception*. New Dehli: Suruchi Prakashan.

Khan, M.A., and Haksar, N. 2016. *Framed as a Terrorist: My 14-year Struggle to Prove My Innocence*. New Delhi: Speaking Tiger.

Khan, M.W. 2002. *The True Jihad: The Concepts of Peace, Tolerance, and Non-violence in Islam*. New Delhi: Goodword Books.

———. 2009. *Islam and World Peace*. New Delhi: Goodword Books.

Kulkarni, P. 2017. 'How Did Savarkar, a Staunch Supporter of British Colonialism, Come to Be Known as "Veer"?' *The Wire*, 28 May.

Lesley, H. 2013. *The First Muslim*. London: Atlantic Books.

Madhok, B. 1969. *Indian Nationalism*. New Delhi: Bharati Sahitya Sadan.

Mahmood, S. (ed.) 1998. *From the Heart: Tahir Mahmood's Select Speeches on Religion, Law and Literature*. New Delhi: Academy of Law and Religion.

Mahmood, T. 1995. *Uniform Civil Code: Fictions and Facts*. New Delhi: India and Islam Research Council.

Mukul, A. 2015. *Gita Press and the Making of Hindu India*. Noida: HarperCollins.

Prasad, C.B. 2006. *Dalit Phobia: Why Do They Hate Us?* New Delhi: Vitasta Publishing.

Rai, V.N. 2016. *Hashimpura 22 May: The Forgotten Story of India's Biggest Custodial Killing*. Translated by Darshan Desai. New Delhi: Penguin Books India.

Raza, M. 2012. *In Search of Oneness: The Bhagavad Gita and the Quran through Sufi Eyes*. New Delhi: Penguin Books India.

Sahgal, N. 2017. 'In "New India", No Place for Others'. *The Tribune*, 13 December.

Salam, Ziya Us. 2016. 'Code Red'. *The Hindu*, 23 March.

Salim, A. 2013. *Vanity Bagh*. New Delhi: Macmillan.

Sarkar, S. 1983. *Modern India: 1885–1947*. New Delhi: Macmillan.

Sarkar, T. 1999. 'The Gender Predicament of the Hindu Right'. In K.N. Pannikar (ed.), *The Concerned Indian's Guide to Communalism*. New Delhi: Penguin Books India.

Savarkar, V.D. n.d. 'Care for Cows, Do Not Worship Them'. In his *Vigyananishtha Nibandh*. Mumbai: Svatantryaveer Savarkar Rashtriya Smarak Prakashan.

Sharma, J. 2011. *Hindutva: Exploring the Idea of Hindu Nationalism*. Noida: HarperCollins.

Singh, B. 2007. *The Jail Notebook and Other Writing*. New Delhi: LeftWord Books.

———. 2015. *Why I Am an Atheist*, edited by Bipan Chandra. New Delhi: National Book Trust.

Smith, V.A. 1919. *The Oxford History of India*. Oxford: Clarendon Press.

Srinivas, M.N. 1980. *India: Social Structure*. New Delhi: Transaction Publishers.

Tahir-ul-Qadri, M. 2010. *Fatwa on Terrorism and Suicide Bombings*. London: Minhaj-ul-Quran International.

Thapar, R. 1990. *A History of India*. England: Penguin UK.

The Kashmir Monitor. 2016. 'Call Me Shaikh, not Shubham'. *The Kashmir Monitor*, 12 May.

Truschke, A. 2016. *Culture of Encounters: Sanskrit at the Mughal Court*. New York: Columbia University Press.

———. 2017. *Aurangzeb: The Man and the Myth*. New Delhi: Penguin-Random House.

Vasfi, S.A.S. 2016. *Hindutva and Minorities in India*. New Delhi: Uruf Enterprises.

Zaheer, N. 2015. *Denied by Allah*. New Delhi: Vitasta Publishing.

ABOUT THE AUTHOR

Ziya Us Salam is a noted literary and social commentator. He has been associated with *The Hindu* for the past 18 years. He has been *The Hindu*'s Features Editor for North India editions for 16 years. At present, he is Associate Editor, *Frontline*, and writes on sociocultural issues for the magazine besides doing book reviews.

His book *Till Talaq Do Us Part*, a study of various divorce options available in Islam, was released in early 2018. His book *Delhi 4 Shows*, a study of cinemas since the talkie era began, was released in 2016. He has contributed to the following anthologies: *Being Young in the Worlds of Islam* and *Past Tense—Living on the Edge*. He has edited an anthology titled *House Full: The Golden Age of Hindi Cinema*. He was a jury member of the International Film Festival of India (non-feature film, 2011), Best Writing on Cinema (2008) and Vatavaran. His book *365 Tales from Islam* will be out shortly.